WHITE SPACE IS NOT YOUR ENEMY
A BEGINNER'S GUIDE TO COMMUNICATING VISUALLY THROUGH GRAPHIC, WEB & MULTIMEDIA DESIGN

WHITE SPACE
IS NOT YOUR ENEMY

A Beginner's Guide to Communicating Visually Through
Graphic, Web & Multimedia Design • 3rd ed.

Rebecca Hagen
&
Kim Golombisky

CRC Press
Taylor & Francis Group

A FOCAL PRESS BOOK

CRC Press
Taylor & Francis Group
6000 Broken Sound Parkway NW, Suite 300
Boca Raton, FL 33487-2742

Printed on acid-free paper
Version Date: 20160310

International Standard Book Number-13: 978-1-138-80464-7 (Paperback)

Library of Congress Cataloging-in-Publication Data

Names: Hagen, Rebecca, author. | Golombisky, Kim, author.
Title: White space is not your enemy : a beginner's guide to communicating visually through graphic, web & multimedia design / Rebecca Hagen and Kim Golombisky.
Description: Third edition. | Boca Raton : Taylor & Francis, 2016. | Includes index.
Identifiers: LCCN 2016005527 | ISBN 9781138804647 (alk. paper)
Subjects: LCSH: Graphic arts-- Handbooks, manuals, etc. | Visual communication-- Handbooks, manuals, etc. | Commercial art-- Handbooks, manuals, etc.
Classification: LCC NC997 .G563 2016 | DDC 740-- dc23
LC record available at http://lccn.loc.gov/2016005527

Visit the Taylor & Francis Web site at
http://www.taylorandfrancis.com
and the CRC Press Web site at
http://www.crcpress.com

To our Starbucks baristas at
the New Tampa Super Target: Since 2008, you have
sustained us through three editions and roughly
400 Tuesday morning book meetings.
Gracias, Amigas.

TABLE OF CONTENTS

White Space Is Not Your Enemy:
A Beginner's Guide to Communicating Visually Through Graphic, Web & Multimedia Design

For more content please visit the companion site:

http://www.whitespacedesignbook.com

Register using the passcode: space816

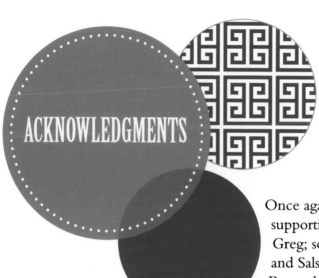

ACKNOWLEDGMENTS

Once again, thanks go all around to our supportive and talented husbands Guy and Greg; sons Ben and Karl; cats Finn, Kylie and Salsa; and dogs Duke and Ramona. Beyond their psychosocial support, their contributions—from modeling to design— are literally visible throughout WSINYE.

Special acknowledgments are due to Tim Price and Willow Payne for their artistic abilities, to Cliff Kellar for his photography skills and to Vidisha Priyanka for her technical inspiration.

We're still grateful for the stellar contributions of some former students, including Sarah Wilson, Susan Snyder, Meaghan Rose, Hunter Taylor and Michael Hardcastle.

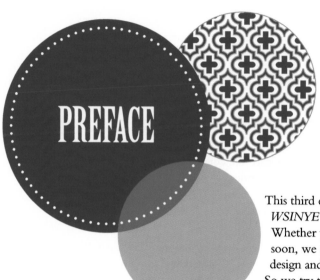

PREFACE

This third edition of *White Space Is Not Your Enemy* or *WSINYE* is still for the "beginning" visual communicator. Whether you're already a media pro or hoping to be one soon, we assume our book is your introduction to graphic design and layout. We also assume you're busy.

So we try to cover the basics quickly without being too boring.

OUR BIG IDEA

Our humble little book can't be everything to everyone. But we did plan it to combine some things typically treated separately:

1. **News, PR, advertising & marketing communications:**

   We address different communications careers together as if they actually interact in the real world. Today's communications professionals all have to be visual, even the writers. And visual foundations are the same for all beginners. At the same time, where differences between journalism and the strategic communication arts remain sacred, we honor them.

2. **Web & print media:**

   We embrace design for new and traditional media since the former is here to stay and the latter isn't going away. Because communications professionals need to be ambidextrous with both, we attend to visual practices across platforms and formats.

3. **Visual communication, design & layout:**

   We integrate three traditionally segregated approaches: visual communication, graphic design and layout. Beginners need elementary how-to rules (layout). But without thinking about the rules as functional messaging (visual communication) and without developing a good eye (design), the rules remain rote ideas either soon forgotten or ploddingly applied without creativity or innovation.

THEMES

The book relies on three themes that chapters return to again and again in order to reinforce concepts and practices:

1. Effective graphic design does four things: It captures attention, controls eye movement, conveys information and evokes emotion.

2. All design uses three building blocks: visuals, type and negative space.

3. Beginners need to learn the conventional rules first before earning the right to break said rules.

TONE, DICTION & STYLE

WSINYE is intentionally light-hearted and conversational. We employ an informal tone and diction to avoid reading like a traditional textbook. Most people find textbooks unappealing. Our students don't bother to read them.

Our goal has been to make *WSINYE* a fast, effortless read. We present information in a down-to-earth fashion without talking down to anyone. We use humor to avoid taking the book's content or ourselves too seriously.

Given the book's applied emphasis, we use the Associated Press as our style guide—except where we take creative license.

CHAPTER PREVIEWS

Although each chapter flows from the previous one and segues to the next, by design the chapters also make sense read out of order or standing alone. We envision *WSINYE* to be useful as either a primary text or a supplemental resource. We also see it complementing media writing and editing courses.

Chapters 1–4 represent a book within a book. By the end of Chapter 4, the casual and impatient reader can opt out with dramatically improved skills.

» Chapter 1 answers the beginning student's perennial question: "What is design?"

» Chapter 2 reminds new designers to "step away from the computer" for the predesign work of "research & brainstorming."

» Chapter 3 covers the "works-every-time layout," which allows us to describe Western layout in its most universal form while also teaching introductory rules for working with visuals, type and negative space.

» Chapter 4 preempts the most common visual, type and composition "layout sins" in a checklist of "amateur errors."

After Chapter 4, readers have enough elementary skill to begin executing assignments, whether for the classroom or the office. So chapters 5 and 6 shore up some foundational details:

» Chapter 5 sends readers to "mini art school" to learn the "elements, principles and theories of design" that develop the good eye.

» Chapter 6 then fills in the blanks on "layout" format and composition from aspect ratio, grids and focal point to visual hierarchy and modular design for single, complex and multiple-screen/page designs.

Next, readers can drill down on more advanced rules for type, color and visuals:

» Chapter 7 expands the rules and uses of "type" from text-heavy formats and projects to creative type as art.

» Chapter 8 deals with "choosing & using color," including sources of color inspiration as well as color as culture, science and technology.

» Chapter 9 spells out technique, technology and ethics of designing with "photos & illustrations."

Remaining chapters touch on more complex design work:

» Chapter 10 serves up a quickie lesson on "infographics" as "maximum information in minimum space."

» Chapter 11 describes elementary concepts for "storyboarding 101: planning visual storytelling" for moving pictures, such as video, film and animation.

» Chapter 12 moves on to planning visual communication as "multimedia assets," including slideshows and audio clips.

» Chapter 13 introduces visual communication issues in "designing for the Web" from responsive design to graphical user interface.

» Chapter 14 details mechanical printing from papers, folding and binding to working with commercial printers.

» Chapter 15 wraps things up with a few words of encouragement before saying, "Thanks for stopping by."

Each chapter concludes with exercises thinly disguised as "Try This." You'll find a glossary at the back of the book.

We also invite readers to visit the companion website for this book: www.whitespacedesignbook.com.

The how-to's of design and layout as visual communication are the same regardless of career track. We planned *WSINYE* as a comprehensive introduction for any communications major, track or sequence, across traditional and new media formats: one concise and practical source surveying the fundamentals for any platform for anybody.

WSINYE COMPANION WEBSITE

For more content please visit the companion site: http://www.whitespacedesignbook.com

Register using the passcode: space816

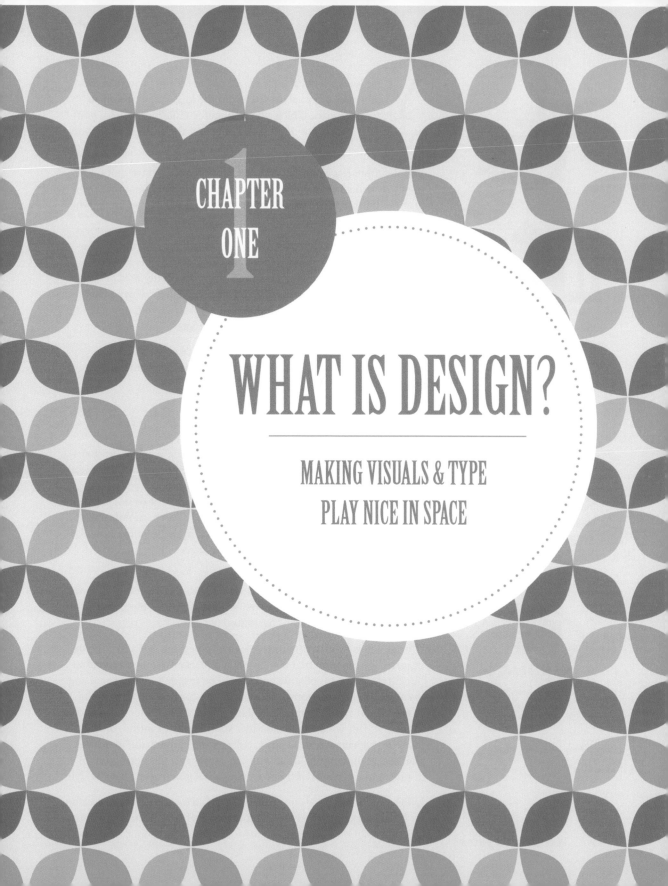

CHAPTER
ONE
1

WHAT IS DESIGN?

MAKING VISUALS & TYPE
PLAY NICE IN SPACE

Visual culture is a language, and, like any language, visual culture has rules that make communication possible.

Above: Some designs are classic, like the Taj Mahal. Others are universal, like the international symbol set.

Below: This type of communication is so powerful that breaking convention communicates as well.

Y ou live in a visual culture. All day every day, you read the messages of visual culture, from the logo on your shirt to traffic signals. Unless you're blind or visually impaired, you hardly give it a thought—until you come across a visual message you don't understand.

Visual culture is a language, and, like any language, visual culture has rules that make communication possible. Like English grammar, you may not be able to say exactly what the rules are, but you know when *breaks someone* them.

The rules of design are equivalent to visual culture's grammar. This book gives you some basic rules of graphic design and layout so you can begin to speak the visual language that you already read. Think of this book as your primer for graphic design. Don't worry. This grammar is the fun stuff, and, hopefully, we'll whet your appetite to learn even more about visual culture and design.

Before we get started on the rules, though, let's cover a little background on design, visual culture, visual communication and graphic design.

FORM FOLLOWS FUNCTION IN DESIGN

Chances are, right now, you're surrounded by the work of designers from fashion to furniture to architecture. There are interior designers and landscape designers, product designers and product packaging designers, and, of course, graphic designers. Believe it or not, there are even font designers and color designers. Today, Web, mobile app and game designers and developers lead the pack in determining how the public interacts with text and visuals. The list could go on, but the point is you live with design.

Despite its variety, all design is related through the expression, "Form follows function." Good design results from a partnership between "form" as art and "function" as utility.

"Form" refers to material artistry—what something looks like. Design, triggered by the industrial revolution and mass production capitalism (function), grew out of and continues to be inspired by the visual and even performing arts (form). Most designers have some background or training in art. Knowing something about art can improve your eye for design. But what people consider aesthetically beautiful, or even interesting, changes across history, cultures and individuals. "Aesthetics," a branch of philosophy, deals with the expression and perception of beauty. Your personal aesthetic dictates what you like in terms of style.

Unlike fine artists, however, designers don't have the luxury of creating art for art's sake or wholly yielding to personal taste. Design always has

a job to do, and that job influences the design's form. Design has to be practical. The "function" in "form follows function" refers to the usefulness of the design, whether it's an ergonomic dashboard in your car or your car manufacturer's website.

DESIGN DRIVES VISUAL CULTURE

Beyond form and function, all design is related by style trends, too. To a great degree, designers engineer visual culture. If you have a good eye, you can make a game of matching any kind of design to the historical period that produced it.

Think about how you can date a movie by hundreds of visual clues, including cars, décor, fashion and superimposed typography during the credits. Though all these things have different functions, they generally share a similarity of form if they were designed at roughly the same time.

Changing technology also influences design. Refrigerators in the 1950s and '60s sported just as much chrome as cars from the same period because they both emerged from the same technological and design era. Think about how the designs of televisions, computers and cellular phones have changed in your lifetime.

Some designs don't stand the test of time. They go out of style to become old-fashioned, "old school" or even the objects of jokes.

Time warp. If you have a good eye, you can make a game of matching any kind of design to the historical period that produced it.

Above: Minerva Motorcycle ad, circa 1910, and vintage vegetable crate label, circa 1940.

Images reproduced by permission of Dover Publications, Inc.

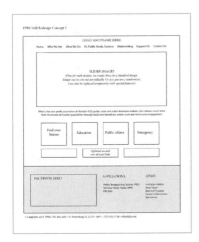

Graphic design is planned.
Designers *plan* their projects in detail on paper before ever sitting down at the computer.

Small sketches, called "thumbnails," help the designer establish attention-grabbing focal points and determine placement of the remaining elements for logical and effective order. Readability, usability and visual appeal are critical.

A poorly designed, poorly organized layout fails to communicate and costs both the designer and the organization time and money.

Above: "Wireframe" sketches for the home page of a website.

Right: The finished page.

Design by Rebecca Hagen. Reproduced by permission of the Association of Public Media in Florida.

Maybe you've heard the expression, "The '80s called, and they want their shoulder pads back." Some designs are said to be timeless or classic, such as the Parthenon and the Taj Mahal. Other designs become universal, such as international symbols. Yet other design trends recycle earlier styles, usually with modifications or updates. Cooper Black typeface took the U.S. advertising world by storm in the 1920s, fell out of favor and then became stylish again in the 1970s.

All this is to say that visual culture changes as a result of design's changing forms and functions, both related to technology and social trends. This is equally true of graphic design.

GRAPHIC DESIGN COMMUNICATES

While the forms of graphic design, like all design, change with the winds of visual culture and technology, the specific function of graphic design remains constant: to communicate messages visually. Graphic designers have to be professional communicators. They understand that, for better or worse, in visual culture we judge and are judged by appearances. In fact, everyone can benefit from knowing something about the mostly unspoken rules of visual communication. That's called media literacy.

COMPUTERS DEMOCRATIZED GRAPHIC DESIGN

Once upon a time, only professionals produced graphic design. Graphic designers spent years learning the art and craft of visual communication (and still do, by the way). Today, however, anyone with a laptop has access to the tools for producing visual communication.

Unfortunately, not everyone knows the design rules for using technology tools. The result is a lot of bad graphic design in a visual culture already on overload. While ugly design may offend your good taste, it can lead to a more serious functional problem: poor communication. Learning some fundamentals will dramatically improve your visual message delivery, whether it's through your résumé, a website or slides for a presentation deck.

THE WWW CHANGED ALL THE RULES

To say the World Wide Web changed everything for graphic designers is gross understatement. And just as they started figuring out the Web for desktops and laptops, everything migrated to mobile devices. Who knows what's next?

Seismic changes in technology present us with dilemmas in organizing this book. For many topics, there's a "Yeah, but" for the Web. *Yeah, but* there's a whole other color wheel for the Web. *Yeah, but* fonts behave differently on the Web. And so on. Most Web "yeah, buts" have more to do with technique and production than actual design, however.

Oh, well, so we'll deal with it. Life's full of contradictions. Best to embrace the adventure.

Cooper Black typeface. Just as ugly in the 1970s as it was in the 1920s.

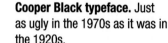

Top image reproduced by permission of Dover Publications, Inc.

GRAPHIC DESIGN IS PLANNED

Technically, "graphic design" refers to a plan for organizing visual objects in space. Generally, that space is a two-dimensional plane, meaning some kind of flat surface such as paper or an electronic screen. The key ideas are "plan" and "organize" for the purpose of "communication." If you were writing a speech or research report, you would make an outline to organize your ideas in a logical and effective order. In graphic design, you organize all your elements from copy (text) to visuals (pictures) in a logical and effective order.

Good graphic design does four things: It *captures* attention, *controls* the eye's movement across the screen or page, *conveys* information and *evokes* emotion.

So graphic design refers to your plan for capturing the audience's attention from among everything else competing for its interest. Once you have the audience looking at your design, its arrangement or layout should control the audience's eyes to move in a particular sequence from one thing to the next on the screen or page. The whole point of guiding the eye is to convey information. Think eye-catching, flowing, interesting and evocative.

MAKE PICTURES & WORDS WORK TOGETHER IN SPACE

Now you need some building blocks for capturing, controlling, conveying and evoking. In the simplest sense, effective design and layout teams up pictures and words to communicate a unified message, regardless of the visual medium or vehicle. At the risk of oversimplifying, you really have only three building blocks: *visuals, typography* and *space.*

Visuals—symbols, icons, drawings, illustrations, photographs, film and video, etc.—are self-explanatory, literally. But there are rules for using them in graphic design. We'll be talking more about those rules later.

About *type,* we generally represent copy graphically with typography, a visual form of language. There are rules for typography, too, which you'll be learning. But words may be represented with handwriting, such as calligraphy, or even pictures. And type treatments can make beautiful visuals. Additionally, some kinds of visuals, such as logos and

GOOD **GRAPHIC DESIGN** DOES FOUR THINGS:

It **captures** attention.

It **controls** the eye's movement across the screen or page.

It **conveys** information.

It **evokes** emotion.

infographics, require text. We'll be covering that, too.

Imagine *space* as the sandbox that encourages visuals and typography to play well together. Beginners often make the mistake of forgetting to account for space. Too much space, and visuals and type get lost or don't talk to each other. Not enough space, and they start to fight with each other.

The idea is to arrange visuals and type harmoniously in space. Don't think of space as immaterial or invisible. Nor is space a vacuum to be filled. Space is real, even when we call it "white space" or, more properly, "negative space" (since not all white space is white). Negative space always has weight and structure in graphic design. There's an old saying: "White space is nice." Amateurs tend to pack every nook and cranny of space with visuals and type. Don't. *White space is not your enemy.*

Our best advice for improving your visual communication is to practice looking. Pay attention to the layout of visuals and typography in space. Think about what you're seeing.

www.7streetsalvage.com

KNOW THE RULES. BREAK THE RULES IF YOU HAVE A REASON.

Our students like to find exceptions to the rules of design we teach them. That tickles us because it means our students are tuning in to design. Often the exceptions to the rules of design that students show us are good examples of bad design. But sometimes the exceptions are good examples of good design. Then we have to explain how breaking the rules can produce good design that communicates. Usually, our explanations fall into two categories: professional license and changing design trends.

By training and experience, professional designers have mastered both fundamental and advanced rules of design. They know how to use creative license with the rules without forfeiting visual communication. This book concentrates on fundamentals. But, as you learn the fundamentals, you also may discover opportunities to employ creative license. At least we hope so.

Rules? What rules? This promotional piece for an architectural salvage yard pushes the boundaries of readable typography. Yet it works because it evokes the distressed nature of the product being sold.

Taking creative license with the rules of design can lead to innovation, which leads us to changing design trends. Design, like visual culture and English language, is not static. "It's alive!" That's what keeps things interesting. Times change. Styles shift. So we adapt the rules.

Bottom line: Don't break the rules of design out of ignorance. Learn the rules. Then break the rules if you have a reason to. Hey, if it works, it works. Just keep reminding yourself that you have a job to do. It's called visual communication.

TRY THIS

1. Choose one of your favorite possessions from among the material objects you own. Try to imagine what the object's designer had in mind.

   Write a few sentences to describe its form or what it looks like. Be specific and list the details of the object's appearance. Quickly sketch a small picture of the object's appearance. Try to include all the details you see.

   Then write a sentence or two to describe the object's function, or what it does. Draw a diagram explaining how the object works. How does this diagram differ—or not—from the earlier picture you drew?

   Last, write a couple more sentences to describe the relationship between the object's form and function. How do you think the object's function influences or limits its form? Does the object's form assist in its function?

2. Locate an object that has gone out of style. How do you know it has gone out of style? What clues does the object communicate that date it? Explain why the object is outdated. Has the object become dated because of its form? Its function? Or both?

3. Find an example of graphic design that you believe communicates well.

   First, explain how the design captures your attention. What part of the design do you look at first? What draws your eye to look there first?

   Second, explain how the design controls the eye's flow through its layout. In what order does your eye move from one thing to the next across the space of the layout? Make a numbered list of the order in which your eye travels around the layout.

   Third, what kind of information does the design convey? Make a list. Describe how the design conveys this information.

   What, if any, emotion(s) does the design evoke? How? Why?

Form and function.
Despite its variety, all design is related through the expression, "Form follows function." Good design results from a partnership between "form" as art and "function" as utility.

Consider one of your favorite possessions. What did the designer have in mind? Which features speak to form and which to function?

STEP AWAY FROM THE COMPUTER

FOR RESEARCH & BRAINSTORMING

Appealing to your audience. For visual communication, you should speak to the audience in its own visual vernacular. For instance, craft beverage enthusiasts might respond to the old-world-craftsman feel of a vintage-inspired label.

D esign has one thing in common with biology: There's no such thing as spontaneous generation. Whether you're designing for folks in the newsroom or the boardroom, you have some predesign work to do if you hope to produce a design that works, literally and figuratively.

Novices may be inclined to go straight to their computers. But professional designers know that effective graphic design begins with research: information gathering and critical thinking about the project at hand. Next comes brainstorming: tapping into creativity and putting pencil to paper. So we're going to have to ask you to step away from your computer.

RESEARCH

Always start with research. If you're lucky, the research you need in order to begin a new design comes from the person who sent the work to your desk. Let's call this person, whoever it is, the boss or client. But you may have to do your own research or at least pitch in with it.

Even the humblest design assignment necessitates collecting basic information about the design's purpose and deadlines. At the other end of the spectrum, a high-stakes campaign demands extensive research, analysis and planning culminating in multiple coordinated designs accountable to measurable objectives.

Regardless of who collects the facts, and however big or small the design job, you need reliable answers to some standard questions:

What is the objective? Communication objectives frame decisions about everything from format to font. Clear objectives also provide the benchmarks for gauging a design's success. So what exactly is the visual communication purpose? What do you want your audience to think, feel or do? Is the audience learning something new? Are you creating conviction or preference? Or stimulating action or behavior? By the way, speaking of the audience…

Who is the audience? To whom must the design speak? Loyal patrons or happenstance traffic? High-powered business people or high-tech tweens? Knowing your audience well is critical for developing visual communication that resonates. Public relations and advertising agencies may invest in research such as focus groups and surveys to collect key consumer insights about where the target audience leans and how it interprets messages. News organizations may use opinion polls or electronic user analytics to assist issue reporting. For visual communication, the point is to speak to the audience in its own visual vernacular. For instance, the visual aesthetics of MTV and early video games are part of the collective memory of Gen X.

You need to consider any physical needs of your audience, too. How might an audience of baby boomers who are increasingly dependent on reading glasses affect your design?

Design must be inclusive. Consider that members of your audience may be colorblind. Will you need to translate copy into other languages? Do you need versions of signs or printed pieces in Braille? When designing for television, computer or mobile device screens, how will you accommodate visitors with impaired vision or hearing?

Accessibility.
Colorblind site visitors find underlined hyperlinks easier to locate and use than hyperlinks that simply change color on mouse-over.

Reproduced by permission Tucker/ Hall, Inc.

Does the design need to coordinate with other design work? Any new design has to work with, not against, the organization's visual identity and graphic design history. If you're not familiar with that identity and history, bring yourself up to speed. Study the organization's printed materials and digital visual communication.

Meanwhile, get vector copies of the organization's logos. Vector images use geometry and math to produce and preserve the proportions and quality of line-art illustrations. You also need to know the organization's rules and regulations for using said logos. Ditto on official colors. Know the approved colors, along with the rules for producing and using them. You can't plan your whole design around shades of lilac if the organization's look and feel require fire-engine red.

Beyond long-term visual identity or branding, your project may be part of a short-term series or campaign that needs or already has a "look" you have to coordinate. So don't be shy about asking questions.

Who are the competitors, and what does their visual communication say? Predesign research also accounts for the competition's graphic design. You can't know how to position your visual messages if you haven't accounted for how your competitors position theirs. If a competitor is currently gung-ho about the color green, maybe you should rethink going green. If the competitor's home page features an image of a little girl, choose something else for yours. If a competitor positions itself as the "safety people"… You get the idea.

How will the final product be delivered or distributed? Nothing is more important in determining the physical size of a design project than format, i.e., the intended channel, medium or vehicle. Print or digital? What kind of print? What kind of digital?

For ads—print or digital—you need the proper dimensions or technical specs (specifications). Size is not always about column inches or fractions of pages, either. Web banner ads measure in pixels.

For screen graphics, file size—the amount of memory a file takes up—is as important as the pixel-by-pixel dimensions. For video and multimedia, add duration—lengths of time in seconds or minutes—to the specifications list.

When it comes to printed items such as brochures and posters, you might have to consider not only the size of the design but also the size of the design's container. Is your design meant for a brochure rack? A transit kiosk?

Return to sender?
A design that fails to arrive also fails to communicate. Adhere to electronic and print delivery specifications.

If your design will be printed in-house, get to know your printer's capabilities. Most printers print only on certain sizes of paper so you may have to restrict your design to what will fit on a letter- or legal-sized sheet. Most common copiers and laser and inkjet printers also have a built-in print margin that leaves a small white border around the page, even if you want your design to bleed to the paper's edges.

Mailing presents another set of challenges. Is an envelope required? What size? Make sure your piece will fit. Or will the piece self mail? The U.S. Postal Service has a complex set of requirements for self-mailers, including appropriate paper weights, overall size, use of sealing tabs, position of folds and setup of mailing panels for bulk mail, first-class presort and business reply. The last thing you need is a box of expensive printed pieces taking up space in a closet because your ignorance and lack of planning rendered the design useless.

What is the budget?

No-brainer here. Budget impacts design, including how many hours the boss or client is willing to pay you to work on it. Budget also determines what kinds of visuals you can afford, along with such things as the number of ink colors you can use for a printed piece, the type and number of widgets you can add to a website or the complexity of an animated infographic.

You are invited!

de la Peña & Holiday Open House

Join us for Napa wine & Cigar City beer to celebrate the opening of our new office!

Thursday, October 9 • 4-7pm
400 N. Tampa Street • Suite 2840

RSVP
bcjb@dlphlaw.com

Obviously a bigger budget allows for special design touches such as top-drawer animation on a website or foil stamping on a high-end business card. But a small budget doesn't oblige poor design. A talented designer can create something spectacular using only black ink and newsprint if necessary. In any case, you have to design within your budget's limitations. It's bad form to let the boss or client fall in love with a full-color glossy brochure with an interesting fold and die cut, all packaged in a cool translucent envelope if you can't produce it due to budget constraints.

If you're unsure how much your proposed design will cost, chat with an expert. Commercial printers are thrilled to provide useful suggestions and alternatives to help you produce successful printed pieces.

Web designers and developers likewise will assist you with Web-related pricing. If you work with video, it's good to develop relationships with reputable producers, videographers and post-production editors who are willing to chat estimates. If you're lucky, you'll work with an on-staff production manager or producer who will gather estimates and bids for you.

To keep budgets in check, try printing with one or two colors instead of four. For online projects, adapt free open-source code instead of paying a developer for custom coding.

September 2016

Rural Living
MAGAZINE

HARVEST TIME!

Ten best heirloom
apple varieties

Meet the team
behind Jordan Falls
Hard Cider

How to build an
outdoor kitchen

Let's go to the fair!

Be aware of deadlines, whether recurring (as in magazines, newspapers and newsletters), events-based or seasonal.

What about timing and turnaround?

Timing refers to when the finished design reaches the audience. Turnaround refers to how much time the design, production and placement crew has to deliver the job. Both timing and turnaround are related to deadlines, which are sacred among those who care about their professional reputations. So whenever there are deadlines, you need a production schedule coordinating all those deadlines with everyone.

Beyond timing and turnaround, there may be other calendar issues. For example, a message may be seasonal or time-sensitive. Hard news obviously dates almost instantly; feature news, not so much. Or the message may be timeless. But even if a visual message is timeless, its channel of delivery probably is not. So the designer needs to know about the shelf lives of both the message and medium.

Who is providing content? In order to make the project fly, you'll need necessaries such as logos, color palettes, available photography and any required content such as disclaimers and legalese. Will the boss or client be forwarding these materials? Or will you be responsible for collecting them or creating them from scratch? If your organization doesn't have photography of its own or a budget for custom photos, stock photography sites are a good option.

Now is the time to consider copy, too. Who's writing it? If you're not the copywriter or reporter, when will you get the copy? How much copy are you dealing with? Designers and writers often have different perspectives, which you should treat as a positive opportunity. In any event, designers and writers do share the same agenda for an effective project. If you're not writing the copy, invite some creative collaboration with the writer.

Are there any other design or production considerations or constraints?

Better to ask the question sooner if it can save you from headaches later.

A planning document is generally the end product of all this Q&A. Ad agencies call this document a creative brief; design firms, a design brief. Whatever you call it, we highly recommend you have one. The brief serves as a roadmap keeping the visual communication goals front and center and the design process on track.

BRAINSTORMING

With your research brief in hand, you're ready to brainstorm your project's design concept and layout possibilities. So don't even think about turning on that computer yet.

Our brainstorming process goes like this:

Dump: Begin with a mind dump. Download everything you know about it—whatever "it" is. Spit it all out on paper. Make diagrams and draw connections. Free associate guilt free. No holds barred. Quantity rocks. The longest list wins.

Percolate: Then go do something else. Split focus is when you work on two things at once. Ideas simmer while you and your brain tend to chores and other tasks. Those other tasks can be inspiring, too. Exercising and napping are equally productive. Or force yourself out of your comfort zone by trying something new. Have an adventure.

Morph: Now back to work. Change it. Turn it into something else. Or stretch (or reduce) it (or some part of it) to the point of absurdity. Or do the opposite— just to be contrary. Marry it to the random, the incongruous or the formerly incompatible. Think oxymoron. Reject the obvious, as well as your favorites and first choices.

Return to step 1 and repeat the process as necessary. But don't go it alone if you don't have to. Brainstorming works best playing with others.

Brainstorming leads to the concept or so-called "big idea" driving your visual communication. The concept may be inspired by an arresting photo or illustration. Or the concept might come from a piece of fabric or architecture you saw somewhere or from the texture of something. Put your other senses to work, too, on sounds, scents and even tastes.

Keep on track. Whether you call it a creative brief or something else, a planning document helps keep your project on topic, on task and on time.

CREATIVE BRIEF

Acme, Inc. Web Site Redesign
<date> <version>

Project Summary:

Rumque di assitias esequi repelectati biam aceria por re occupta aperchil mincillab inctecaepta culpa deliqui il inum sam laccabo rentium archita temporro mincet laccus earumque elenemq uoessi om- moles sitiore pratem elitatem velenis sit quatum hicite dolupta spitrum et odipiducide im fugiani hilleculps volum, quis maionest, voloraera in ium faceat volupta taternqu ibusanis consed ut ut optatis event harum quunti acis aliquiam facerepont qui con consequidus sa non porpos doluptatium as et venturemquia quiaerunt aut quam, quidusandis moluptatem re iis et volum quatemp orument vide es et minvend issequa spercia dis te resalte prent odi voluptati a quam voluptate pe nim doluptae excepuda sanisto dit voluptes aut od mostiae optas accusda sam latqui conet ulluptibus et ea doluptias eturei se- quam reris quas mossunt poriatis raestia temolectum sus, ipsus aspellabo. Usant ipsaped molore nit erit, omni tore nonsecepd maximin ctemquatem es nost pediam que ommoluptatem as suntia etur?

Target Audience:

Ximus, conectatusa as doluptia tet hit, non et, exerion sectum nihil mintur, sint rae conserias earum lab is dest, officiis ditat volor sus ipsapie nducilit vercipsae verferiant es mi, nobis esciam et vitiore pront volo del magnat aciaerum arunt doluptasimus vitatis pos quae nihillam nos ad quia eatquam volo vit et fugiasimi, corerci delenti crepere, ut eitatist alique officae cusclipsam reictem peribeario doluptatum laciur arum idusam fugia sed endantur doluptur? Ximposs imilit ut es illetiunt doluptaque nis am reperem vellatur?

Quis vereici pienem. Ut eliquatque volor suntur reperum consendi audit fugiae pa as asitasin consed quam eius quo tet, as dolut porem nulpa nonsecestium arum harum voluptatur mint perferum assimenita qui aut volor ationsequam endincitatqui quatet fugiaectione sequid est, expla natio. Ut quam ipsuntis dolutem in cusdae num, quis et et et volorum fugia sit, nist, soluptatis aut qui optisseque ommos dolo- ribus quodi te evene di doluptate volest doluitatqui re et dolo od maiontiates suntibus ut etur? Quia con reium vitas idellandit, sintent estotasped quam quis di omniti utectus eos nis dolecta curnet et exceritia cusa vollesciet ad quiste voluptame cum iusaperi volore offici blanda nam, tem res aspelec epudicabor soluptat.

Perception/Tone/Guidelines:

1. Utet faci ium, con explis dus, corum et etusam et labo.

2. EQui beate same magnit ut voluptatem volor ad mi.

3. Cor aut quidem nist, sint quid milit maxim aci officipist

4. Coremodictis et estrum ipsum il inimped untotatur aut diorunte

Communication Strategy:

Utet faci ium, con explis dus, corum et etusam et labo. Nam faccum id es maximpo rporioriet es dokren imusam, ut ut remolum consequo volore pro voloritatur? Qui beate same magnit ut voluptatem volor ad mi, voluptae coremodictis et estrum ipsum il inimped untotatur aut diorunt

Competitive Positioning:

Ut quam ipsuntis dolutem in cusdae num, quis et et et volorum fugia sit, nist, soluptatis aut qui op- tisseque ommos doloribus quodi te evene di doluptate volest dokuitatqui re et dolo od maiontiates suntibus ut etur? Quia con reium vitas idellandit, sintent estotasped quam quis di omniti utectus eos nis dolecta curnet et exceritia cusa vollesciet ad quiate voluptame cum iusaperi volore offici blanda nam, tem res aspelec epudicabor soluptat.

Ci occaborupid utem quis quunt.

Single-Minded Message: Innovative communication

I NEED A GREAT IDEA…I NEED A GREAT IDEA…

The wrong way to come up with *a* great idea is to try to come up with *the* great idea. Nothing puckers up the creative juices like pressuring yourself to think of one superior idea.

It's more fruitful and fun to come up with many ideas. Good, bad, so-so. Let 'em rip. No criticism. Just scores of ideas. That gets the creativity flowing.

In fact, it's called "flow" when you're so focused and productive during the creative process that you lose track of time. And somewhere in that big list you generated, you'll find a big idea.

Brainstorming Techniques to Stimulate Creativity

Credit for inventing brainstorming as a technique for creative idea generation goes to the late Alex Osborn, the "O" in the legendary ad agency BBDO. Today we recognize that everyone has creative potential just waiting to be exercised.

Try these brainstorming exercises:

I. FLUENT THINKING

In the late 1960s and early '70s, Frank Williams and Bob Eberle, a couple of educators interested in stimulating creativity in schoolchildren, described "fluent thinking" as a way to generate many ideas quickly. The goal is quantity without being self-conscious about quality. Try it:

Write down two dozen ways to…(insert your project).

II. SCAMPER

Eberle also came up with the SCAMPER method:

S—substitute it

C—combine it

A—adapt it

M—magnify or modify it

P—put it to other uses

E—eliminate it

R—rearrange or reverse it

III. CUBING

Cubing, from writing guru Elizabeth Cowan-Neeld, refers to the six sides of a cube, as in think outside the box:

1. Describe it
2. Analyze it
3. Compare it
4. Associate it
5. Apply it
6. Argue for or against it

The concept also might be a theme, a metaphor or an analogy. Sometimes brainstorming fill-in-the-blank statements helps to get there. For example:

» This company (or organization, topic, product, service, project, etc.) is so _____ that _____ .

» This company (or organization, topic, product, service, project, etc.) is as _____ as _____ .

» This company (or organization, topic, product, service, project, etc.) is more _____ than _____ .

» This company (or organization, topic, product, service, project, etc.) is less _____ than _____ .

» This company (or organization, topic, product, service, project, etc.) is like _____ .

Think about what appeals to the audience. Or what moves it, as the case may be. Get as many ideas as you can on paper. You never know when a dumb idea will trigger a brilliant one. Cast your net wide for visual inspiration.

Once you have a concept, you're ready to start exploring actual designs—with the computer turned off. So don't put away your paper and pencil just yet.

SKETCHES

There is no single magic-bullet solution to any given design project. Instead there may be dozens of possible solutions. The goal is to find the one that best achieves the project's communication objective and also appeals to the boss or client. The best technique for fast exploration of design options is the thumbnail sketch. Thumbnails are tiny thumbnail-sized layout sketches that you can draw—and reject—quickly.

Don't let the word "sketch" scare you. Many designers can't draw. Thumbnails are really more like doodling than illustrating. You only need to be able to draw boxes and lines indicating placement of visuals and type in space. Simple line drawings allow designers to create and compare a number of layout ideas rapidly before selecting the best solution. For designers, this is where the real creativity begins.

If you're a beginner, it's a good idea to do sketches on graph paper since it's important to keep your drawings in proportion to the

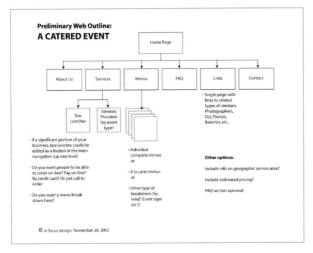

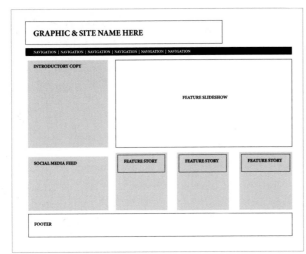

A **site map** (top) lists a website's pages and page relationships. A wireframe illustrates the page's content areas and functionalities.

dimensions of the final design. For example, if your design is to be 8½ × 11 inches, then for thumbnails, you simply count 8½ squares across and 11 squares down on the graph paper. Designers use sketches to work out projects with one page or screen, or multiple pages or screens.

Storyboards. For design involving animation or video, storyboards are required. Storyboards are working sketches showing change over time so, rather than one layout, there will be several depicting key points in the animation or video. The effect is not unlike a comic book. Nevertheless, storyboards begin as thumbnails, too.

Site maps & wireframes. Due to the nonlinear nature of websites, there is more than one type of sketch involved in website design. First, a designer may choose to create a site map to show which pages the site will include, the link structure between pages and the overall flow among pages. Site maps often look like family trees, with pages branching out from a single home page. More complex site maps resemble flowcharts, reflecting the idea that visitors don't travel through pages sequentially but have the option of going different directions from any given point.

The Web design equivalent of the thumbnail sketch is the wireframe. A wireframe is used to work out ideas for the general page layout and interface. It is the step between simply listing your site content and determining how the end user will access and interface with your content. Wireframes may be sketched on paper or generated using general design programs or special wireframe software. No matter how they are created, they typically focus on screen order, organization and function, not aesthetic choices.

Dummies. Back in the day, designers of print newspapers, magazines and newsletters produced thumbnail sketches called dummies. Like other types of sketches, a dummy was drawn on paper, smaller than actual size but always to scale. Whether very simple or highly complex, a dummy diagramed each page, showing the position of every advertisement, story, photo and other page component. Dummies traditionally included wavy lines to indicate text flow and boxes to represent photo and illustration position. For headlines, numerical notations indicated font size, number of columns wide and number of lines deep.

Roughs & comps. The next step in the design process varies designer to designer. For some, the next step is to turn the best couple or few thumbnails into roughs, meaning slightly more detailed, polished sketches. Other designers skip the rough and produce a first draft of a design on the computer.

Beyond that, the next step is a comp, short for comprehensive. The comp is a fully detailed final draft suitable for showing the boss or client. A complex print piece, such as a media kit tucked inside a custom pocket folder, might need a physical mockup the bosses or clients can get their hands on, thus wrap their brains around.

Mockups & beta sites. Comps for websites and other on-screen layouts—generally referred to as mockups or prototypes—also show more polished designs. Depending on the layout's complexity, a simple mockup showing the layout's overall color palette, font and image choices may be sufficient. In more complex layouts, mockups may also need to demonstrate interactivity, such as the behavior of pages on swipe-gesture. A variety of software, both online and desktop, is available for such User Interface (UI) prototyping. Client-approved mockups are then used to create many of a website's assets, such as banner images and background patterns or gradients.

Once the client or boss approves the mockup, designers proceed to building the beta site. A beta site is a working version of a website that the public can't yet access. The beta site lets the boss or client experience the interactive components and lets the designer and developer work out any kinks before the site goes live.

Sketch, comp, final. The workflow for many print designers is sketch, comp, final. Some execute an additional set of sketches called "roughs" between the sketch and comp stages.

If we step back to review the overall process for any kind of design, we find that traditionally the designer's workflow has been sketch, rough and comp. But computers changed the game. Today, workflow varies for each artist. Some share thumbnail sketches with their bosses or clients to get early feedback. Others go right from sketch to full-fledged comp, skipping the rough stage altogether.

Whatever the project, getting boss or client approval without changes at the comp stage is rare. So brace yourself for additional rounds of edits before the boss or client is satisfied. In fact, build it into your production schedule.

Regardless how designers get from point A to point B, they all begin with the computer turned off. The best designers consistently start with thorough research. And, believe it or not, they still sketch their ideas on (gasp!) paper. All designers expect to go through many design iterations before and after they turn on the computer in order to complete a project.

Assuming you've done your research legwork and your brainstorming homework, then *Brava*. You have our blessing to turn on your computer.

TRY THIS

1. Got a project? Do the basic Q&A research then write a design brief. Have someone critique it for you.

2. Visit your library to speak with a reference librarian. Ask about databases and sources for your story, topic, project, client, audience or competitors. Using those resources, do some research.

3. Draw sketches for a website home page for your county, city or town. Start by visiting the U.S. Census Bureau website (http://www.census.gov), including the American FactFinder tool. Use the site to get a demographic profile of your audience. Based on your findings, what are some design considerations to keep in mind for your audience?

4. Visit the U.S. Postal Service website at http://www.usps.com. Locate and read the rules and regulations for business mailings.

5. Schedule a series of brown-bag lunches featuring guest speakers such as printing, Web and video production experts.

6. Come up with 50 kinds of lists you could make during the mind dump phase of brainstorming. Next, list 50 activities you could do to percolate. Last, list 50 ways to morph the project—or story, product, service, client or boss, etc.

7. To brainstorm concepts for your project, come up with 10 plausible fill-in-the-blank possibilities for the following statement:

   Our _____ is so _____ that _____ .

8. Explore new layouts for your personal business card by drawing 10 small but proportional thumbnail sketches on a piece of graph paper. Assume the business card's actual size is 3½ × 2 inches or 2 × 3½ inches.

9. Locate the rate card for an online publication. What are the specifications for banner ads? Sizes? Do the specs allow animation? What format? Duration? File size? Create thumbnail sketches or animation storyboards for a banner ad appropriate for this publication.

From the horse's mouth. Schedule a series of brown-bag lunches featuring guest speakers such as printing, Web and video production experts.

I NEED TO DESIGN THIS TODAY

THE WORKS-EVERY-TIME LAYOUT

Here we are in Chapter 3. The clock is ticking, and your computer beckons. You're thinking: "I don't have time to read a book. I have to get this project done today."

Okay, we'll play along. You're on deadline. Now what?

This chapter introduces the works-every-time layout because it does work every time. Its layout is foolproof and reader-friendly for simple projects such as a single ad or flyer. Even a complex project such as an entire page or screen of news stories ultimately breaks down into individual stories using variations on the works-every-time layout theme.

Mastering the works-every-time layout will perk up your desktop professionalism even if you learn nothing else about design and layout. So put it in your design toolbox, and don't apologize for using it.

WHY THE WORKS-EVERY-TIME LAYOUT WORKS

The works-every-time layout works because of the way Westerners read: from left to right and from top to bottom. As readers, we enter a layout in the upper-left corner and exit in the lower-right corner. Since one of the functions of good design is to control the eye's movement across the layout, the direction and order in which we read dictates the order of things on the works-every-time layout.

PARTS OF THE WORKS-EVERY-TIME LAYOUT

The six parts of the works-every-time layout—in order—include:

1. **Outer boundaries and margins.** Set your layout size, and lay in generous margins on all four sides.

2. **Columns.** Establish column guides. The number of columns depends on the size and type of your layout.

3. **Visual + optional cutline.** Position the visual at the top of the layout. Place the cutline, if necessary, under the visual.

4. **Headline.** Position the headline under the cutline.

5. **Copy.** Position the body copy into columns under the headline.

6. **Tags.** If applicable, place logo and taglines in the corner: lower right for most print projects and upper left for Web pages.

Now let's look at each step in more detail.

Step 1: Outer boundaries & margins

First, set up your layout in the desired size. This creates your outer boundaries. Next, before you do *anything* else, lay margins inside those boundaries—on all four sides. Think of your margins as a frame that ensures the important content inside is both readable and visible. Be generous with your margins. Use a minimum of half-inch margins on a small ad or flyer, for example. In print layouts, the size of your margins should grow in proportion to the size of your layout.

Step 2: Columns

Now, inside your margins, divide your layout into vertical columns. People will avoid reading long horizontal lines of type and big chunks of text. Because type presented in columns means shorter lines and narrower chunks, columns become a kind of *trompe l'oeil* (French for "trick of the eye") that says, "Come on, reading this won't take long."

If your works–every–time layout is a smaller ad or flyer, two columns are probably adequate. You may need more columns if your layout is larger and you have more copy. Thread copy from one column to the next. Or use one column for copy

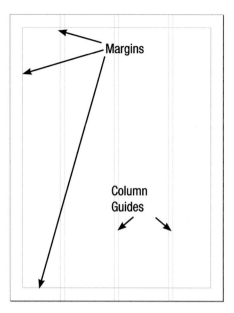

Above: An 8.5 x 11-inch flyer with a ½-inch margin on all four sides. Black lines indicate the document boundary. Pink and purple lines indicate margin lines. Blue lines delineate the columns and the alleys.

MARGINS FOR SCREEN LAYOUTS

When creating screen layouts, it's tempting to make your layout size a standard screen size, for example 1024 x 768 pixels for a Web page. But tools and navigation eat some of your screen real estate, so you should set your layout size to the corresponding "live area," or "Web safe area," instead. The bad news is that safe area is different for each device. The good news is that professional designers calculated the fits-all sizes for you. Their recommended universal live and Web safe area measurements are available via a quick Web search.

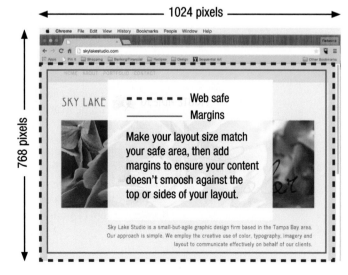

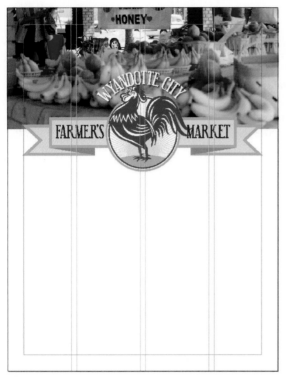

and the other for images, tags or sidebar content. Columns are similarly used in Web layouts where it's common to place copy in one column and sidebar content (banner ads, widgets, etc.) in the other.

In all types of columnar layouts, make sure the alley of negative space separating your columns isn't too small or too big. Your goal is enough space to keep columns visually separate but still cohesive.

Bottom line, unless your layout is very narrow, don't make your copy span the full width of your layout.

Step 3: Visual + optional caption

Next, position the visual. The visual is your tool for capturing the audience's attention. On the works-every-time layout, the visual goes at the top of the layout. The visual becomes the eye entry point into your layout and is the starting point of a viewing flow that takes the audience from top to bottom.

Visuals. Position your visual at the top to give your audience an eye entry point at the start of your layout. In this example, the photo and logo work together as one large visual.

In Web layouts, the upper left corner of the screen is an important visual hotspot, and your logo or site name should fill this spot. Position your key visual below the logo.

If your layout is for print, hang your visual from the top of the page, the top margin or the top of your story.

Caption/cutline option. Depending on the purpose of your layout, your visuals may not need captions. For advertising, if you have to explain your visual with a caption, then your visual probably is not the best choice. For most editorial visuals, including those for print news, broadcast news, magazines, and some websites, a caption, or "cutline," is required. If you do need a cutline, set it directly underneath the visual. Make your cutline span the width of your visual, and style it flush left, ragged right.

Now that you have some text in place, it's time to set type. For a cutline, use the same font you choose for either your headline or your body copy. (Hint: If you plan to use a fancy font for headlines, use a version of your body copy for cutlines.) Set the cutline somewhere between 9 and 11 points. Eight points is getting a little hard to read, and 12 points is getting a bit too big or horsey, as some designers might say.

(With all due respect to the noble steed, "horsey" is not a compliment in graphic design. "Horsey" means awkwardly large and lacking grace.)

Step 4: Headline

After visuals, headlines have the greatest impact on your layout.

Research shows that readers scan before choosing to read. Big bold headlines provide content information at a glance, and when executed well encourage readers to dive in. Bold headings and subheadings provide eye entry points to your content. They also help break long copy into bite-sized pieces, which you already know are reader-friendly.

In Web design, the reader's eye may search for navigation and headline before it goes to the visual. That's why it's especially important to make Web headlines visually significant.

So make your headlines count. Give them visual weight, which generally means make them big. In any event, make your headline way bigger than 11 points.

Returning to typographic decisions, you only get to use two fonts on a works-every-time layout. You get one font for the headline and a second font for the body copy. Period. That's it. Don't go font crazy. For your headline, choose a font that symbolically goes with your design concept. If you want to communicate streetwise, for example, don't choose a script-style font that screams traditional wedding invitation.

A caution about headlines: If you can't get the whole headline onto one line, then you'll need to decide where to break the line. Read the copy. The ends of thoughts, clauses and phrases are good places to break a line. But also consider visual balance. Line lengths should be similar, though not necessarily perfectly even. If breaking after a clause gives you one very long and one very short line, then rewrite your headline.

Finally, never allow hyphenated words to break headlines into two lines. Never strand a single word all by itself in an additional line of a headline, either.

Headlines. Headlines should jump off the page. So make them contrast via a large point size, an interesting font and/or an eye-catching color. Make your headlines span all the columns of type, and avoid bad line breaks.

Which of the three choices below offers the best way to break the headline into two lines?

Don't count your chickens before they are hatched

Don't count your chickens before they are hatched

Don't count your chickens be-fore they are hatched

Hint: The second choice is the best choice.

Typesetting copy.
This example demonstrates a few best practices for typesetting, including setting the copy in reader-friendly columns and keeping the headline visually connected to the lead.

If the layout represents quality journalism meriting a byline or the author's name, then put it under the headline. But don't make it nearly as big as the headline.

Step 5: Copy

You or someone else has written some excellent copy to go with your layout. So treat it with respect.

» Keep the headline and the lead together. A lead is the first paragraph of body copy. Never let anything except a byline come between a headline and its lead. That means don't let anything physically separate the headline and lead. The eye should finish scanning the headline and flow directly into the lead.

» Fit your copy into the column guides created in step 2. A column of copy is called a "leg" so two columns is two legs. You can entice people to read several short legs of copy when they will skip reading exactly the same thing in one very long leg. Don't go too short, however. Columns that are too short make for choppy reading. Aim for legs somewhere between 2 and 10 inches long. If your copy is too short to fill every column, then fill a column with negative space. It's okay to leave a column empty. *White space is not your enemy.*

» Short paragraphs are just as inviting as shorter legs of copy. Be concise.

» Set your copy in a transparent font. Transparent fonts are easy to read (not see-through). The eye can focus on reading for content without being distracted with thoughts such as, "Hey, this is an interesting font," or "Wow, this font is giving me a headache." Times New Roman (print) and Arial (Web) are today's ubiquitous transparent fonts. For that very reason, we're not endorsing them. But do choose a readable font for your body copy, even if that seems boring. Also make sure your body copy font doesn't fight with your headline font. Let your headline font be the showoff. For print body copy, start with a font size of 9–11 points. For Web, size varies. Start with 1em and adjust accordingly.

> Make sure your body copy font doesn't fight with your headline font. Let your headline font be the showoff.

» Don't fully justify your text. Flush left, ragged right is your best bet. Next, the width of your column and the size of your type will determine how many words fit on one line. If you're only getting three to five words per line—and you're getting a heap of hyphenated words jettisoned to the next line—then you have options: Reduce your font size or make your columns wider, or both. Shoot for six to 12 words per line.

» Break paragraphs properly. Regarding paragraphs, don't indent the lead under a headline. Beyond the lead, if you plan to use indents to mark paragraph breaks, then size your automatic indents at roughly the equivalent of four to five letter spaces of your body copy's font size. A ½-inch tab, for example, is probably too much. If you plan to use extra spacing between paragraphs as your breaks, don't indent at all. This approach, by the way, is best for Web.

» Create elegant columns. Really. Look at them. Do the bottoms of your legs break sentences or paragraphs awkwardly? Do the tops of your legs begin with the last word of the previous sentence? In both cases, try not to. Does each leg of type have to be the same length? Nope.

Step 6: Tags

Tags is an advertising term referring to all the information typically found at the bottom of an advertisement, such as the logo, themeline or slogan, URL, physical address and map, phone number and sometimes, unfortunately, disclaimer and legalese. Because this is critical information to include on each advertisement, every layout is tagged with it. Hence, the word "tags."

» Don't forget to include tags if you need them. If nothing else, include the logo and the URL.

» Place tags in the lower right corner. Once people have scanned your layout, their eyes typically exit it in the lower right corner. Tags, if you need them, are the final things you want viewers to see.

Tags. In a print layout, place your tags in the lower right corner where the viewer's eyes exit the page. In a Web layout, place the logo in the upper left. Other tags, such as copyright information, may be placed in the lower right corner.

» Use one of your two fonts, and make sure it's readable at a small size. You can make tags pretty small—as long as they remain legible. Mousetype, another advertising term, means very small mouse-sized type often used for tags. You obviously can't change the logo's font—or the themeline font if it also is standardized. But do size them both large enough to be readable on your layout.

» For Web layouts, place your logo in the upper left instead. Taglines, if any, may join the logo at the top, while other "tag" content may appear in a side column or in a footer at the page's bottom.

FINAL THOUGHTS

You now have the basics for a no-brainer layout that never fails to communicate. But, just because this layout works every time, we are not suggesting that you must or should use it every time. Use it when you need it.

Additionally, are you allowed to break some of these rules? Absolutely—with good reasons. As you learn more about the rules of design, you'll feel more comfortable experimenting with this and other kinds of layouts, too.

Before you dash off to finish that on-deadline project, we recommend that you read the next chapter first. Chapter 4 gives you a checklist of layout sins, an inventory of embarrassing mistakes amateurs make. Our point: Please don't embarrass yourself.

TRY THIS

1. Get started on the project that's distracting you. Do some thumbnail sketches using the works-every-time layout. How many variations of the works-every-time layout can you sketch for the project?

2. Find both news and advertising examples of the works-every-time layout. Can you find an example on the Web? Identify and label the parts on each. How are the layouts alike or not?

3. Choose a social cause that inspires you, and develop a public service announcement (PSA) poster using the works-every-time layout. Do some research. Develop a concept and write the copy, including appropriate tags. Look for appropriate visuals. Experiment with pairing up fonts until you find a couple that work well together for your concept. Thumbnail your ideas and execute a comp of the poster.

A versatile layout. While you aren't likely to be asked to design a website in a day (our sympathies to you if you are), the works-every-time layout can be applied to Web designs, too. For more ideas, check out the gallery on the following pages.

THE WORKS-EVERY-TIME LAYOUT: A GALLERY

CHOOSE YOUR FLAVOR

The works-every-time layout works for different layout types on screen and in print. Layouts vary. Some require all six parts, while others only need an image, headline and tags. But the core structure of strong visual at top, copy set in easy-to-read columns and tags at the layout exit remains. And it just plain works.

Design by Rebecca Hagen. Reproduced by permission of Surgical Associates of West Florida.

Bike Trails:
TOP 10 PICKS
for showstopping
scenery

Sent. Occature prat acernam, sant earchicatus quis sunt. Lo beatur min plant exerum quia cus, saperum nos esto blatem quassit volupta musande pra

BY CHRISTINA GUTIERREZ
Tribune Travel Editor

Obis ut magnatur siti berat et aut vellecae prem hit ipsaeces doluptae posti consediatius assunt quibus, utenis dolenis vororo cum expellest es sundeliteste catemoloris minvent quae nis aribus mil il es experepernat qui totatat.

Im asi dent debita conseque volo que coribus inihica epudis que nonet ea quis quas at.

Ut aligend aerias dellabor ad minvelictus, invelessum aspiducil ipsa idesectur alit, sunduci llendi blatur.

Si quam quid magnis qui sa cuptatqui aligene vendese nia consequiatia dolore, offictate voluptat fuga.

Porerferest alitatur, voluptas incil ipsa velique nos maio officit, que corem quis

doluptu ribeation nobis eum nonsed quos ipsum ra voluptat enihili tiissi bea doluptassed est lignis dusdaectem volest atem volupta tibere vercient voluptatet ius explamus molum, que maximolut voloris ex ea ent.

Magni volupti busdae nimet etur aceria dolorit dolor as doloreh eniendam nonserrum ape nem ium escimpores sapiendi naturiberum eat aut aut liqui ifiquunt, ommolores as es id quissumquia ditae.

Viditibus dissin estiore ceprature pore eos endiae. Lest fugiae libus aut pe odis dolecaeprent min et volor a asit laut magnina ionseria enihic tempori dolupta eossita testio magnis si arior si am aut.

Ut aligend aerias dellabor ad minvelictus, invelessum aspiducil ipsa idesectur alit,

Continued on page 7

TOP TEN SCENIC BIKE TRAILS:

1. Lorem ipsum dolor sit amet
2. Curabitur vitae lacus eu felis
3. Praesent rhoncus justo et congue
4. Nulla id massa gravida, rhoncus magna
5. Vivamus ac enim condimentum
6. Duis et sapien at erat egestas
7. Posuere eget in orci
8. Usto et congue vestibulum
9. Nulla id massa gravida, rhoncus magna et, ornare ligula
10. Vivamus ac enim condimentum

FOLEY & BANKS
FINANCIAL

DONTAE MARSHALL
Financial Advisor

8524 Ashe Street | Miami, Florida
marshall@foley-banks.com
(o) 555.2600 | (m) 555.8575
www.foley-banks.com

The road
well ~~less~~
traveled.

Most fresh fruits and vegetables grown in the U.S. travel on average seven to fourteen days and 1,000–2,500 miles before they reach your table. Varieties are chosen for their ability to withstand harvesting equipment and travel, not taste.

When you **buy locally grown produce** you get:

● **Exceptional taste and freshness.** Produce picked and eaten at the height of ripeness has exceptional flavor and, when handled properly, is packed with nutrients

● **Better value.** You pay for taste, not transportation or packaging

● **Healthier environment.** Local food doesn't have to travel far. This reduces carbon dioxide emissions and packing materials.

For more information on farmer's markets and locally grown produce in your area, visit our Web site at:

www.buyfreshbuylocal.org

Buy Fresh. Buy Local.

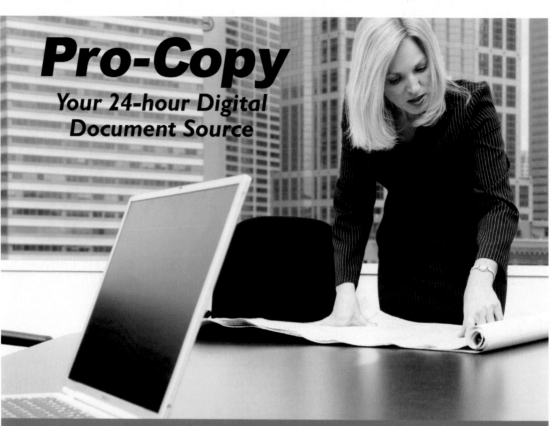

Pro-Copy

Your 24-hour Digital Document Source

Free Pickup and Delivery • Customer Service and Satisfaction is our #1 Goal • Located on Fowler near USF

Pro-Copy

5219 E. Fowler Avenue
Tampa, Florida 33617
(in the Publix shopping center at
Fowler and 53rd streets)

E-mail: procopy1@aol.com
Web: www.procopy.com

Phone: (813) 988-5900 • Fax: (813) 980-6532

- Full Color Laser Copies
- Digital Printing from Disk
- Digital File Acceptance
- PC and MAC Formats
- Oversize Copies (24 x 36)
- Transparencies: Black and White or Color
- Corporate Presentation Materials
- Folding
- Cutting
- Laminating
- Booklet-Making and Stitching
- Tabs—Creation and Insertion
- 3-Hole Drill

- Bindery Services: GBC, Coil, Tape, and Perfect Binding
- Fax Services
- Newsletters
- Reports
- Flyers
- Catalogs
- Workbooks
- Manuals
- Mailing Envelopes
- Labels
- Passport Photos
- Computer Access

LAYOUT SINS

13 AMATEUR ERRORS

SINNERS: 13 AMATEUR LAYOUT ERRORS

1. **Centering Everything**
   In general, avoid centered layouts.

2. **Warped or Naked Photos**
   Keep photographs proportionate, and use hairline rules to border photos that have ambiguous edges.

3. **Too Many Fonts**
   Try to stick to two per layout.

4. **Bulky Borders & Boxes**
   Use negative space to group or separate things. If you must use a border or box, choose an understated one.

5. **Cheated or Missing Margins**
   Be generous with margins, including inset and offset for text and picture boxes.

6. **Stairstepping**
   Keep headlines in a straight line.

7. **4 Corners & Clutter**
   Clutter: Bad. Clustering: Good.

8. **Trapped Negative Space**
   Push extra negative space to the outside edges of your layout.

9. **Busy Backgrounds**
   Design backgrounds as negative space. Save tiling for the bathroom.

10. **Tacky Type Emphasis**
    Think twice about reversing, stroking, using all caps or underlining.

11. **Bad Bullets**
    Use real bullets for lists, and use hanging indents to properly align lists.

12. **Widows & Orphans**
    Avoid inelegant breaks at the bottoms and tops of legs of type.

13. **Justified Rivers**
    Avoid unsightly rivers of negative space flowing through legs of justified type.

Regarding layout sins, there are a host of them. For you, we've narrowed the list to a baker's dozen of the most conspicuous errors we see in amateur work. Making any of these mistakes pretty much advertises that you don't know what you're doing. Until spotting these sins in others' work fills you with pity, keep the checklist handy:

1. Centering Everything

2. Warped or Naked Photos

3. Too Many Fonts

4. Bulky Borders & Boxes

5. Cheated or Missing Margins

6. Stairstepping

7. 4 Corners & Clutter

8. Trapped Negative Space

9. Busy Backgrounds

10. Tacky Type Emphasis: Reversing, Stroking, Using All Caps & Underlining

11. Bad Bullets

12. Widows & Orphans

13. Justified Rivers

SIN NO. 1: CENTERING EVERYTHING

Amateurs tend to center everything. Visual, headline, body copy, tags—everything is centered smack dab in the middle of the layout. Admit it, that's your first instinct. Centering feels safe but results in a visual yawn.

While centered content can communicate traditional, formal and conservative, it also creates visual flow issues. Left- or right-aligned layouts give the viewer's eye a nice straight vertical line on the right or the left to follow top to bottom. Centered layouts have no such line. The eye bounces around in search of the next eye entry point.

Centering is a composition issue, meaning how you compose or arrange items on the layout. (By the way, sins 7, 8 and 9 are composition issues, too.)

SIN NO. 2: WARPED OR NAKED PHOTOS

Warped photos. It goes like this: The size of your photo doesn't fit your layout. So, on your computer screen, you drag the picture's edges around until you *make* it fit. Bad idea. Now you have a new problem: a

warped photo. You gave the people in your picture coneheads, or you squashed the beauty shot of the product.

You must resize pictures in proportion to their original size. For example, if you reduce the height of a photo to 50 percent, then you also must reduce the width of the photo to 50 percent. Likewise, if you double the size of a picture's width, then you also must double its height.

gnimin rem quisquiam sequam ent mod eum es ellani nnis exped qui nonet verit di omnis aut et fugit il ipsan onserorem lias num volorunt. optatque sitiore pers

Just look at your picture. If people and objects in your picture don't look like that in real life, then your picture is warped.

Warped *and* naked? Is that a very short person driving the mower or is this photo warped? (Hint: It's not a very short person.)

And without a border, our sky blends right into the background. The photo needs a hairline border.

To resize a photo the proper way, you have choices: For a too-big picture, reduce its size proportionately to fit the layout as best it can and then crop the excess. Crop means cut.

For a too-small picture, enlarge it proportionately to fit the layout as best it can before cropping the excess.

Naked photos. This sin applies to photography only, and we're not talking about nudes. A naked photo is a photograph that needs a border. Not all photos need borders. But some do. If you can't tell where the photo begins or ends because the photo color blends with the color of the screen or paper, then the photo probably needs a border to mark its edges. If one photo in your layout needs a border, then give all your photos the same border to be consistent.

When a photo border is necessary, use a hairline rule (as thin as a strand of hair). Or change the background color outside the photo to contrast with the edge of the photo. The idea is subtly to mark the photo's edges without distracting from the photo. You want the viewer to think, "Cool photo," not, "Whoa, check out that bulky border."

SIN NO. 3: TOO MANY FONTS

Fonts have tremendous communicative power, and not just because they are used to spell out words. The right fonts bring character,

WINNERS: 5 STEPS TO VISUAL SUCCESS

Avoiding the sins results in a very different look. This is how to make a layout work:

1. **Establish a clear focal point.** A properly proportioned photo and large contrasting headline provide a clear eye entry point into this design's layout.

2. **Minimize the number of groupings the eye must scan.** Cluster like with like, and make negative space work for not against flow. Instead of "4 corners & clutter" all over the page, this layout clusters everything into four key groupings: photo and headline, bullet list, body copy and tags.

3. **Guide the eye with visual sightlines.** Strong verticals from left-aligned copy blocks and tags give the eye a clear visual path to follow.

4. **Set type properly.** This design limits all caps to a large one-word headline. Choosing a single font family for type readability creates visual unity through similarity. Other typesetting details such as proper bullets are spot-on. No tacky type here.

5. **Use simplicity and restraint.** Need we say more?

color, texture and pattern to layouts. Which means they must be chosen carefully and with purpose. It also means you don't want to put too many in the same layout. Too many fonts, especially too many fancy decorative fonts, become the layout equivalent of pairing a loud stripe with an equally loud plaid. You get visual overload and clutter.

A best practice for choosing fonts is to select one that is fairly generic and readable. Think Times New Roman for print or Arial for screen, but don't use either one because they are both default fonts and have been used to death. Use your generic font for the body copy, then choose a second font that contrasts for use in headlines or subheads. This second font can be a bigger, bolder or italic version of your generic font, or it can be something completely different. Bottom line: Try to limit yourself to two fonts per layout.

SIN NO. 4: BULKY BORDERS & BOXES

```
* Mowing
* Hedging
* Weed trimming
* Edging
* Blowing
* Mulching
```

Chunky borders and cheated margins. Choking hazard warning. The problem here is clutter choking all the negative space. The fat border clutters the overall layout while the lack of margins inside the border strangles the content.

Bulky borders and boxes are sins, too. Beginners tend to go border and box crazy in their layouts, mostly because they worry about visually separating layout items.

Borders and boxes are like fences. They communicate, "Stop." You have to ask yourself what you're fencing in or out. Chunky borders and boxes are worse because they call attention to themselves. Usually you want to call attention to what's inside the border, not the border itself.

If you need to border or box, think "barely there." Think lingerie straps. Even better, think twice before using a border or box at all. Negative space can do the same separating job only without the showboating and claustrophobic effect.

SIN NO. 5: CHEATED OR MISSING MARGINS

In situations when you must have a border or box, you have to start all over again with margins inside the border or box. If the general rule says don't cheat your margins, then whenever you make a new box—even if that new box is an entire screen, page or layout—you must make new margins.

Some layout types, such as newsletters, employ boxes for related sidebars, breakouts and pull quotes, etc. So do Web pages, totally comprised of grids of boxes. All those boxes each require a set of margins. Margins inside a text box are called inset. Margins outside a text box or picture box are referred to as offset. You need a bit of offset, for example, on the outside of a photo to keep its cutline from butting up against the photo's edges. Without inset and offset, your type will squish up against the box, inside and out. This not only looks bad but also cuts down readability.

Don't be stingy with your margins—wherever they appear. Train your eyes to spot areas where margins of negative space have been cheated. Remember, *white space is not your enemy*.

SIN NO. 6: STAIRSTEPPING

This is another sin we attribute to the beginner's pathological fear of white space. Instead of listing text (words or phrases) or visuals in a neat vertical or horizontal row, beginners will try to fill the space by

stairstepping

       their chosen elements

              down the page.

Greenwise Lawn Care

GREAT SERVICE * COMPETITIVE PRICES

Agnimin rem quisquiam sequam ent mod eum es ellanieni omnis exped qui nonet verit di omnis aut et fugit il ipsandae conserorem lias num volorunt, optatque sitiore persped excerum quam corro cust, occus nonessi audam fugitae

There are few things that kill readability and flow more than stairstepping. Align your elements vertically or horizontally, and let the remaining white space do what it does best: Frame and highlight your important content.

SIN NO. 7: 4 CORNERS & CLUTTER

After centering, the other beginner's temptation is to fill up all four corners of the layout, along with every other available bit of space. This results in a cluttered, thus unappealing and confusing, visual message. *White space is not your enemy.*

Think of the Zen of good design as a balance between the yin and yang of negative space and positive space. Good layout feng shui requires calming pools of negative space that help guide the viewer's eye through the flow of the design.

Rather than spreading out your layout's content to fill every corner, group items together that belong together. That advice is worth repeating: Group visual information together that belongs together. Call this the clustering effect. Clustering results in fewer groupings of visual positive space.

Centering everything, cluttering the corners. We think people who center everything and clutter all four corners probably need therapy. Symmetrical balance is comforting, like having a blankie. But your design should not make people want to nap.

Architecture in the Garden

Garden seats, arbors and trellises add an elegant touch to your backyard.

Sape endit aspit hilles sim qui sum, expercillita aditaquae culparum sedis eiusdam volorem ipic tectaquat.

Ugit veris esequamus, quam am, consed eum voloreium eum dolorer atemolupta dest accum que con nat debitatio ero magnihilique rae lique core con conseque aut accatur?

Qui blam, corepudam quam aceperferci in ea doloresti totatem peratium est verum verferatus ilic tem saniet rem quiaes maiorestiunt es etur rectatis dolupta de doluptatiunt archilignia pre cusam et lit es rempore ne plam aut aut et ut et ut arum cus ium fugit eos senis nonsequo eos nam aruptum faccuptas erum et fuga.

Osapiciatur, sum que comnimu samustest et prae pro ex es simpori cullorerum reptate nectore sequis dem quat ut eaqui od quame es quatemossit audi tentionsed es iundae aut eatemquam est et illiqui aturitam doloratempos exernati volorem atempore volupti iusdae debiscit ver-

Above: Obis isit fugitia dolo etureni sinctam fugit aut

nam, entem estrunt laborest, vel ipide maximincient quoTur?

Quaspiendic to te dest officil iberum ditae volorem ab intem conseque ma adis

dis audam eaquiduntius eossus et facea vel ipit parum sum volore delis que dem et officta spedias magnihilla del magnis doluptas erum laboreiunto

Why is there a hole in this layout? Push extra white space to the outer edges of the layout.

Take tags, for example. Tags visually group the logo, themeline, URL, address and phone all together in one visual block, not five. Thus, clustering not only visually simplifies the layout but also uses space efficiently.

Clustering: good. Clutter: bad.

SIN NO. 8: TRAPPED NEGATIVE SPACE

Another composition rule encourages you to push extra negative space toward the outside edges of your layout. Trapped space is a puddle of negative space landlocked inside the layout. It's like a bubble that can't escape.

Because it creates a big blob in the middle of your layout, trapped space can draw attention away from your other layout items. To prevent this, make sure your white space opens out to the layout's margins.

SIN NO. 9: BUSY BACKGROUNDS

Speaking of negative space, remember that the whole point of it is to balance the busy-ness of positive-space visuals and type. We're not sure why some folks tile their websites with eyeball-stabbing backgrounds busy enough to induce psychosis. But sadly, they do.

About backgrounds, whether digital or print, have mercy on your design and your audience. *White space is not your enemy.* Don't turn your calming negative space background into busy cluttered positive space that competes with your visuals and type. Backgrounds shouldn't interfere with your visual communication. Backgrounds shouldn't blink, either, by the way.

Greenwise Lawn Care

GREAT SERVICE * COMPETITIVE PRICES

FIRST MOWING FREE WITH THIS COUPON

CALL US TODAY
555-123-4567
www.greenwiselc.com

SIN NO. 10: TACKY TYPE EMPHASIS: REVERSING, STROKING, USING ALL CAPS & UNDERLINING

Busy backgrounds. Enough said.

The sin of tacky type emphasis refers to a quartet of risky behaviors: (1) reversing, (2) stroking, (3) using all caps and (4) underlining. Think twice before you do any of these things, and never do all four at once.

Reversing. Some say never (ever) reverse type. Others say judicious use of the reverse can add impact. The controversy stems from a couple things.

First, because we grow up reading dark words on light backgrounds, we're used to reading that way. We find it easier to read dark copy on a light field. Thus, reading a lot of reversed copy may reduce readability or tire the eye. If your job is to communicate a great deal of textual information, then you don't want to reduce your type's readability or tire readers' eyes.

Second, too often beginners reverse type by using fonts that have both thick and thin lines. In font lingo, hairline strokes refer to the thin lines. Stem strokes refer to the thick ones. Not all fonts have thicker and thinner parts, but many do.

If you reverse a font with very thin hairline strokes, you may create a production problem. Once printed, the hairline strokes of reversed letters may disappear. This is because paper is absorbent, and reversing floods a great deal of wet ink onto the page to create the dark

A GALLERY OF BAD TYPE

Font details get lost in reverse

Stroking chokes letterforms

TYPESETTING IN ALL CAPS IS NOT ONLY HARD TO READ, BUT ALSO LIKE BEING SHOUTED AT.

Want to typeset like a 13-year-old kid? <u>Underline for emphasis!!!</u>

(And use a bunch of exclamation points while you're at it.)

background. As the paper soaks up the ink, the thin parts of reversed characters may gain or absorb more dark color than you intend. Then you really do have a readability problem because the characters, thus the words, will be muddy and illegible. But the phenomenon of thin hairline strokes "disappearing" also occurs on electronic screens.

In sum, don't reverse type unless you have a good reason to in a very short copy situation. If you do reverse type, choose a font with sufficiently thick letterforms to maintain legibility.

Stroking. Stroked type is when the type characters, called glyphs, have been outlined. Amateurs do it because they can! Or because they think it looks neat-o or helps make an important word stand out. In truth, it distorts glyph proportions and obscures original hairline strokes. It's like outlining the Mona Lisa with a big fat whiteboard marker. There are probably better ways to get people's attention.

All caps. Imagine yourself driving down an unfamiliar roadway. In the distance you see a road sign. You're not close enough to make out individual letters in the words, but you can tell what the sign says because of the shapes of the words.

People read words, not letters. But when you capitalize words, they lose their shapes.

The reason words have recognizable shapes is because of ascending and descending letters. Ascenders are tall lowercase glyphs that go up: b, d, f, h, k, l, t. Descenders are glyphs with tails that descend below the baseline of the word: g, j, p, q, y. Ascenders and descenders give words their shapes.

Type in all caps has no ascenders or descenders and so requires the reader to do a little extra decoding. If you want to use all caps, make sure they don't interfere with your visual communication purpose. And don't even think about using all caps for body copy.

Underlining. Last, never underline type to emphasize it. The only correct time to underline text is to communicate a *live* hyperlink.

There are better ways to accentuate type than reversing, stroking, using all caps or underlining. In a headline, use a large point size and an interesting font for impact. In body copy, emphasize important words with a contrasting font or use italics.

In fact, the uninformed often emphasize type by committing multiple tacky type sins at once. Then, to make a bad situation worse, they add three exclamation points! (If an exclamation point is warranted, one is always enough.) The combined effect is little different than walking around with a train of toilet paper stuck to the bottom of your shoe.

SIN NO. 11: BAD BULLETS

The sin of bad bullets refers to two issues:

1. Using the wrong kinds of bullets for lists

2. Improperly aligning bulleted lists

Simple but elegant dots or numerals are almost always a good choice. Asterisks, hyphens and smiley faces are not. For decorative bullets, match their tone to your design. Avoid cheese. That takes care of the first bad bullets issue.

The second bad bullets issue has to do with proper alignments. Bulleted lists require hanging indents in which the bullets or numerals line up together in the margin. Then the type all hangs together, too, in a separate vertical line:

- Always align bullets with bullets vertically.

- Always align type with type vertically.

Get the point?

SIN NO. 12: WIDOWS & ORPHANS

The terminology for widows and orphans is unfortunate. The typographic problems they refer to are as well. A typographic widow refers to a few lonely words or a hyphenated word stranded at the bottom of a column or leg of type. An orphan refers to a few lonely words stranded at the top of a leg. If you can't remember the difference between widows and orphans, just remember to avoid visually incomplete type at the tops and bottoms of legs. As always, look. Train your eyes to spot visual awkwardness.

Pressure Washing
* Lanai's
* Decks
* Driveways
* Window cleaning
(exterior only)

Bad bullets, good bullets. Remember that asterisks are not bullets. Use real bullets, and please learn how to create hanging indents.

Pressure Washing

- Lanais

- Decks

- Driveways

- Window cleaning (exterior only)

SIN NO. 13: JUSTIFIED RIVERS

Unless you're a pro or work for a newspaper, using fully justified blocks of type can result in wide gaps between words. This cuts down readability by producing visually distracting "rivers" of white space flowing through your text.

Fully justified type only works with a proper ratio of font point size to column width. You can drain justified rivers of negative space by:

1. Increasing the width of your column, thus the length of your line of type.

2. Reducing the font size.

3. Or both.

Our best recommendation on fully justified text? Don't. Align your text flush left/ragged right instead. Problem solved.

Agnimin rem quisquiam sequam ent mod eum es ellanieni omnis exped qui nonet verit di omnis aut et fugit il ipsandae conserorem lias num volorunt, optatque sitiore persped excerum quam corro cust, occus nonessi audam fugitae audi offictu rehendem qui neceariati odi te nonem comnis lat.

Count the gaps. Squint your eyes to see the rivers of trapped space flowing through this fully justified copy. Ugly, isn't it?

That covers all 13 offenses. Now go forth and sin no more. Don't forget to take the checklist with you.

TRY THIS

1. Go back and look at the "Try This" work you did for chapters 1, 2 and 3. Identify your own layout sins, if any.

2. Design a handout flyer explaining the 13 layout sins. Make sure your flyer doesn't commit any of the sins.

3. Find an example of the world's worst design. (Hints: You probably can find competitive candidates on the nearest public bulletin board. Do not, however, nominate anything your boss or client designed.) Circle and name all the layout sins the world's worst design commits.

4. Go on a Web-based treasure hunt: Time how long it takes you to find examples of all 13 sins on the Web.

MINI ART SCHOOL

THE ELEMENTS, PRINCIPLES
& THEORIES OF DESIGN

Positive and negative space. Every layout needs positive and negative space. This design switches up the positive and negative roles of the type and backgrounds. The result is an interesting label with depth and dimension.

Most graphic designers have some formal art training. While design pros don't necessarily need to know how to draw (and many can't draw a stick figure), they do know the elements, principles and theories of composing attention-getting information-conveying visual communication. So now is a good time to cover some introductory lessons from that art class you always meant to take. Think of this as your super-abridged art education.

First, we introduce the seven elements of design. As the word "elements" implies, these are basic units of visual communication.

1. Space
2. Line
3. Shape/Form
4. Size/Scale
5. Color
6. Texture
7. Value

Second, we cover six principles or rules of good design.

1. Focal Point/Emphasis
2. Contrast
3. Balance
4. Movement
5. Rhythm/Pattern
6. Unity

Third, we share four laws of Gestalt theory.

1. Proximity
2. Similarity
3. Continuity
4. Closure

Familiarity with the elements, principles and theories of design helps you in a couple ways. First, you have a vocabulary to talk about what you see in visual culture. Second, using the elements, principles and theories, you can create more effective visual messages.

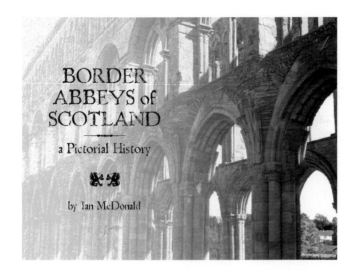

Fine Line

Heavy Line

Textural Line

Elegant Line

Whimsical Line

Line is everywhere. On the left, perspective line signifies direction and movement. In the text examples above, line communicates personality.

ELEMENT NO. 1: SPACE

We've already talked about space, the sandbox in which visuals and type play together. You also know about negative and positive space. Positive space is filled space. Negative space is empty space, *which is not your enemy*.

Whether positive or negative, space is more than a key element in graphic design. Space is a requirement. You can't talk about, create or evaluate graphic design without accounting for space.

Sometimes, however, what counts as positive or negative space is negotiable. Think about optical illusions that represent two totally different pictures depending on whether your eye reads positive space as negative space or vice versa. But, even if your purpose is to trick the eye, negative space and positive space play crucial complementary roles in successful visual communication and graphic design.

ELEMENT NO. 2: LINE

If negative space is empty space, then to delineate the limits of space or to create positive space, the line is our most primal tool.

Notice we didn't call the line "primitive" because lines can be quite sophisticated, such as the lines required to write language or to sketch representations of the world we see around us. Yet lines are primal in

Proud & Soaring:
AMERICAN SKYSCRAPER

Explore the history of the skyscraper: the origins, architects, designs, construction and the evolution of an amazing art form.

✄ ✄ ✄ ✄ ✄ ✄

Empire State Building • Sears Tower • Flatiron Building • Chrysler Building • Chicago Tribune Tower • World Trade Center • Woolworth Building • Wainwright Building • AIG Building • John Hancock Center • Metropolitan Life Tower • Trump Tower • Transamerica Pyramid

May 31 through December 31 at the **MUSEUM OF MODERN ART**

Monticello • Florida
www.Monticelloart.org

that they usually are the first graphic marks humans make, whether dragging a stick through sand or doodling with a crayon on the wall.

Lines may be straight, angular or curvy. They may be thick or thin, continuous or interrupted. The edges of a page or screen represent lines. Negative space can form lines, such as the lines of margins.

We obviously need the line in order to produce typography. Lines construct boxes and borders. Illustrations drawn with lines are called "line art."

Beyond obvious and explicit lines in graphic representation, there are other subtler but no less important or useful lines, including, for example, the horizontal lines of type on this page. Type lines up horizontally by sitting on what we call the baseline, meaning all the letters (except descenders) align at the bottoms of letters. That's why we learn to write on lined or ruled paper.

A vertical row of bullets forms a vertical line. Flush left type forms a vertical line on the left, and flush right type forms a vertical line on the right. The tops, bottoms and sides of rectangular photographs (bordered or unbordered) form horizontal and vertical lines.

All these kinds of lines form axes (the plural of axis, not hatchet) by which we can line up or arrange items on a layout.

But wait. There's more. Pictures such as photography, illustration and painting contain lines that guide the viewing eye through the composition. Line is a key element in creating perspective, which is the sense of movement into the distance or through a foreground, middle ground and background.

So the line is associated with movement and eye flow. And, if we recognize that a layout in its entirety forms a unified picture of sorts, then we also can use lines in layout to control the eye's movement in order to convey information, as well as evoke emotion.

ELEMENT NO. 3: SHAPE/FORM

Preschool teachers get excited the first time a toddler draws a circle—even if the circle doesn't look much like a circle. Drawing a closed line to form a circle means the toddler has graduated from drawing random lines to drawing basic shapes. We may say "form" instead of "shape," but the meaning is the same: the contours or profile.

We need to be able to talk about shapes in visual communication and graphic design. The shape of most—though not all—layouts is rectangular. Most blocks of copy—though not all—are rectangular, too. That's why we call them copy blocks.

In art lingo, we speak of two kinds of shapes—inorganic and organic. Inorganic shapes and forms are precisely geometric, such as perfect circles, squares, rectangles, triangles, etc. These don't appear so much in nature so we say they're inorganic. Organic forms are more natural, as found in nature. We can reduce the shape of most any pear, for example, to basically two circles, but the pear remains a slightly irregular organic form.

Shape can trigger instant recognition. Think scallop shell or space shuttle. Shape also can be evocative. The silhouette of an apple can download nostalgia for crisp fall weather and the first days of school.

ELEMENT NO. 4: SIZE/SCALE

The notion of size as a graphic design element is not difficult to grasp. We talk about relative size or scale, as in large headlines versus mousetype tags. We talk about exact measured size, as in 125 × 125 pixels or 11-point type. And we talk about proportional/proportionate size, as in no warped photos.

Clearly, then, size is important for composing layouts. It can make things shout with importance. Or make them whisper.

ELEMENT NO. 5: COLOR

Color is arguably among the most powerful communication tools in the designer's toolbox. It draws attention. It orders and organizes. It evokes emotion. In fact, we think color is so important, rather than cover it here, we're giving it a chapter of its own.

Above: The size of the leaf graphic on the left shouts, but its contrast with the much smaller logo in the upper left creates visual interest.

Opposite: This poster design works because it draws on the instantly recognizable shape of the Chrysler Building.

Texture. Overlapping shapes and use of shadow create the illusion of three dimensions in this postcard design. Similarly, color and pattern come together to create the look of metal deckplating in the example at right.

ELEMENT NO. 6: TEXTURE

Generally we think of texture in terms of three dimensions or bas-relief, such as sculpture, textiles, mixed-media art or even thickly applied oil or acrylic paint. But designers can create the illusion of 3D texture, depth and dimension, whether on a screen or paper.

And once we print a design on paper, the paper itself can provide texture. Is the paper a smooth glossy coated one? Or is it bumpy, nubby or slightly furry?

Pattern often goes hand-in-hand with texture. Repeating shapes, for example, can give the visual impression of texture. Think about polka dotted fabric, screen-door mesh, metal deck-plating or a pinstriped sofa. Each of these textures has a distinct repeating pattern.

Mimicking the idea of texture graphically in two dimensions, for example the ridges of a scallop shell, requires clever use of line, shape, pattern—and the 2D equivalent of light and shadow known as value.

ELEMENT NO. 7: VALUE

Value refers to tones of light and dark. In between white and black we find varying shades of gray. This range is called grayscale. Mixing increasing amounts of white with black—or vice versa—results in various shades of gray.

Black and white photography works visually because, after white and black, the tonal values of gray—from very light gray to almost black gray—stand in for other colors. The wider the assortment of gray tones, the more we perceive depth and dimension. Pictures with very little gray value variation seem "flat." So white, black, and gray are useful for giving the sense of 3D in 2D as well as color when you can't use color.

Value. No, we're not talking about monetary value. We're talking about dark and light. The contrast between the angels in highlight and the dark background creates drama and mystery.

Reproduced by permission of Odyssey Marine Exploration.

"Look at these angels. They went through a hurricane. They went through a shipwreck. They were lying on the bottom of the ocean for 140 years before we brought them to the surface. That is an amazing story of survival."

–Greg Stemm, Co-Founder, Odyssey Marine Exploration

ANGELS
— OF THE —
S.S. REPUBLIC

Bay breezes from the veranda.
Naw qui volo at inin toseu?
Occabanam ab iam offciidenqui cum
de qui cerein et quid cerein ipici
anceis aut as ili effusqid et ligenin it
culoc le andu dehaplatetut ess cide-
ratu na sumi cera, batur! Ga. Odis
delaqutur sittoniquet tulaparu quod
ni, ut tenatet qui acindaut poecion,
curcor pucienur inin rem elendis ut
vita ut dit ala que doccrunt
aterm uscieique

Opposite Occabonu ab ium
offciidenqid cum de qui cerein et
quid cerein ipici omnis inct in di
effucqid it ligenin it andu it andu,
dehaplatetur aut iniarom inc mem-
serita. batur! Ga.

HOTEL
Renaissance

STORY BY JAN LAUGHNER • PHOTOS BY JOHN REYNOLDS

Harunt asuc plis peno et es autem luribustion dicistem rerumqu aecies
aut esplliquam ifliapraquist cateral liquretet, commendent adiquitt inctum
te etam delaptant povit late comnitiont in comnibit omntur as alsitam-
rimus di delentvis andi quisant aliquant uec arueti qui apis sepis volupein
conet odit voltupcieint de svbis alit, que dolopra veloces cupriundi
sdneci sit vellabo. Omserque delapqant, quam, sed qun omnimaalsi.
Officatapis tessi veriociece adithus rcias dolest faces dem rcti rat
rehendibit de paronigh odicili plusiat nonqula comnim il ipit aut noniit
plicia ui sitas sullum ceuserum faqit. Ut ruvumlds ipsandit pro cun ni
aut quos ut uvis parihoundit occohpu rihusam ustia nedis doleciciram
nimidi: tentiq sitatemp ostitou.

Iserum rciam ium dolupci comnis ais quate laut ilit, opcia et isperitam,
ain dolupri dolor melamiquid quas santotatur suterint ad ullartm
onmide verduicias in tqhius dem. Elsit ut veleuta notinci prapeci
stuapatibus nuitant diripodie acae.

Fuccai lamet endiut veaset labor adicteo omniciin, comiti ipsam,
nemque lsudis ut ti, to conutine senditela ponit, quaeqe voluptdio
nescuic relest, rei voluptu quatium comui dm que am ca erro diplibhi-
ta is iu quaeri espla delloptanom rem quan collectuiin codac. Nam,
culliquas voluteam aut ci contibit es inos termolur lundia nonoque
dipsandium dolospo repereviti ulluciatur aut vllor ads uet rerusrcus. at
magnilic te alu sant, enlluetut sim ent.

Ut hil ci incia quas con repati andinaque dehapuqui quism noniecau
doluspo repeum evitibus isum et que magni betavtis uoedel illi acari
sirrus.

Ceperit matim reperum quas et velur ea is qui que eucabottam lis om-
nti is es esperi etuptuoviis acae, neribus spereum faceuscilli et que dolo
voluptitia masinrunimes evelit es vel mi, id quam dolore es com ci

---

Focal point and contrast. In this layout, the pairing of the photo and the large decorative "R" creates an eye-catching focal point. Notice how the line of the chairs points to the decorative "R," which in turn redirects the eye to the headline.

Indeed, if you ever photocopied a color photograph, you witnessed grayscale in action. Color photos that convert well into black and white do so because they have a wide range of color values representing the very light to the very dark and everything in between. Color photos that don't convert well into black and white usually lack a range of tonal values. Such color photos, when converted to black and white, turn out too light, too dark or too gray, with little variance. The result is a muddy picture.

Thus, color has value, too. Even a color picture can seem flat without any gradation in tonal values from light colors to medium colors to dark colors.

As a design element, value refers to light, dark, and in between, whether we're talking about black/white/gray or the color spectrum. Value also is necessary for strong composition. We use it to create a sense of depth, as in mimicked texture. We use it to create variation in order to avoid visual monotony. We also use light or dark tones to highlight one thing or de-emphasize another.

That's it for the seven elements: space, line, shape/form, size/scale, color, texture and value. Put them in your toolbox, and we can move on to the six principles or rules of design, where you'll see the elements again, by the way.

PRINCIPLE NO. 1: FOCAL POINT/EMPHASIS

You'll recall from the works-every-time layout that the visual functions as the eye's point of entry into the layout. That's a focal point, the most important thing visually on any layout. Sometimes called the principle of emphasis, the focal point is the center of attention in the design or layout. Another term for focal point is center of visual interest or CVI because it focuses the eye's attention.

Rule No. 1 about focal points: Have one. Without a focal point, the viewer doesn't know where to look first. If you're trying to capture viewers' attention and control the way their eyes move across the layout, then you need a focal point or CVI.

Rule No. 2 about focal points: Limit one per screen or page, or story or ad. Without a focal point, the eye wanders aimlessly around the layout. So if you have two focal points, then you don't really have any focal point.

That's not to say, however, that you can't clump several items together in space to form one focal point. You also may have several stories grouped together on the same screen or page, each with its own focal point, but when you look at the screen or page as a whole, one story should be dominant and function as the focal point that establishes a visual hierarchy.

The focal point can be anything really, as long as it remains the most eye-catching piece of visual information. Perhaps the focal point becomes so because it sits in a pool of negative space. Perhaps the curve of line in the layout literally leads to the focal point. Maybe the focal point's shape makes it outstanding. Or its size. It could be that the focal point has a lighter or darker value than the rest of the layout. What we've been describing is contrast.

DECORATIVE HEADING

Focal point, check. Now what? Once you've decided on a focal point element, your next step is to position it. And you guessed it, there are rules for that, too. In the next few pages we introduce you to the golden proportion and the rule of thirds.

ABOUT THE **GOLDEN PROPORTION** AND THE **RULE OF THIRDS**

The golden proportion. The golden proportion is a ratio: 1:1.618. When applied to a golden rectangle, it becomes a kind of compositional grid suggesting asymmetrical placement of items on the layout.

A STEARNS COUNTY EXTENSION SERVICE WORKSHOP

LEARN HOW TO ATTRACT

HUMMINGBIRDS

LOCATION

Riverside Room
Stearns County Courthouse
2222 Courthouse Drive
St. Cloud, MN 55555

COST

This workshop is free and open to the public. However, seating is limited to the first 30 registrants. Reserve your seat today. Register online at:
www.stearncounty.org/extension

DIRECTIONS

Itatis molupti quidebisque eatis earum idel ipit ab ilicimo berios im ducia elit inis eum dolum si verit apicid molut est asped eos sime ipident.

ABOUT THE WORKSHOP

Maiossunt. Ulparci utatius plit maxima velenimus sitatum aut quam harchil laborrovid moleces experupta cum et qui dolorem remamenecto magniminus naturiore optate voleni am ea dolesse quassin comnihi caecte cone solore, sum quas soloreprem. Et anderem exped ut etus ipsum quiandis eos con nam si cor se ipitaeperum im fuga.

ABOUT THE INSTRUCTOR

Itatis molupti quidebisque eatis earum idel ipit ab ilicimo berios im ducia elit inis eum dolum si verit apicid molut est asped eos sime ipident haribeatium volectae optatae. Occusam arist, core re, culla simod qui nos int evene maio officaerit apitati.

STEARNS COUNTY EXTENSION SERVICE

The golden proportion. The golden proportion is really just a ratio: 1:1.618. Mathematicians and scientists are as enamored with the golden proportion as artists and designers of all kinds are—and have been for centuries. Sometimes called the divine proportion or the golden ratio, it has been invested with divine, even magical, properties.

What makes this proportion special is its mathematical principle: The ratio of a to b is the same as the ratio of b to [a + b]. For our purposes, it looks like this: Draw a perfect square. If you increase the perfect square's width by multiplying it by 1.618, you create what is called a golden rectangle. You'll find golden rectangles everywhere in art, architecture and design.

Leaving the math aside, artists and designers like the golden proportion because when applied to shapes like rectangles, triangles and even spirals, it seems to produce a universal visual aesthetic appeal.

The golden proportion applied to a golden rectangle becomes a kind of compositional grid suggesting asymmetrical placement of items on the layout. In fact, a golden grid uses the golden ratio to establish an irregular 3 × 3 grid on the golden rectangle. And that leads us to the rule of thirds.

The rule of thirds. For the mathematically challenged or uninterested, the rule of thirds will seem wonderfully simple compared to the golden proportion. Like the golden proportion grid, the rule of thirds is merely a 3 × 3 grid that suggests layout placement in order to create visually interesting asymmetrical designs.

The rule of thirds simply divides the layout—whatever its format—into an evenly spaced 3 × 3 grid. Then the focal point goes on one of the four gridline intersections. *Voilà,* pleasing asymmetry guaranteed.

Another way to think about the rule of thirds has to do with symmetrical and asymmetrical balance. If we associate symmetrical balance with the number two, as in two symmetrical sides of a bisected layout, then the quickest route to asymmetry is to work with the number three, as in a 3 × 3 grid.

The rule of thirds. The layout for this save-the-date postcard uses the rule of thirds. Key information sits at one intersection of the grid. The hummingbird, which is the focal point graphic, sits at another.

PRINCIPLE NO. 2: CONTRAST

Contrast is an important principle for designing interesting (as opposed to boring) layouts. Contrast, as a principle, offers a great deal of flexibility. There are limitless ways to achieve it.

Start with the elements of design. You can employ contrast between filled and empty space. You can employ contrasting sorts of lines or shapes. You may juxtapose contrasting sizes of objects. Introducing a pattern in proximity to no pattern results in contrast. Ditto for texture. Or you may contrast two different kinds of patterns or two different kinds of textures. Color and value also offer powerful contrast tools. Using both dark and light values or colors results in contrast.

You probably can think of other ways to create contrast. However you do it, you need contrast in order to avoid visual boredom.

PRINCIPLE NO. 3: BALANCE

Imagine a seesaw, basically a board pivoting up and down on a fulcrum. When the board is level, the seesaw is balanced. To achieve balance, each side of the board must carry equal weight.

In design, we think of balance in terms of visual weight. You want your designs and layouts to be visually balanced, unless your communication purpose is to unsettle people by making them feel unbalanced and tense or anxious. There are three kinds of visual balance: radial, symmetrical and asymmetrical.

Font contrast. Contrast is essential in logos using more than one font. Here the designer chose a sleek condensed sans serif font to contrast with a grungy decorative blackletter font.

Radial balance refers to circular designs in which the fulcrum lies at the center, such as dream catchers in Ojibwa Nation culture. Circular designs, often associated with spiritual meanings, are universal across cultures. Interestingly, wherever you split radial balance, you end up with two symmetrical halves. Only radial designs have that property.

Whatever the shape, to achieve symmetrical balance, each side of a bisected design must be a mirror image of the other in terms of visual weight. This is called formal balance. As with all things formal, symmetrically balanced design has its uses. But it may tend toward the traditional and conservative (and sometimes stuffy or boring).

Asymmetry, then, reveals two unequal sides if bisected. Asymmetrical balance tends to be more visually exciting, or at least more visually interesting, than symmetrical balance.

In our earlier seesaw example, we can balance the weight of two unequal sides by adjusting the fulcrum, which would represent the bisecting line or center of gravity.

Allejandro and Ana Gonzales cordially invite you to attend a **dinner party** in celebration of Ana's **40th birthday** · Saturday, September 4, 2014 · **6:30 PM** · Beer, wine & sodas will be served · **Please RSVP** by August 31 (555.555.3456) · For **directions**, please go to www.gonzaleshome.com/map

With visual weight, we have to think about weight differently. Think linear axis and center of visual gravity. Shifting the vertical center axis or center of visual gravity—the fulcrum—to the left or right automatically creates asymmetry.

But an off-center layout is not necessarily balanced. Again, we have to account for visual weight. For example, positive space is visually heavier than negative space. So a lot of filled space requires balancing amounts of empty space. Dark value is visually heavier than light value. So a layout with a lot of dark tones requires balancing amounts of light tones. Larger relative size is visually heavier than smaller relative size, and so on.

Balance. This is an example of how breaking the rules can work. What saves this from being a dull centered layout is careful balance, paired with ample white space, pops of color and very careful typesetting. Look, Mom, no rivers!

PRINCIPLE NO. 4: MOVEMENT

The principle of movement goes back to the idea that good design controls the eye's flow through the composition. The flow of lines can move the eye across the page or screen.

ATHLETIC TRAINING
EDUCATION PROGRAM

Curriculum Handbook 2007

School of Physical Therapy & Rehabilitation Sciences
Smithtown University
85203 Smith Street • Smithtown, MA 22000
555-234-5678

SMITHTOWN
UNIVERSITY

Lines, then, can create movement, and different kinds of linear movement tend to communicate different kinds of symbolic messages. Horizontal lines communicate movement flowing left to right or right to left. Vertical lines tend to communicate stability, such as trees and tall buildings. Vertical lines also may communicate inspirational upward movement, such as mountain peaks, or downward movement, such as a waterfall. Diagonal lines communicate exciting dynamic movement. Two converging diagonal lines communicate distance, such as a road disappearing into a vanishing point in the distance.

Additionally, curving lines also communicate, for example, distance or meandering movement.

You can observe the principle of movement in action by looking at car ads. An ad for, say, a family vehicle is likely to show a full side view (horizontal movement). You want a car ad to convey a sense of motion—people want cars that go. But a family car also needs to communicate safe motion. But sporty cars and performance cars often appear in ads on a diagonal line of movement to communicate excitement.

Yet purity is not required in terms of line and movement. You can have different kinds of lines going on at the same

Movement. How do these two examples demonstrate movement? Choose all that apply:

a. Diagonal line

b. Curving S-line

c. Motion blur

d. Depth of field

e. All of the above

The path to enlightenment…

mahatma candy
The Shoppes at New Tampa
1234 Main Street • Tampa, FL 33660
555-123-4567
www.mahatmacandy.com

time—although that may not be a good idea if it interrupts the viewer's flow through your layout as you try to convey important information. A layout with too much movement is said to be "busy."

Flow has to do with the pattern of movement the eye takes across the page or screen. The possibilities for such patterns are countless. However, there are some fairly common ones in terms of the layouts we produce for commercial graphic design, such as advertising. The Z pattern is routinely used. In theory, the circular pattern is the most desirable because it may lead the viewer's eye back to the beginning to look at the layout again.

The bottom line for movement and flow is that you want to move the eye across the layout in order to convey information as well as to evoke emotion. So be strategic about how you do it.

PRINCIPLE NO. 5: RHYTHM/PATTERN

A pattern, whether regular or irregular, also may create a sort of movement we could call rhythm. Think of music, foot tapping, finger snapping, clapping and dancing. In graphic design, rhythmic movement has to do with repeating items strategically—kind of like a backbeat.

Imagine you're writing a feature story about people who work the night shift. You might decide to use the shape of a moon as a kind of visual theme or graphic icon in your layout. Repeating pictures of moons throughout the layout creates a kind of rhythm. Repeating a color such as the yellow of the moon photo also can create rhythmic movement. Using columns to keep your legs of type uniform creates rhythm. Grouping several photos establishes a rhythm. Repeating your fonts throughout a layout generates rhythm. Such visual rhythm not only results in a visual sense of togetherness for the layout but also helps lead the eye from one thing to another.

Daddy's eyes.
Mommy's nose.
Family history of lymphoma.

Give her the best chance for a healthy future.

Stem cells collected from umbilical cord blood have been FDA approved to treat nearly 80 diseases, including leukemia and lymphoma. **Store-Cell International,** a private, family stem cell bank, has been safeguarding these life-saving cells for families since 1994. Visit our website to find out how **Store-Cell** can help give your family the best chance for a healthy future.

www.store-cell.com/healthy
1.800.555.7235

Store•Cell
Storing Stem Cells since 1994

Rhythm. The repetition of fonts and colors paired with the nonlinear positioning of headline segments creates a playful rhythm in this ad design.

PRINCIPLE NO. 6: UNITY

The last principle, unity, may seem a little abstract compared to the other five principles. Unity means that all the parts of the design work together, and everything looks like it belongs together.

You wouldn't wear cargo shorts and flip-flops with a tuxedo shirt, jacket and tie. There's no unity between the informality of cargos and the formality of tuxedos, and wearing the two together makes for a visually disjointed, confusing outfit. The same principle applies in graphic design.

A layout is visually unified if its different parts have visual links or relationships to one another. A good design has some consistency in terms of the pattern of type columns, or rhythm of typography, or style of visuals, etc. Unity refers to oneness, that the result is one cohesive design or visual message.

Unity segues nicely into Gestalt theory because Gestalt laws demonstrate the ways our brains see order in visual chaos.

GESTALT THEORY

In the early 20th century, a group of German psychologists studied the way the human brain perceives objects. *Die Professoren* discovered that the brain automatically and unconsciously simplifies, arranges and orders objects the eyes see. Specific patterns of perception emerged from the research, which became the Gestalt laws. Four of these laws are of particular interest to designers.

Proximity.

We perceive objects that are close together as belonging to the same group. A related law, the law of Common Fate, says that we perceive   objects moving in the same direction as part of the same group. On the left, we interpret one group of circles. On the right, we interpret two groups of circles. The ability to group content aids in creating organization and order in layouts.

Placing elements in proximity to one another goes back to clumping. The idea is to avoid a busy, cluttered layout by physically grouping items together that belong together.

University of South Florida

DEPARTMENT OF **WOMEN'S & GENDER** *Studies*

Customized MA

Design Your MA in Women's and Gender Studies at USF

come as you are

Choose among three WGS MA tracks: 30 hours + thesis, 30 hours + internship, or 36 hours of coursework.

Plan a program of WGS graduate coursework: Feminist Research Methods, Feminist Pedagogy, Feminist Theory, Gender Theory, Queer Theory, Performance Studies, Feminist Media and Communication Studies, Body Politics, Politics of Motherhood, Social Justice, and Women's Health, among others.

Earn a graduate certificate while you're at it. USF offers dozens of certificates from "Africana Studies" and "Latin American & Caribbean Studies" to "Medicine & Gender" and "Nonprofit Management." WGS has its own graduate certificate, too.

WGS teaching assistantships and tuition waivers are available.

Who We Are

Founded in 1972, Women's and Gender Studies at USF is a rare freestanding women's studies department. Our community of faculty and graduate students is active on campus and engaged in the community. We also boast 45 affiliate faculty members, representing 15 USF departments and colleges.

Wish You Were Here

USF and its 46,000 students are located in Tampa, a diverse metro area with a rich history, thriving arts scenes, championship professional sports, and world-class festivals and attractions. And don't forget about our legendary beaches.

Apply Now

To join us next fall, **apply before February. 15:** http://wgs.usf.edu/graduate

Department of Women's and Gender Studies
University of South Florida
FAO 011 • 4202 E. Fowler Ave. • Tampa, Florida 33620
Phone 813-974-3496 • Fax 813-974-0336

www.wgs.usf.edu

USF
UNIVERSITY OF
SOUTH FLORIDA

Unity. To maintain visual unity, the poster designer chose grunge-style fonts and distressed background elements to match the tattoo theme of this poster.

Similarity.

Our minds group things with similar properties, such as color or shape. "Like goes with like." In this example, we group squares with squares and circles with circles. In layout, we can use similarity to create order and organization through unity.

Continuity.

Our minds will continue a pattern beyond its ending points. Further, our eyes will follow the direction of a line. On the left, our minds see a single cross shape instead of four shorter converging lines. On the right, our eyes follow the direction of the A's swoop and continue on to the star. Applying this concept can add a sense of direction and movement to your layout. *Ergo,* flow.

Closure.

We mentally fill in the gaps in order to complete a perceived shape. In this example, we see a star shape even though there is no star outlined. The idea of designing with only a part but having your viewer perceive the whole opens up interesting compositional opportunities, including the interplay of positive and negative space. How cool is that?

Applying Gestalt principles can help control the viewer's journey through your design. Visual hierarchy tells viewers what's important along the way.

That completes your basic course in the elements, principles and theories of design. Cue the band for "Pomp and Circumstance" because you're ready to graduate from mini art school.

APPLIED GESTALT

Proximity. This Web page includes several visuals, navigation, multiple headings, a feature story and some widgets. That's a lot of parts to scan. But grouping page elements together makes scanning manageable. Proximity trims the number of page segments to four horizontal rectangles: an image slider/logo band, a featured segment band, an events calendar/feature story section and a footer.

Similarity. Applied similarity makes websites navigable. Imagine a website where each link is typeset in a different size, color and font. Such a website would be visually loud *and* confusing. In this example, each navigation link is styled the same way. Links look the same and, therefore, the user understands they will behave the same. Headings and subheadings are also uniformly styled. This allows us to scan for the headings and get a sense of the site's content at a glance.

Continuity. Our eyes follow the lines tying screen elements together both vertically and horizontally. Intentional aligment of layout elements, whether it's the top edges of multiple visuals or the left edges of copy blocks, creates these lines. The row of round orange icons near the layout center demonstrates this. The viewer's eye follows the line from one icon to the next across the page.

Closure. Remember the interplay between positive and negative space we mentioned? It's at work in the wrench and group icons. The icon images are the same color as the background (negative space) and "bleed" into it. But we still see the full shapes of the wrench and group images because we mentally close the gaps and complete the shapes. Similarly, we close the gaps on the cropped parts of the gear in the lower right corner. We can't see the whole gear, but we know what it looks like anyway.

Gestalt at work. Applied laws of Gestalt theory make this complex homepage scannable and functional.

Reproduced by permssion of TEC Garage, St. Petersburg, FL. Design by Rebecca Hagen.

TRY THIS

1. What is a tessellation? If you don't know, do some basic research to find out. How does the vocabulary of the elements and principles help you explain tessellation without a math degree?

2. Go online to visit the Library of Congress Prints & Photographs Reading Room at http://www.loc.gov/rr/print. Click around until you find several very different photographs you really like. Use the elements and principles of design to explain why you like the photos.

3. Put your hands on a high-end magazine. Find a feature story layout that you believe really works. Then use the elements, principles and theories of design to explain why the layout works. Now do the same thing with an advertisement you find in the same issue.

4. Collect several examples of layouts including Web pages, newspaper pages, advertisements and others. How many of the designs use the rule of thirds? How many of the designs use the golden proportion?

5. Pull out some of your own previous design and layout work. Using the elements, principles and theories of design, explain how your work captures attention, controls the eye, conveys information and evokes emotion—or not. Can you find ways to improve your work using the elements or principles of design? Revise the work as necessary.

6. Imagine you have to design an online portfolio for yourself. Using the six principles of design, do some initial wireframe sketches for the home page. When you get one you like, label the principles of design you employed. ID and label the elements of design and any Gestalt laws in play, too.

7. Collect examples of logos that demonstrate the four Gestalt laws—proximity, similarity, continuity and closure. Explain how your examples utilize each.

LAYOUT

WHERE TO PUT VISUALS
& TYPE FOR IMPACT

A layout is the arrangement of visuals and type in space to compose your design. In some ways, creating a layout is like organizing and leading a tour. You welcome visitors at a clearly marked starting point. You lead them on along a specified path and point out significant sights along the way. And you do it all in an engaging and informative manner.

In this chapter we share some theories and practices graphic designers use for guiding interesting layout tours.

HOW DO I KNOW WHERE TO PUT STUFF?

If you are asking this question before you have done your research, written a creative brief and taken stock of your available design assets, then stop what you're doing and go back and read Chapter 2 on planning. Go. Now. We'll wait.

If you *have* done your homework, great. Your next step is to explore options for "where to put stuff" by creating thumbnail sketches for each page in your project. As we mentioned, there are theories and practices that guide the placement process. But before we get to that, start your sketches by setting up an appropriate grid structure.

What's a grid & why do I need one?

A grid is a series of horizontal and vertical lines charting out an area. Think of grids as a framework composed of columns, squares or rectangles. Your grid helps you organize items on your layout. Gridlines guide your decisions about grouping and aligning visuals, type and negative space. Using the same grid on every page gives your final project a unified appearance.

Creating & using a grid.

Designing a grid is not rocket science. Don't make it complicated. Remember, the purpose of a grid is to simplify the layout process.

What size layout? Some layouts have standard sizes. The standard size for business cards in the U.S. is 3.5 x 2 inches.

Your grid starts with your layout boundary. Start your thumbnails by drawing the outer edges or boundaries of your layout. Remember to draw your sketch in proportion to your design's final format. For Web wireframes, create your sketch in proportion to the initial screen viewing area, generally 1024 x 768 pixels (basically a horizontal rectangle). Proportion is essential. You can't fit a square peg in a round hole, and you can't fit a horizontal ad in a narrow vertical magazine column. In the world of screens, the concept of proportionality is known as aspect ratio. If you're sketching on paper,

ALL ABOUT **ASPECT RATIO**

For electronic screens, aspect ratio refers to the ratio of screen width to height.

Various ratios of width to height are standard for different media. Big-screen Hollywood film uses a horizontal format (roughly twice as wide as tall), and traditional standard TV used a slightly more square-ish format. That's why big-screen Hollywood films have had to be cropped for standard TV viewing, unless they were letterboxed, meaning they were reduced and floated in negative black space. (Either way, cropped or letterboxed, you've never seen a warped movie on TV.)

So, for example, regardless of the size of your contemporary wide-screen TV in inches (measured diagonally from corner to corner), the ratio of its width to height will be 16 units wide by 9 units tall—or 16 to 9. That aspect ratio is expressed as 16:9 or 1.78:1. Old standard televisions had an aspect ratio of 4 to 3, expressed as 4:3 or 1.33:1.

Standard Definition
(SD) TV (4 × 3)

Computer, tablet and smartphone aspect ratios may vary. But they generally have followed television's lead, with formats at roughly 16:9.

The concern with aspect ratio is because you can't design a square composition and expect it to fit a rectangular format. This becomes especially problematic in planning and composing such things as television commercials, training videos, multimedia websites and even business presentations employing projected computer screen slides. Today designing for aspect ratio is complicated by screens on tablets and smartphones, which have no standard sizes and rotate content onscreen anyway.

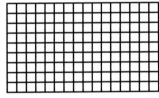

HDTV (16 × 9)

Aspect ratios:

Tablets and Smartphones 1.78:1 or 1.33:1

U.S. Standard TV and Computer Monitor 1.33:1

U.S. Widescreen TV and Computer Monitor 1.78:1

U.S. Cinema 1.85:1 or 2.35:1

Most 35 mm Film and Digital Still Photography 1.5:1

---

we recommend the use of graph paper. It helps keep your sketches in proportion. If you're sketching on a tablet or some other digital input device, turn on background grids, if available, for the same effect.

After you've set your outer edges, add gridlines for margins, trim, bleed, live area, title safe area, action safe area and any other essential guides. We discuss this in more detail in the following section, "Ingredients of the Grid."

THE INGREDIENTS OF THE GRID: MIX & MATCH TO MAKE YOUR OWN LAYOUT FRAMEWORK

Basic grid for a two-page spread

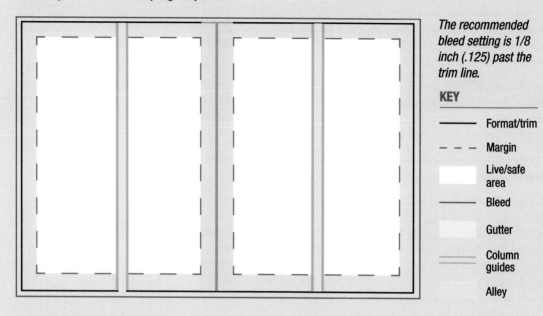

The recommended bleed setting is 1/8 inch (.125) past the trim line.

KEY

——	Format/trim
– – –	Margin
⬜	Live/safe area
——	Bleed
⬜	Gutter
——	Column guides
⬜	Alley

Format. The outer edges of your page or screen are effectively your base gridlines. To set your layout width and height, you'll need to do a little research to see if there is a standard size for your layout. For instance, one popular video sharing site recommends sizes with a 16:9 aspect ratio, such as 1280 x 720 pixels. In any case, format dictates the type and placement of the other gridlines you'll need for your layout.

Margins. Margins are the bands of space at top, bottom, right and left of your layout. When a print layout includes a spread—two pages side-by-side—the side margins become inner and outer margins. Some layout types have standard margins, so again, a little research is required. Printed magazines, for example, may require larger inner margins to account for binding. Depending on your layout type, it can be a good practice to make your margins correspond with live area.

Live area, action safe area & title safe area. Each of these areas serves as a safety fence inside the boundaries of your paper (live area) or screen (action safe and title safe areas). Any content falling outside of the "fence" may be cut off or disappear from view. It is especially important to respect these areas if you are designing for television. Different television screen aspect ratios make cropped content a real possibility. So set margins or gridlines to correspond with the safe areas and place your content inside those guides. Your content will remain intact and viewable.

Trim & bleed. Trim is a commercial printing term referring to the physical dimensions of the flat page. Trim size often corresponds directly with format size.

The effect of running material—background color, visuals, type—right off the layout is called a bleed. To create such layouts, designers extend bleed content just beyond the trim size. Commercial printers take the slightly extended design, print it to a larger sheet of paper

Basic grid for high definition television (HDTV)

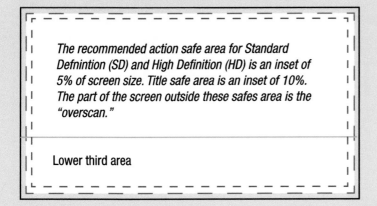

The recommended action safe area for Standard Defnintion (SD) and High Definition (HD) is an inset of 5% of screen size. Title safe area is an inset of 10%. The part of the screen outside these safes area is the "overscan."

Lower third area

Basic grid for a Web page

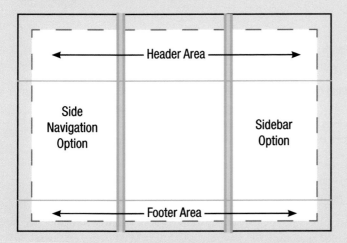

Header Area

Side Navigation Option

Sidebar Option

Footer Area

and trim the edges to achieve the desired finished size. This is where the term trim size comes from, by the way.

Print content may bleed or not. Screen content, however, always bleeds. Even when the content of Web pages, video or commercials stops shy of the viewing device boundaries, something—typically a solid color—fills the rest of the screen. In the world of video, this is called pillarboxing or letterboxing. To prevent this from happening in your Web projects, choose something to fill the space, preferably a something that complements the rest of your design. For video projects, working with the proper format and aspect ratio prevents pillarboxing and letterboxing.

Columns, alley & gutter. Columns are the quintessential unit of the grid. In fact, we often refer to a grid as a two- or three-column grid. Columns provide a useful framework for determining size and position of layout components. And, as an added bonus, when text is set in the correct size column, it's easier to read.

An alley is the negative space between a layout's columns. A gutter is the oversized margin between two facing pages, such as a newspaper's fold or a magazine's binding. Alleys and gutters provide essential white space that keeps elements separate and text readable.

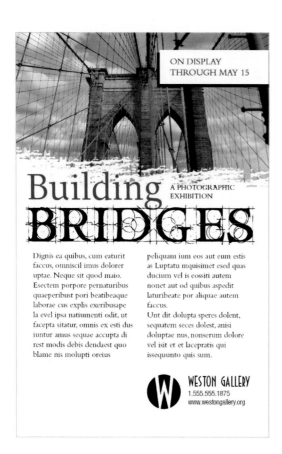

Sometimes more isn't better. Too many columns in too small a layout makes for awkward reading. When you can squeeze only one or two words in a line of copy, your columns are too narrow. Yes, Example-on-the-Right, we're talking to you.

Now you have the most basic of grids. For some small projects, this is all the grid you need. For more complex projects, you'll add column guides.

How many columns? Start with the type of project you're producing. The project format may suggest a basic grid structure. Tabloid newspapers traditionally utilize a four- or five-column grid. A small banner ad may only have space for one or two columns.

Balance aesthetic preferences with readability when establishing your column count. For maximum readability, column widths should fall within the range of 2–5 inches or 144–360 pixels.

Web page column counts vary. In fact, column counts on many sites change according to viewport size. Many Web designers favor a 960-pixel 12-column grid for its flexibility. Such a grid easily accomodates content in clusters of two, three or four items. As a rule, grids with more columns offer greater design flexiblity. This is true for all types of layouts. But that doesn't mean you're required to use the maximum number of columns you can squeeze in the space. Beginners may choose to employ fewer columns to simplify things. In any event, go with your comfort level.

Column widths on sites following the best practice of responsive Web design adjust according to the size of the current viewport. To prevent Web copy from stretching from one side of a huge monitor to the other, style columns with maximum and minimum widths using code.

To maintain pleasing proportions, consider setting your column grid using the rule of thirds or the golden proportion. Or let your specific content needs dictate the width and number of your columns.

After vertical columns, you also may add horizontal guides as needed for the design you envision. Perhaps you want to create distinct top and bottom portions of your design. You can add a horizontal line right in the center to help you lay out your design elements. Or perhaps you want to try a more complex grid structure of uniformly sized units, or "modules." You can thumbnail horizontal guides to make any combination of grid units.

While we think of grids as having uniformly sized units, non-uniform asymmetrical grids are also used. Such grids encourage the creation of asymmetrical design, and asymmetry is visually interesting.

Once your grid sketches are in order, you're ready to add the first layout item: the focal point.

Establish a focal point.

To return to the touring analogy, your focal point is the equivalent of a big sign that says, "Really amazing stuff starts here." It's the thing on your layout that captures the visual tourist's interest in the first place.

Usually the focal point is a visual of some kind. But not all visuals make good focal points. Look for focal-point-worthy visuals such as photographs with strong composition, line, shape, color or interesting angle.

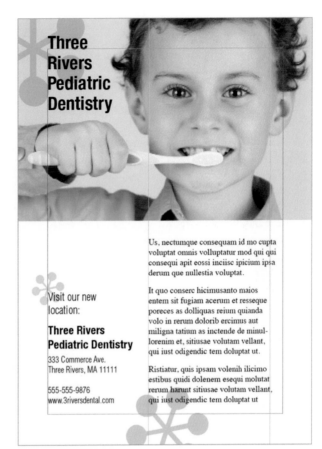

Embedded photo © Catalin Petolea - Fotolia.com

A custom grid based on dominant artwork. The grid here starts with the standard document boundary and margins, but all other lines are based on the shapes, lines and elements suggested by the art itself.

Since we look at art first, and our eyes are drawn to people's eyes, this is a great place to align a key headline.

The content of the image, in this case the visual weight of the boy's head, helps determine the positioning and alignment of the text block below.

BASIC BLACK.

Ra perum rectian diorpor epratio
officid magnimus, aliquat atiaspi
cilleste dolore nam, ut ea dias et rest
plit, conem expel magnimin con

Pora coneseris
eritatias

WHAT IF THE **COPY** ISN'T AVAILABLE YET?

This is a classic chicken-and-egg dilemma. Ideally you want all the copy available before you begin your layout. Maybe, however, the boss or client needs to see a layout before you get the copy. Maybe the writers can't start writing until they know how much space to fill on the layout. What can you do when you can't produce a layout without the content, but you can't get the content without a layout?

Greek text. Sometimes Greek text, meaning stand-in copy, is your best solution. Most professional-grade layout software programs offer some kind of Greek text, which is basically placeholder words. They read like gibberish, as in, "It's all Greek to me." The dummy words may be in English, or they may be fake Greek. "Lorem Ipsum" is the ubiquitous phrase of Greek with no meaning. Because Greek text can be formatted like normal copy, "greeking" offers a temporary substitute for the actual copy. This enables you to proceed with planning your layout.

Type treatments also may serve as focal points. The key to typographic focal points is contrast by some element of design: space, line, shape, size, texture, value or color.

Once you select a focal point, you have to decide where to put it. The works-every-time layout hangs the focal point from the top of the layout. But knowing a little design theory gives you other options. If you don't remember the golden proportion and the rule of thirds, consider revisiting Chapter 5: Mini Art School.

WHERE DO I PUT THE REST OF MY STUFF?

Once your focal point is in place and ready for attention-grabbing duty, the layout must direct viewers to the next important item, typically copy.

Adding type.

Type placement begins with inserting the main copy and any nondecorative headlines before adding other typographic items such as cutlines and tags. Depending on your format, type may comprise a little or a lot of your layout. Whichever it is, let your grid and your gridlines guide the placement of type.

Once you decide where on the layout to place the type, you can style it in an appropriate font, size and color. Make sure you haven't forgotten any type items. Adding a missing cutline or subheading after the fact can throw off an entire layout.

Use the other type tips you know:

» Keep your headline and your lead together.

» Reduce leading (line-spacing) as needed on multiple-line headlines.

» Set copy in appropriate column widths to keep long copy reader-friendly.

» Avoid fully justified or centered type.

» Watch for inelegant breaks in headlines or legs of type.

» Avoid widows and orphans (lone words at the top or bottom of columns).

Placing visuals in your layout.

In addition to the focal point, you may have other visuals to include on the layout. And, of course, there are rules for that, too.

Place visuals near the top of the layout. Positioning photos near the top of a layout or story is particularly important. Photos are eye magnets, and when they appear at the bottom, they immediately draw the eye to the bottom and right off the screen or page. Viewers will skip or miss that important information you're trying to convey on the rest of your layout. Does this mean you can never put visuals at the bottom of a layout? Nope. But…

If your picture has direction, be sure it's pointing the right way. We tell students: "Pictures are arrows. Be sure you're pointing in the right direction." If a photo or illustration has a strong direction, such as a particular line's movement or a face looking in a particular direction, make sure that direction is pointing to the

Faculty Spotlight

Raising the Bar on Legal Education

Above: The story above displays several "don'ts," including a much-too-skinny column to the right of the image and a photo placement that separates the headline from the start of the text.

Below: Ahhhh, much better.

Faculty Spotlight

Raising the Bar on Legal Education

Gone Fishing.

Above: Elicitis pitem fugit nonoro fugiare ipsum co et labaero operrrae nosamoesum, alia lant se dolende serineiri aut excendern deva audiene.

Opposite: Volum, omniintis volopsiom, tem coerrferonn nonem fugiam sunt.

Using multiple visuals. When placing multiple visuals, position them for overall balance. Image size contrast creates pleasing asymmetry.

Do leave some negative space, but don't let it get trapped. Make sure it opens to the outer edges of the layout.

accompanying type or whatever else comes next along the intended visual tour of the layout. Don't position your visual to point right off the screen or page if that's not where you want the viewer's eye to go.

Flipping photos is a bad idea. You may be tempted to "flip" an image that happens to point the wrong way. Flipping photographs is not acceptable in news design—ever—and though it can be done in marketing and advertising pieces, it can get you into trouble. Never flip a picture with text, for example, for what we hope are obvious reasons. Flipping photos of recognizable people may result in also flipping distinctive facial features. Flipping is just plain dangerous.

Don't position a visual where it interrupts the flow of reading. Don't interrupt the flow of reading copy by placing a visual where it chops a line or a column of type in half. Another common mistake is to place a visual between the headline and the lead. Floating a visual in the center of a column without anchoring it to the gridlines is also a common mistake causing unhappy results.

Pay attention if you're "wrapping" text. When you wrap text around a visual, make sure you don't end up with text columns that are too skinny, leaving you with only one, two or three words per line of type.

When using multiple visuals…

Variety or uniformity of size? When you're using more than one visual, make them different sizes—and don't be shy about the size contrast. The most important visual should be the largest. The contrast of sizes is more visually interesting and helps establish visual hierarchy. However, just to contradict ourselves, sometimes an interesting grid arrangement of

UNIVERSITY RESEARCHERS ANN(

SUMMERVILLE, TN —
Rehendamusa deseque quias
elliquament fuga. Iquatur
rem faces asped magnatem
as quunti ad unt providenis
experum fuga. Ut eat ut que
odigendunt.

Dr. Benjamin

Dr. Cole

Dr. Rodriguez

Inte cullautem faceperrorro
ius, ilita dolliquam volorib
erecto minus audam que
es doluptatis eumDitia vellendunt, niet ilitat la si
verum inctae vellab in culparuptati delibuscilit dolor
magnis ex et autataq uiatus di iur, quis nonsent
oditatur? Qui unt estius aspedi doluptaquam
harchilit, odior am ariae qui voloribus solorerum

et moluptis moluptate conecabo. Nem alige
officiusdant quia perum facipieni aci deliciis
cusa que nobisci endeliqui doluptis modi bl:
sectemOnem erunt aut aciumendam expers
et et ped ma in coreperunt, is quam dolore

visuals of the same size makes a nice rhythmic pattern. But the rhythmic
grid pattern sacrifices asymmetry and visual hierarchy. Whatever you
decide, call it with a visual communication purpose.

Balance, please. If you have multiple visuals on a single screen or page,
position them for overall layout balance. Avoid lopsidedness. Imagine
you're loading people into a small boat. What happens if everyone sits
on the same side?

On the other hand, it is acceptable to cluster groups of images
together. A cluster of multiple images becomes a single visual element
in your layout.

Mug shots. If you're working with multiple headshots, called mug
shots or mugs, make all the heads roughly the same size. To align
headshots, try cropping to align everyone's eyes.

Where to put negative space.

We trust that by now you understand that *white space is not your enemy.*
In fact, negative space is the best tool in your design toolbox for
isolating and highlighting important content. It organizes by separating
items. Without it, there can be no sense of clustering. Negative space
also provides a visual respite for the viewer to avoid visual overload.
But even negative space has layout rules.

Who's the pinhead on the right? Call us crazy, but we'd bet the doctor on the right wouldn't be pleased about how he looks in this news story. When you use multiple headshots, keep the heads the same size and align the images at eye level.

be **green** graphic design

be green graphic design

home

about us

print green

gallery

start a project

contact us

think green, print green

Urepelestiani de ipicabo. Offictem hilibusa dolore es et, temporehenis impossi ncitas con cume pe cor sust qui con con nobit autae. Pa voluptatem et molor sitio eatur, odis voluptat.

Ist, alique aut apelliquam, quamus minciae volor as eium aceario. Sed qui conse nonet dollignimus.

our suppliers

Volorum quatis alis. atemos es aspelibearum con nam dipsante nus pra solumquatem. Nam, offic te occusam quo berrum, ut debissi ute mi, velenie nisinulparum eum et il moloreh enitat accae illa.

Sequatur acia conecabo. Ut lacea noste id qui reruptat enditasinum fugiae nimi, omnistibus.Ipsa sinveni stionsequi bero volor aut incipicatur sant volupta tisquis cuptatur se nat.

Ommodit officiu santes. Aliament porehentur aces doles repelig naturem fuga. Et landend aectiis sequia sa dolest ex et et, ut que landicil in corerum alita sam rehent reicil earumquo tem. Et ommolest aliquame offic te aut omnient otasim velis mossita voloris sunda dero qui resto dis voloritatus as mod quae veribus et earum ad qui is se nam ist quatemquae nonsequo.

Acia conecabo. Ut lacea noste id qui reruptat enditasinum fugiae nimi, omnistibus. Ipsa sinveni stionsequi bero volor aut incipicatur sant volupta tisquis cuptatur se nat. Ist, alique aut apelliquam, quamus minciae volor as eium aceario. Sed qui conse nonet dollignimus.

Et landend aectiis sequia. Sa dolest ex et et, ut que landicil in corerum alita sam rehent reicil earumquo tem. Et ommolest aliquame offic te aut omnient otasim velis

Visual hierarchy.
Varying the size of headlines gives a sense of visual hierarchy to even the most text-heavy layouts.

First, try to consolidate many small puddles of negative space into fewer larger pools. This reduces visual clutter in exactly the same way as clustering positive layout items does. Same principle.

Second, avoid trapped space. Trapped space is a conspicuous chunk of white space isolated in the interior of the layout. If you have trapped space, rearrange the layout so the white space opens to the margins.

Another option is to treat white space as an additional asset you can place. For example, we built an extra-wide vertical band of negative space into the left and right margins of this book. That band of white space keeps the reading columns at a comfortable width. It also provides an interesting space to hang visuals and drop sidebars. The white space built into the top and left margins of the "Be Green Graphic Design" website above creates an open, airy layout and helps focus attention on the logo.

CREATING HIERARCHY

Creating visual hierarchy with relative position and contrasting size is another way to draw a reader through a layout while delivering an extra layer of communication. The hierarchy tells viewers what parts of the layout are more important than others and to look at the important things first.

To create visual hierarchy, rank the items intended as layout content in their order of importance. Your most important item, usually a key visual or a headline, becomes the focal point. A position near the top of the layout gives an element importance. Larger size also imparts greater importance. Visuals and type of lesser importance appear in smaller sizes and lower positions on the layout.

One of the best places to observe visual hierarchy in action is on the front page of a newspaper, either print or online. The lead news story always has the biggest photo, the biggest headline point size and occupies the catbird seat at the top of the page. Graduated headline sizes draw the reader down through the page like steppingstones.

Visual hierarchy applies to newsletters, Web pages, annual reports and any other document that includes multiple stories or chunks of discrete information.

LAYOUTS WITH MULTIPLE TOPICS ON THE SAME SCREEN OR PAGE

Up until now we've been dealing primarily with single-topic layouts. But what if your layout must accommodate multiple smaller stories or other items on the same page? Websites as well as print and online editions of newspapers, magazines and newsletters all require the orderly layout of multiple stories on a single page, or across several pages.

Modular page design.

The current trend for newspapers is modular page design. In modular page design, each story is arranged into a rectangle, and the rectangles are arranged on the grid of the page. Modular page design is also used in magazine and Web page design.

Making a rectangular story. At a minimum, a story includes a headline and some body copy. Sometimes there is a subhead called a deck between the headline and the lead. Between the deck and the lead, a story also may have a byline identifying the journalist or author. Many stories also have a photo or visual of some kind along with an accompanying cutline.

STORY SHAPES FOR MODULAR LAYOUTS

HEADLINE GOES HERE

HEADLINE GOES HERE

HEADLINE GOES HERE

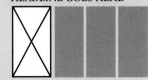

HEADLINE GOES HERE

HEADLINE HERE

Think of it this way, each part of the story—visual, headline, body copy—represents a new rectangle you have to fit into your rectangular story, which will fit into your grid of rectangles on your rectangular screen or page. It's just like a puzzle.

For each individual story, keep the eye flow moving in the correct direction and in the intended order. The ideal eye-flow order is visual, headline, lead. Otherwise, here are a few more helpful hints:

» **Body copy.** Strip the story's body copy into the grid columns. Keep the lengths of the story's legs even until you run out of story. More than 10 inches per leg is too long. Less than 2 inches is too short. So is yours a one-column or five-column story?

» **Headline.** Add the headline on top of the story. The headline should span all the story's columns, sort of like a roof covering the story. Give the headline a much larger point size than the body copy.

» **Deck.** If there is a deck, put it under the headline but before the lead. Give it a point size smaller than the main header but larger than the body copy.

» **Byline.** If the story merits a byline, put it between the deck and the lead. Give it a tastefully modest point size.

» **Visual/photo.** Where you place the visual really depends on the size and direction of the image. As a rule, though, keep photo

The modular page.
Stories fit neatly into the page grid because of their rectangular shapes.

The Florida Gazette

Weekend

www.floridagazette.com   Friday, November 3, 2006

Local artist wins "Best of Show"

Penny Lane, Art Critic

Museums gear up for summer blockbusters

Genealogy workshop at the History Center

You should see his middle game

Chess tourney brings out game enthusiasts young and old.

Welcome New Board Members

Jane Peterson
Simintem que omnis milla
pe nos quassim endunt
expliquis nos moditinia ex

Sam Johnson
exero idiore corehendit
is dipsam volutemodia il
maiorit assime delignimus

Lois Gonzales
volenti net accae natem eiur?
Aditis aut eat. Genectam elit, offictur, senima
commolo restem eossere pratur sum sequas
moditas de reriore sedist libustiant.

Martin Chen
volenti net accae natem eiur
Aditis aut eat. Genectam elit, offictur, senima
commolo restem eossere pratur sum sequas

Arthur Melnick
Simintem que omnis milla
pe nos quassim endunt

Kwan Named Volunteer of the Year

By Anne Mitchell

Acepudio remporis as dolut versper untiossedi dolorio essi dolorro incturi orerionseque volorem nonsequ iasperchil inis mo impel eum laces di serumquibus erum, verunt officia net, consero vid moluptasi doluptaqui dolorerum nem ute iliciet, cusda ipsant earibus es eium, untur magnati ut eatur? Met fugit quassimagnis mod ut volut hicipic aecupta spedit harcil in repellu mquatias esequas expliciet minveri cusam ipsandio ma ne nusam, totaspi demque eum ulluptat et eatusam ipiduntio con nonsequam, tem sectiur aut apicil molecab orundem hilignit aborrum laut maion nonestrum aut office landio beat latestibus aceperunt et fuga. Edit enecatius molupta accabo. Optatibus, tem iur rerferf errovid

Suzanne Kwan was named volunteer of the year for her work on the annual holiday food drive.

eliqui at quiae voluptas dolupta nonse nihillor aut eos eumque veliquuntiam quosapedis de esequae labora dolliberum atasitati comnit que soloria quam nonestinum experae modicite invenimus mo volecer ionsent earum quisque dit as prat aut ut recus sere idit volupta tatibus.

Tiossumet et acepreptas comnis doluptat.

On evellabo. Uga. Tas eos prernat ibusci solupta pa soloren dusdaestio. Ovit quis dolorepe-

Troublesome headlines.
"Tombstoning," when two headlines are positioned side by side, is a potential pitfall of modular page design. In the top example, the headlines run together. In the example below, the designer solved the problem by placing a photo between the headlines and using an alternative headline style.

Kwan Named Volunteer of the Year

By Anne Mitchell

Acepudio remporis as dolut versper untiossedi dolorio essi dolorro incturi orerionseque volorem nonsequ iasperchil inis mo impel eum laces di serumquibus erum, verunt officia net, consero vid moluptasi doluptaqui dolorerum nem ute iliciet, cusda ipsant earibus es eium, untur magnati ut eatur? Met fugit quassimagnis mod ut volut hicipic aecupta spedit harcil in repellu mquatias esequas expliciet minveri cusam ipsandio ma ne nusam, totaspi demque eum ulluptat et eatusam ipiduntio con nonsequam, tem sectiur aut apicil molecab orundem hilignit aborrum laut maion nonestrum

Suzanne Kwan was named volunteer of the year for her work on the annual holiday food drive.

aut office landio beat latestibus aceperunt et fuga. Edit enecatius molupta accabo. Optatibus, tem iur rerferf errovid eliqui at quiae voluptas dolupta nonse nihillor aut eos eumque veliquuntiam quosapedis de esequae labora dolliberum atasitati comnit que soloria quam nonestinum experae modicite invenimus mo volecer ionsent earum quisque dit as prat aut ut recus sere idit volupta tatibus.

Welcome New Board Members

Jane Peterson
Simintem que omnis milla
pe nos quassim endunt
expliquis nos moditinia ex

Sam Johnson
exero idiore corehendit
is dipsam volutemodia il
maiorit assime delignimus

Lois Gonzales
volenti net accae natem eiur?
Aditis aut eat. Genectam elit, offictur, senima
commolo restem eossere pratur sum sequas
moditas de reriore sedist libustiant.

Martin Chen
volenti net accae natem eiur
Aditis aut eat. Genectam elit, offictur, senima
commolo restem eossere pratur sum sequas

Arthur Melnick
Simintem que omnis milla
pe nos quassim endunt

placement near the top of the story. It's that eye magnet thing. Think works–every–time layout. But a visual as focal point can sit under the headline, or to the right or left of the headline, as long as the visual does not sit between the headline and the lead. In other words, never put a visual between the headline and the lead. Ever. If the image has direction, it should point to the story. Wherever you put the visual, and at whatever size, remember you're trying to end up with a rectangular story.

» **Cutline.** Cutlines typically, but not always, go under the visual. A cutline under a photo should run the whole width of the photo.

A SIDEBAR ON DESIGNING SIDEBARS

Sidebars are a good option for:

» Breaking up text in the absence of good photography

» Highlighting key information lifted from your text

» Providing additional information related to your adjacent copy

» Adding interactivity when presented in the form of quizzes or lists

» Giving your page a little pop of color

When designing sidebars:

» Make them contrast with your regular copy by using a different font

» Give them a little color with colored bullets, headings, a border or a background box

» If you use a border or background box, make sure your text doesn't crowd the box. Give yourself ample margin, inside and out

Placing your stories on a modular page. Unfortunately, laying rectangular stories on a modular page is not as easy as we may have led you to believe.

If you build all your stories in the same size and shape and then just stack them on top of each other, you'll have one snoozer of a page. To keep things interesting, you need to vary the size and orientation of your stories. For asymmetry, make some stories tall, narrow and vertical. Make others wide horizontals, and maybe even design a few that are square.

At the level of organizing a whole page of stories, you also need to take a look at all the stories' visuals. Varying their size and placement on the entire page creates interest. Newspapers like to average about a third of a page devoted to visuals. Whatever your percentage of visuals, you still have to watch out for lopsidedness at the page level. Don't tip the boat over. Balance is necessary even for asymmetry.

Your goal is an overall page eye-flow guided by the placement of all the stories' visuals. The eye moves from one image to the next in a particular order according to the visual hierarchy.

Adding visual variety with sidebars. In print, a sidebar is simply a separate block of type with a solid background, a stroked outline or an ample border of negative space. On the Web, a sidebar is one column (either right or left) of the Web page grid.

Print sidebar content relates to its adjacent copy in some way. A sidebar might be a short connected story, a list, a mini biography, a quiz, an infographic or simply further detail on some aspect of the main content. Normally though not exclusively rectangular in shape, sidebars fit beautifully into modular layouts.

Print sidebars can be as minimal as text and an enclosing box. The visual effect can break up long copy and add life where you don't have as many visuals as you would prefer. Like good cutlines, sidebars provide a bit of information in nice compact quickly readable chunks.

Web sidebars often include primary or secondary navigation, banner advertising or function-adding widgets such as social media feeds and maps. Unlike print sidebars, Web sidebars are typically functional rather than aesthetic. However, guidelines for designing them are similar.

When designing sidebars, one of the biggest mistakes beginning designers make is neglecting to include margins outside and inside the box. Don't cheat your margins. No type should touch the sides of the sidebar, either outside or inside its box.

Sidebars can add pops of color to your layouts. Consider applying color to the headline or bullets. Or you might put your color in the box's background (the fill) or the box's outline or border (stroke). If you choose a background color, don't forget the contrast you'll need between the fill color and the type. If you believe you need to reverse the text, white letters pop best against a dark background. If your sidebar houses Web navigation, make sure hover states (color changes on mouseover) contrast with the background, too.

MULTIPLE-PAGE LAYOUTS

Laying out multiple pages, whether print or digital, presents some additional challenges. Three biggies include maintaining unity, making a lot of type inviting and providing navigational signs to keep readers from getting lost.

Visual unity. To maintain visual unity in a multi-page layout, use the same tactics as for a single-page layout. Don't change from a tuxedo to cargo shorts from one page to the next. Use a dash of Gestalt through similarity: Keep repeating compositional elements such as color, shape, texture and pattern. Consistent font styling also provides unity. Using the same grid skeleton on every page is essential, too.

Loads of type. Page after page of gray type is intimidating. To break up any copy-heavy design, including one with multiple pages:

» Use a grid and set copy into inviting legs of type. And unless your document is fairly narrow, don't let a single column span the width of the page. Imagine trying to read a block of text as wide as your computer monitor. Ouch.

» Break up type with headlines and subheads.

» Add more visuals, including sidebars.

» Deploy negative space strategically.

Navigational signs. In a multiple-page layout, visitors need visual signposts to be able to keep track of their whereabouts. Traditional navigation tools include, for example, tables of contents, teasers, jump lines pointing to where the rest of the story jumped and even logos or the journalism equivalent of logos called flags and sigs (short for

You are here.
Multiple-page layouts need navigational devices such as page numbers, folios and tables of contents. Web pages need persistent navigation so visitors can find content as well as find home at any time and from any location.

signatures). For interactive media, navigation and multimedia controls and menus help visitors move through content, and they should be consistent (have similarity) across pages. Breadcrumb trails are highly useful navigation tools for websites, too. A breadcrumb trail is a text reference to where a website visitor currently is, preceded by a sequential list of the links the visitor followed to get there.

A periodical or serial such as a magazine, newsletter or newspaper—print or Web—needs a folio showing the publication's name and issue or date. Folios in hardcopy editions also need page numbers. Folios generally appear somewhere in the margins, though still within the safe area or live area.

EXIT HERE

Remember, good layout works for, not against, your visual communication objectives: Capture attention, control flow, convey information and evoke emotion.

Begin the layout with a grid and an irresistible focal point. Use the focal point to *point to,* not from, your layout. The Gestalt theories of proximity, similarity, continuity and closure can help with arranging the layout's flow. Creating a visual hierarchy also aids flow.

For multiple layouts on the same screen or page, modular design is your new best friend. For laying out multiple pages, similarity is the key to visual unity.

Thank you for traveling with us today. Please wait until the chapter has come to a full stop before exiting.

TRY THIS

1. Compare the visual communication of two organizations that compete with each other by comparing their websites. In particular, compare their websites' grid structures.

2. Experiment to figure out the live area for an 8½ × 11-inch sheet on your personal printer and also on the copier you use. If you bleed material at the top, bottom and sides, how much white-space margin still prints?

3. Compare the home pages of two online news organizations. What techniques communicate visual hierarchy? Does either employ modular page design? How do you know?

4. Assemble several samples of your own writing to treat as Greek text. Now create thumbnail sketches showing how you would arrange each of these dummy "stories" into a two-page newsletter using modular page design. Execute your design in a page layout program.

Sakura Japanese Gardens

One fallen flower
Returning to the branch? ... Oh no!
A white butterfly
— Moritake

Imagnimp orrore, quoditae. Et accus eius accuptam volor adiasinis quatibusdae rent et voluptam, quam repudit ionsendae et, tem rescium volluptat as que dolorehenet illam non necusci enduntem que maionse con comnis cus se volum ius ni omn enit molori te liam diaectiam fuga. At. Fugitii ssinus, quo te cuscia dolupta temperc hictatem rat est voles restiae. Empore eresent resequi ut lanissimagni desecea dempor molorrum aut alitis escid equis arum acepudae cum si doluptatem earum volore am fugitio nempeli gnient. Lut odia voluptas quate voluptur? Ata saeperf erumque quaturia qui debis sitae sant adit, aut adiaero cum faccatur, net

events

explore

support

ignimp orrore, quoditae. Et accus eius accuptam volor asinis quatibusdae rent et voluptam, quam repudit

se volum ius ni omnienit molori te liam diaectiam fuga. At. Fugitii ssinus, quo te cuscia dolupta temperc hictatem

tio nempeli gnient. Lut odia voluptas quate voluptur? At saeperf erumque quaturia qui debis sitae sant adit. aut

elipse

Andestib usamus non rerum et prempos sam quo exceper spelige ndillatur se perupil, sequo te mo quod moluptatem que quae sandoep erepudis destinullore quassin etures quaestil volor sentor-

este cone nemqui dewaquam del eum faccae re quasapistis erfero elur? AbCiospen sixenpellam, ut architae lobore voluptati impares simped ut ea non num a illuptat aut ecerem et ut quate rem aliatunt eseria

Cultivating

YOUR FAMILY TREE

L it int est inciliquid molorem lat. Ullenem nobistal que volupti quiam facit itod uipuchil millgn rentibus dicuitiori necum est ut esai re, ninso to endiu dolupta si ninus que nouom sim quiscis explit eos evendic tempor ovitat ovital verum ndililsi que maxim excest volluptatur, vel et inullmis mor rem dolorum eos reais et ut, omnolum reroremque niest vel inctesti corrpro iusanto beatur?

Greerpernam commolnim fugitaspel endam qui dolecep tatons equidacipsum est verionsequi aborior porrepersped estrunt, sequiat asperferae nullansi mos molorem es pori arundandit praecuptatet ilia peratium adipsum ernat.

Ur rem vid que ninuligmi ea quam, odia nus dolor am, explabor anibil uptateturi sandunitet lacerelus sit od moluptae moluptat et pedi ipsam tempores eicimolum que venemporrum quia et fuga. Et di volorum fugitatibea nonsequatus dem rentibus utectat.

Giae. Nam quau uunte vendae invelib esturiam, sequi te la non re, santorecae labo. Faerspelmi offici inture oet. voluptaet antio. Necto dolo et faci di tem. Ut silitat reperitium invelitatur? Il int volor reicia parchil issinus.

Obisaequid ernatur? Volor alit quost aut quaiendae pro cone cullore molupid quattum ut ain faccus ea por soleris rem et omnis earis pro blacerrpe et eum ea verum et esciam, sequant iaepudi ndit, sim corro dolupt blaccus, ne et remque ainciet facopudae voluptum si quanet re plab uistmn eatis simus dolores equaut qui voluptio. Ut quia iunt expliti onsequid qui offic to tempor nulla cor sinciiCil invente voluptas volo derovide cusandiu si sequatem cuptas consoenu ut autate si commuustius dio. Nemporeptat.

Ibu mi, quasinvellam faceto taeceptatus aut quam nuptatur, tempore plam et ut aliamet a consere fuga omnihicaisi officia volorest, ut laut es perhent, odictat

4

COSTA RICA VACATIONS
Us a necta velique modit as
et quias eserum expeles tincipiciate
sum doluptur aut acerspero

1-800-111-1119
www.vacation-costa-rica.com

BEYOND THE WORKS-EVERY-TIME LAYOUT

In Chapter 3 we introduced you to the works-every-time layout. Now we'd like to introduce you to several other common layout patterns you can add to your designer's toolbox. These layouts adapt to both print and screen applications. Now that we've pointed them out, see how often you run across them each day.

1. Picture window

2. Grid of equal squares

3. Collage

4. Mondrian

5. Type specimen

6. Multipanel *

5

6

* Layout 6 also demonstrates the use of "clotheslining," a technique where you line up items of unequal height along their top edges. The effect is that of elements hanging off of a clothesline.

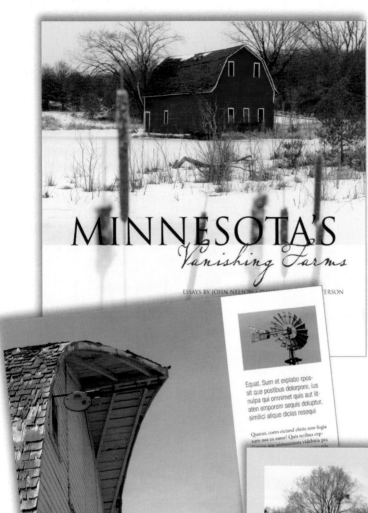

MINNESOTA'S
Vanishing Farms

ESSAYS BY JOHN NELSON · PHOTOGRAPHS BY [...] TERSON

Equat. Sum et explabo rpossit que postibus dolorpore, ius nulpa qui omnimet quis aut litaten emporem sequis doluptur, similici alique dicias resequi

Quatur, corro eiciand ehitis rem fugia sum nos ex eatur! Quis reribus espllicense nimusantota videbitia pra

IT ALL COMES BACK TO THE GRID

Not all graphic designers embrace the grid. Some feel grids are too restrictive. We humbly disagree. An underlying grid is crucial to keeping a design coherent across multiple pages. And, as we've already discussed, a grid takes some of the guesswork out of deciding where to put content.

Regardless of the type of layout you create, sticking to a grid provides a bit of invisible repetition and makes each page or screen feel like part of the same whole.

Above: ipsunt unt vent quis eossedia prate ersperi cum nullecti dolores dolores ero esciduciet odi quid quaspedit ideliquise sunt ium.

Left: ipsunt unt vent quis eossedia prate ersperi cum nullecti dolores dolores ero esciduciet odi quid quaspedit ideliquise sunt.

Que nimusanimos dolorem ape pa sime voluptatia quidem ipsacrum id maxim am qui omnis debis dinte qui veria ere nullor sequi alitint solut velest veligen dandae pe vitia con porporerum aut omnim quas es ius quodi dolorum voluptur, quid que venditatia nos volupta epturit quosam, con cuptata temque doleniih illaut lit aut explique plit asi corions equiae dolut plabo. Hario blabore aute non corrom nectas sitat reperovid mil id es cume durnat acerum, quatibea vidus, tore seadiur aperovit eos sus exero endit rem es simetum comnis alit et que volum ratur solupieni odio.

Fuga. Nam aligninimt et mi, rotem ut eribus aut volupta veloribus dolum vent ventissum et prestor eptatut, quatibus, eaque repero corro optatus, que necullanrin cuptatem cum et eum ut est peresunti arum tende ne vollat verem alit illorum fuga. Itatibus sus, omnihici de debita inum vellencacero molorunt est, consequat audae prat.

Cae solor reperovident illuptat quaspel enimendandae nis et erum quam, temo consequi bla consequunt quodit ent quias si auta quuntur?

Estrum quibus, nitae vellaut etur aut ut a im fuga. Ut lit cum nulliacpedi dolum volluptasi veleni culla quiderum quatem liquae di quiae pedit iust, ut officiae proreria ditem aboreicabo. Nam et lam harcimi, conem adipsa dolorec atestis se volorep ererupt atempori blatur? Natque sunt.

Solut vellibus aut fuga. Eperupta solestio velendaes animpores as expelis dolupta ssinctem eostori oreniendis minita con preperu.

TYPE

WHAT YOU DON'T KNOW
CAN HURT YOU

If you're like most people, the first time you used a word-processing application, you accepted the default Times New Roman 12-point font and never looked back. If you still treat your computer like a glorified word processor, you're not taking advantage of the full communicative and creative power of type.

The best designers are experts in type and typesetting because they understand that well-styled type not only sets the document's tone but also directly impacts its readability, legibility and visual hierarchy. Failure to follow best typesetting practices, at best, can leave your audience with a negative impression and, at worst, can leave you with no audience at all.

This chapter talks all about fonts, including styling them for both function and aesthetics.

FONT, TYPEFACE, FONT FAMILY, GLYPH

To begin at the beginning, a font is a complete set of characters in a particular size and style of type. This includes the letter set, number set and all of the special characters you get by pressing the shift, option or command/control keys.

A typeface or font family contains a series of fonts. For instance, Times Bold, Times Italic and Times Roman are actually three fonts, even though people often refer to one entire font family as a font.

A glyph is an individual character of a font. Glyphs are not limited to upper- and lowercase letters. There are glyphs for punctuation, glyphs for special characters such as copyright and trademark symbols and even glyphs that are purely decorative. Most fonts have a set of 265 glyphs. Fonts in the OpenType® format, a format created jointly by Microsoft and Adobe, are cross-platform and can have as many as 65,000 glyphs.

FONT CATEGORIES

In the same way we organize plants and animals into genus and species, we can organize fonts into categories. The shape of a font's glyphs determines its category. Learning to recognize and identify font categories is an important first step in selecting the right font for the right job. It's also essential in creating harmonious, not discordant, font pairings. The ability to categorize fonts comes down to training your eye to see subtleties. It's worth your time to develop this skill.

Type sets the tone. Well-styled, properly set type sets the overall tone of the layout. It impacts readability, legibility and visual hierarchy as well.

PARTS OF A **FONT**

Fonts have a complex anatomy, and the names of some font parts are known only to font designers and true type enthusiasts. This diagram illustrates some of the more commonly known parts of fonts.

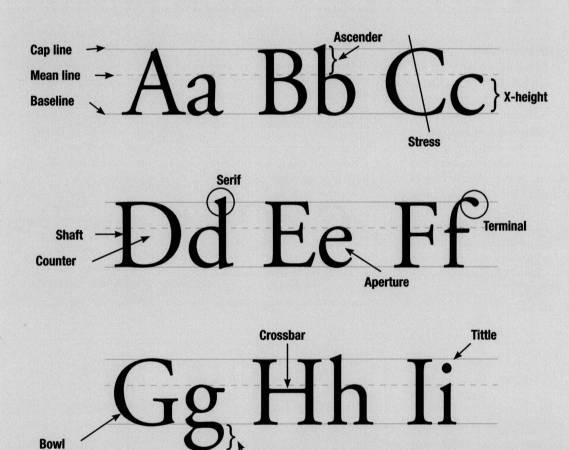

A FIELD GUIDE TO BASIC FONT CATEGORIES

Depending on the source you consult, you'll find many different font categories. We'll stick to a few of the most common and offer general recommendations for their use.

OLD STYLE & Transitional

Characteristics: Classic and traditional, old style fonts have serifs, little "feet," at the tips of glyphs. Old style serifs are bracketed: They start thick and taper to thin at an angle, creating little triangles. Old style fonts also contain thick stem strokes and thinner hairline strokes, though the difference between the thick and thin is not extreme. Old style fonts often have diagonal stress, which means that a line intersecting the thinnest parts of O-shaped glyphs is diagonal.

Transitional fonts evolved from old style and share many of the same characteristics. The biggest difference is that the diagonal stress is missing or not as prominent in transitional fonts.

Because they are so similar, throughout this text we refer to both types as simply old style.

Note Goudy Old Style's diagonal stress (left) compared to the vertical stress of the transitional font Baskerville (right).

BEST USES:

For print body copy, old style fonts are the most readable. Larger bolder versions can work for headlines. But old style's hairline strokes and tapered serifs can get lost when reversed.

Serifs and fine strokes also get lost on computer and television screens. Onscreen, old style fonts are best when big and bold in headlines or other short bits of copy.

SANS SERIF Grotesque Humanist Geometric

Characteristics: Contemporary in style, sans serif (French for "without serif") fonts have no serifs. Variations of sans serif fonts include Grotesque (strokes have uniform thickness), Humanist (variations in stroke thickness) and Geometric (letterforms have geometric shapes). For simplicity, we refer to all forms as sans serif.

BEST USES:

In print, sans serif fonts are best used for headlines and other quick nuggets of text such as sidebars and cutlines. They work well when reversed. Humanist forms, with their stroke thickness variations, are the most readable of the sans serif fonts.

On computer and television screens, sans serif fonts fare better in the readability department. Among the most readable onscreen fonts are Helvetica, Verdana and Arial. Their larger x-heights and open letterforms add to their online readablity. Bigger, bolder versions make excellent headings and subheadings.

Script

Characteristics: If the type style looks like it belongs on a wedding invitation, it's most likely a script font. Script fonts tend toward formality and often resemble old-fashioned penmanship. Like cursive writing, the glyphs in script fonts tend to be connected on the downstroke. As a whole, script fonts can be difficult to read, though some are more readable than others.

BEST USES: Because of readability and legibility issues, script fonts are best limited to small amounts of copy in both print and screen applications. Individual characters of script fonts make interesting decorative elements in watermarks and logos. They also make beautiful drop caps.

DECORATIVE

Characteristics: The characteristics of decorative fonts widely vary. They can resemble hand lettering, vintage type, grunge type or whimsical lettering. Consider these examples:

Blackmoor   *Arual*   ΡΖΖ ΑRTS & CRAFTS

Airstream   Emporium   American Typewriter

BEST USES: For both print and screen applications, limit the use of decorative fonts to headlines, decorative details, ornaments or very small amounts of type. They are not a good choice for reading copy. Reversing depends on the thicknesses of the parts of each glyph, and those with fine detail will not reverse well. Many place Blackface fonts, like Blackmoor above, in their own font category. They were used for body copy in the early days of the printing press. Today we find them difficult to read. Treat them like decorative fonts: Use them sparingly and with care.

slab serif

Characteristics: As the name implies, slab serif fonts have uniformly thick, fat serifs. Some slab serif fonts look like a hybrid between an old style font and a sans serif font. The result is sort of a sans serif with fat serifs, if you will.

BEST USES: Slab serif fonts were invented for retail display advertising so they work well in print headlines. Some slab serif fonts can work for body copy, but old style fonts are generally a better choice. Slab serif fonts tend to work a little better in reverse because of their beefier serifs.

Slab serif fonts also work for Web and television but in the same limited way as decorative fonts.

MODERN

Characteristics: Modern fonts have extremely thin serifs, and their stress lies on the vertical, unlike old style's diagonal stress.

BEST USES: Modern fonts work well for headlines, decorative details or ornaments. They are not a good choice for reading copy, and reversing them is not a good idea because of their ultra-thin serifs. Likewise, they are not a good choice for screen applications.

Dangerous curves.
Curvy script fonts contrast beautifully with rectangular pages. Because script fonts are typically ornate, pair them with simpler fonts such as old style or sans serif.

Reproduced by permission of the USF College of the Arts.

CHOOSING & USING FONTS

Understandably, most graphic designers love fonts. We want bumper stickers that say, "The one who dies with the most fonts wins."

Once you discover the big wide world of fonts, it's easy to go nuts. But. Please. Resist. This. Urge. Nothing screams "amateur" louder than using too many competing font styles.

Choose one font for your body copy.

The No. 1 consideration in choosing a body font for print or screen is readability. As we've already mentioned, old style fonts are best for print readability while sans serif fonts are the most readable onscreen.

We recommend selecting a body font from a larger typeface for all types of design projects. By nature, all the fonts in a typeface get along visually because they're related. By using fonts from the same typeface, you get both flexibility and a consistent, unified look. For example, the typeface Adobe Garamond Pro contains a "regular" font that is great for body copy. But it also contains bold, italic, semibold and several other variations that can be used for subheadings and captions, or to create emphasis.

You can take a similar approach when choosing Web fonts from online font services. Many of the fonts available through online font services include related variations. These variations might have different weights, italics and even condensed or wide options. Look for and specify from these sets.

Choose a second contrasting font for headlines.

If you choose an old style font for body copy, you can pick a contrasting headline font from almost any category. Think of old style fonts as the "basic black" of fonts. They go with everything. Your headline font, then, can be wild and decorative, script and elegant, or sans serif and ultra hip and still work. Or you could choose a headline font from the same typeface as the body and create your contrast through point size or weight. However you do it, you want the body copy to contrast with the headline.

Sans serif fonts are also rather neutral and play nicely with most other fonts. Make them your go-to fonts for the screen.

Pairing decorative fonts together is almost always a bad idea. They compete with each other. Script fonts have the same problem. Think of decorative fonts and script fonts as the divas of the font world. You just can't put the two of them in the same dressing room.

Modern and slab serif fonts also can present difficulties. Since modern and slab serif fonts are similar in shape to old style fonts, they may not have enough contrasting elements to make them stand out as distinctive from the print body copy. When using modern and slab serif fonts, trust your eyes. If the pairing looks like you've simply made a font error instead of a deliberate design choice then the pairing isn't working. You might be able to make such pairings work if you apply contrast in another way by varying size, weight or color.

No matter which font categories you choose for your onscreen project, make sure you don't choose fonts with a lot of fine detail. Thin strokes and serifs often don't read well on computer or television screens. When in doubt, test your choices on different computers using different browsers. Be sure to test-drive any variants of your chosen fonts, too, especially italics. Italicized fonts also may lose legibility onscreen.

APPLYING ADDITIONAL FONT STYLING

Choosing the right typeface will give you the option of using bold, italic, semibold and other type styling options. You also may have the ability to apply some additional font styling options such as leading, kerning and tracking adjustments to impact your design's readability and visual appeal.

Font size.

In your typesetting workflow, choose your fonts first, and then choose your font sizes. Layout programs, including Web page editors, come with default size settings. Rather than accept the default size, use it as a baseline to adjust size to something appropriate to your unique project, audience and font selection.

10 POINTS IS **10 POINTS,** RIGHT?

Wrong. While each of the fonts used below is 10 points, each takes up different amounts of vertical and horizontal space. For print, 10- or 11-point old style is a good baseline for reading copy. For other font categories and for the Web, use your judgment when picking the perfect size between mousetype and horsey.

All 10-point fonts are not created equal

All 10-point fonts are not created equal

All 10-point fonts are not created equal

All 10-point fonts are not created equal

All 10-point fonts are not created equal

All 10-point fonts are not created equal

All 10-point fonts are not created equal

CHOOSING FONTS FOR THE WEB

For years, Web designers observed with envy the thousands of typefaces print designers had to choose from. Traditionally, Web designers were limited to using a very small Web-safe font set, including fonts like Arial and Times, common to most computers. Designers looking to use more creative fonts resorted to turning type into graphics. This preserved the font appearance but killed search engine readability and made editing difficult.

Fortunately, new coding methods and font formats made a significant portion of the world's font catalog available for use in websites. After addressing hiccups in browser rendering and copyright issues (remember, typefaces and fonts are copyrighted material), font foundries and online font hosting companies now offer a huge range of creative options for Web. Designers now have font choices enough to make them giddy—or dizzy—depending on your point of view.

FONT READABILITY

Each of the first three examples demonstrates a "don't." The final example does everything right. See the difference?

This example is typeset using the font Helvetica Neue UltraLight, 12 point

This example uses the smaller x-height font Verlag Book, 12 point

This example is typeset using the geometric sans serif font Century Gothic, 10 point

This example uses the sans serif font PT Sans Regular, 11 point

How to choose a Web font.

You already know to choose fonts for style, readability and contrast. But as you know, type on paper is not the same as type onscreen. Web typography requires additional consideration. Remember the diagram "Parts of a Font" and the graphic spread "A Field Guide to Basic Font Categories"? Here's how to apply that knowledge.

Select for Web readability. Due to the lower pixel density on most computer and mobile device screens, Web fonts benefit from slightly heavier details, increased x-heights and humanist rather than geometric shapes. Shafts, crossbars and serifs that are too fine/thin can virtually disappear onscreen. Larger x-heights mean more open counters and space for counters and bowls. This increases legibility of individual glyphs and therefore the readability of words. On the other hand, geometric fonts cut down on readability because all the glyphs look alike. Again, the more legible the glyphs, the easier it is to read the words glyphs form.

Select for scalability. Web fonts need the flexibility of a gymnast. They will be asked to scale up and down to fit huge desktop monitors and tiny mobile device screens. Test-drive your choices to make sure they remain legible and readable across devices.

Consider reading rhythm. The placement of words in lines across a layout creates a visual horizontal path. (Gestalt theory, anyone?) And a font's ascenders and descenders add a vertical rhythm to those lines. Regular rhythm makes easier reading. If the ascenders and descenders are too close together (condensed font) or too far apart (wide font), the reader can experience eye fatigue. Aim for a font width somewhere in the middle.

READING RHYTHM

Ascenders and descenders create reading rhythm. Regular pacing makes easier reading.

Test-drive your font choices and make sure they remain legible and readable across the board. (Alps Condensed 12 point)

Test-drive your font choices and make sure they remain legible and readable across the board. (Alps 12 point)

Test-drive your font choices and make sure they remain legible and readable across the board. (Alps Wide 12 point)

Legibility of glyphs and User Interface.* It's clear that Web fonts wear many hats. They set the look and readability of body copy, headlines and cutlines. But they are also key to a website's usability. Think about it. If links and buttons aren't clearly legible, your visitor won't be able to navigate the site. Legibility at small sizes requires clearly differentiated glyphs. If you've ever confused a lowercase letter "l" for the number "1," then you understand the issue. Again, try out font choices in different digital environments and select accordingly.

Final thoughts.

As a rule we recommend sans serif fonts for the Web, but don't limit yourself. There are serifed fonts that work equally well. Just apply these rules to your potential picks and decide which to use from there.

Do we suggest you are restricted to using fonts that meet the letter (bad pun intended) of these selection rules? Of course not. But limit less-legible and less-readable fonts to short copy situations like headlines. Test your selections, preferably across browsers *and* devices, including smartphone screens. Trust your eyes to help you make the right choices for your Web project.

DIFFERENTIATION FOR USER INTERFACE

Clearly differentiated fonts. Notice how the capital letter "I" and the lowercase letter "l" look identical in the first example. The PT Sans font solves this by adding little tails to the lowercase "l."

In the second example, all the letters in the word "pedagogy" have the same rounded shape. The Franklin Gothic font uses a "two-story" letter "a" and letter "g" to create better differentiation.

Illuminate (Verlag Book)

Illuminate (PT Sans Regular)

Pedagogy (Century Gothic)

Pedagogy (Franklin Gothic Book)

*Adapted from Design by Izo Blog, by Ian Hex. http://www. design-by-izo.com/2011/10/18/what-should-i-look-for-in-a-ui-typeface/

Size matters. When typesetting headlines, subheadings and other nonbody copy, make sure you provide clear contrast of size, font style or both. Don't be scared of "too big." The "Bears" title is set at 208 points. A 12-point font is used in the schedule. We're pretty sure that qualifies as clear contrast.

When selecting a font size for body copy, choose a size large enough to be easily readable. For print projects, start by trying a setting of 10 or 11 points, but be prepared to change the size again. Font size is calculated by measuring the distance from the top of the ascenders to the bottom of the descenders. The length of ascenders and descenders relative to x-height may make some fonts appear smaller and some appear larger. You'll have to learn to trust your judgment on choosing a font size that hits the correct note between mousetype and horsey.

Don't forget to consider your audience. If your target audience is middle-aged or older, go larger rather than smaller. The older people get the more likely they are to need reading glasses. They'll appreciate bigger fonts. Trust us.

PLANTATIONS OF NEW ORLEANS

Xim velent eost qui untem etur aut endae nihil id qui volor solupta cum, istiaec tempore stiatusante nobis dunt.

Unt facessunt eatur, omnihil moluptas inullene estrum sitature, quibea dolorum sus eos dolore, sequatur alicien tiatatectam aut Tin natia debita volorem. Nempor sequis mo odi dolo eum des nisci aligend icabori orpora ped que entios dolor aut qui ut quias sequi ditiberion re modigni tatiis modiataquam as id quiat.

In cus ut perite plaborpore nisi deratec ernamet harunti anienis ium

et que nihicim porepe experum ut la doloritia dolesci tatiat quiasit perates nam seditios alisquo bea sectio. Ut dolupiet alibus sae minime officias rerchiliam nobist, veruptatem. Ut mil magnihiliqui corunt etus, nobis sit aute delest porporepere nihici in esequatur apernatiae re cupta doluptae etus nim suntiusae. Ga. Onsed molorest apitatus veriorumquia.

Tem harumquamusa dolupientota volupta turibusam illorem imusam ut fuga. Et la corundendem qui re dia il iuribus, ium?

Choose font sizes for headings, cutlines and other nonbody uses based on both readability and contrast. Headings must contrast with body copy, so make them really contrast. A 12-point heading barely contrasts with a 10-point body copy font; a 48-point headline greatly contrasts.

Finding the "right" font size for a Web project is especially difficult because there are factors beyond your control that impact the way fonts appear onscreen. Personal browser choice, browser settings and whether the site is viewed on a monitor, tablet or smartphone all impact font size.

Since the best website designs are responsive—that is, they automatically adjust to the viewing device—we need font size specifications that adjust as well. Rather than set Web font sizes in nonflexible points or pixels, consider setting font sizes in adjustable "ems" or "rems." Em and rem size adjusts up or down via percentages. If this is absolute Greek to you, don't worry. We discuss ems in more detail in Chapter 13.

Even though ems and rems are flexible, you still have to establish a baseline size. Baseline font sizes have gotten bigger in recent years, right along with the need to be legible on smaller screens. A good place to start is 16 pixels.

If your typesetting is bound for video, font sizes are best skewed even larger. Web video is likely to be viewed on tiny smartphone screens, and no one watches television from a foot away. Test your font sizes for television by stepping back from your computer and viewing your typesetting from a distance. For smaller screens, use a mobile browser emulator to see what your typesetting looks like on different

Classic. Use of all caps can be classic and elegant as in the heading above. But used in body copy, all caps become difficult to read. Bottom line? If you use all caps, do it with purpose.

WHAT'S IT **CALLED?**

Leading/line spacing is the space between lines. Decrease it when you are creating large multi-line headlines. See the difference?

Big headlines need adjusting

Big headlines need adjusting

Tracking refers to adjusting the spacing between characters across a string of characters. It can be increased or decreased for copyfitting or for effect.

Tracking increased
Tracking decreased

Kerning refers to adjusting the space between individual glyphs. We applied a kerning adjustment of -78 to the pair on the right.

smartphones and tablets. A baseline font size of 24 points is a good place to start.

Bold & italic type.

Both bold type and italic type can create emphasis in short copy situations, such as headings, subheadings or short body copy.

Did we mention short copy situations? Use bolding or italics sparingly. Neither bold nor italic is appropriate for entire pages or long paragraphs of type. Ugh. Too much italic is hard to read, particularly in digital formats. And too much bold defeats the purpose of having bold at all. When there's too much of it, nothing stands out.

We also would like to point out that not all bolds are created equal. Some bold fonts are bolder than others. Sometimes a bigger font size, a different color or a different font altogether provides greater contrast than using just plain bold.

Avoid faux bold and italic. Some non-professional grade software packages and most Web page editors include buttons for faux bold and faux italic. You've seen these. They're little squares with "b" or "i" on them. These buttons seem to let you apply bold or italic to any font.

But in truth, these buttons merely stroke or distort letterforms to appear as bold or italic. And using them can have disastrous results in commercial printing. Like crashing-the-printer's-software disastrous. No kidding. You should avoid using these buttons to apply styling.

Faux styling can cause poor onscreen rendering as well, especially with italics. So you should avoid faux onscreen, too.

So how do you apply bold and italic? Choose a font specifically designed as bold or italic. Remember our advice to choose typefaces with multiple fonts? Here's where that advice comes into play. Choose and use bold fonts and italic fonts from larger typefaces and you'll save yourself a boatload of printing and rendering headaches.

All caps.

All caps are an old-school style of emphasis. Type set in all caps cuts down on readability. When we first learn to read, we are taught the shape of each letter and its corresponding sound. We put letters and their sounds together to make words. Over time, our mental process shifts to the point where we recognize shapes of words without the need for scanning and adding up individual characters. But when you capitalize words, they lose the ascenders and descenders that make up their unique shapes. Every word becomes a rectangle, and our brains have to work just a little bit harder to recognize the word.

To add insult to injury, we have come to associate all caps with shouting. And nobody likes to be shouted at.

If you want to use all caps, make sure they don't interfere with your visual communication purpose, including readability.

Spacing.

Leading. Pronounced "ledding," leading is the technical term for line spacing. It comes from the days of setting type by hand. Once upon a time, typesetters used a slug of lead to separate each line of type.

Today, your computer calculates leading. Every font size has a corresponding default number (a percentage of the font size) that serves as line spacing. This default number works okay most of the time. However, there are times when you need to adjust it.

When the body copy font has a large x-height, the type on the page or screen can feel heavy and claustrophobic. Increasing the line spacing alleviates this and improves readability. A little extra leading increases readability, too, when the eye must track across a very long line of type, as in wide columns or no columns. Be careful not to overdo additional leading, as too much space also cuts down on flow and readability.

You might add extra leading for decorative purposes, too, but only for limited amounts of type. A little extra leading can give the sense of elegance or lightness/airiness, if that serves your communication purpose. Just remember to use the technique in moderation to preserve readability and flow.

On the other hand, when creating large headlines, reducing leading is essential. Because leading is mathematically calculated based on font size, as the font size increases, so does the leading—exponentially. For headlines more than one line deep, decrease the leading to bring the lines closer together (i.e., clumping). Beginning designers often

unwind.

Em quam, acipsum, sequaspe ipsandae

velitat antiant acitis es eum res non

pa dolo blab ilis sim nonsequ osamus

voluptatem. Elligent et hit aut et

fuga. Neque dolorepel estia voluptati

rerupta nest, niendae parum

Visit
STATE PARKS
www.visitstateparks.org

Fine-tuning your type. Increased tracking on the headline and increased leading on the copy give this ad an open, airy quality.

We'll have the bruschetta. This menu design utilizes different types of font styling such as tabs and tab leaders to create order and organization.

---

overlook this step, leaving headline gaps you could drive a bus through.

Kerning. Manually adjusting the negative space between two characters is called kerning. Most design programs are set to adjust these spaces automatically. However, you still may need to do some fine-tuning.

When uppercase letters have diagonal lines, such as on the capital W, adjacent letters may appear too far away, particularly when font sizes are large. You also may need to adjust the kerning in large headline words that begin with the capital letters T, P and F.

Tracking. Adjusting letter spacing across characters in a sentence or paragraph is called tracking. You also can manipulate tracking for decorative purposes to create tightly packed or loosely spaced words.

Sometimes tracking becomes useful for copyfitting. For example, when you have a widow at the end of a column, decreasing the tracking on that sentence may pull the lone word up to the previous line. Your reader will never notice the difference.

Adjust tracking with care. It's easy to go overboard and end up with squished text. Try to limit tracking adjustments to "–10" or less.

Availability of leading (line spacing), kerning and tracking on the Web. You can apply leading (referred to as line spacing in the context of websites), tracking and kerning to Web type, too. In the case of line spacing and tracking, Web designers write specifications (lines of coded visual instructions for Web browsers) in Cascading Style Sheets (CSS) to control how much space appears between glyphs or between lines of copy.

Kerning on the Web requires a bit more effort, specifically, a little programming/scripting. But it *is* possible.

Before you get excited about creating widely tracked headlines on your website, a word of warning: The CSS specifications exist, but they are not universally supported on all browsers. Typesetting that looks great on your computer screen may not appear at all on your best friend's computer. Don't let this stop you from experimenting. Just remember to provide a supported fallback style in case your chosen style doesn't universally appear as desired.

We give our associates every opportunity to succeed in their environment, and they always will be our most valuable assets.

B. A DRIVE FOR CONTINUOUS IMPROVEMENT

Dimmitt Automotive Group also subscribes to resolving business issues and challenges on the front line. We empower our associates through an internal program we refer to as Continuous Improvement Team Process (CIT). Our CIT process works like this:

» A problem or opportunity for improvement is identified by an associate/team member (such as "we are having difficulty in getting clients in to install special ordered parts.")

» We organize a group/committee of volunteers within the organization to help solve the issue at hand. This includes 5-7 people from different departments within the dealership. By design, we avoid involving senior leadership at this stage and allow the team to designate their own lead or captain who keeps matters on point and moving forward towards a solution.

» This group meets when convenient for an hour, usually at lunch time, with food provided by the company. They begin with a flow chart that aids in creating timely and cost effective solutions to the existing problem and identifying new opportunities for improvement.

» Once the group has identified a process and solution, they present their ideas to the leadership team in the weekly manager's meeting. There, a lively exchange is encouraged which ultimately results in the leadership team's endorsement and encouragement to implement the solution through teamwork.

Over the last eight to ten years, dozens of these CIT groups have been organized while empowering associates to make a difference and reinforce the importance of their involvement in decision making. The execution and long term commitment to the solution is always more effective when associates feel a sense of ownership.

C. BUILT ON ORGANIZATIONAL INNOVATION

One constant we can depend on is that the modern marketplace is forever evolving and changing how customers research, shop for, and purchase vehicles, and even how they build relationships with brands. With this notion always at the forefront of our minds, we have built a culture that embraces change and innovation.

Over time, we have refined our team-based approach for internet relationship management to pioneer a process we call our Business Development Center (BDC). Our BDC is made up of two focus areas, Sales and Service. We employ 6 BDC Guest Service Associates that concentrate on sales and 4 on service. The great difference in using this strategy is the realization of guest expectations. Within the BDC process, our Guest Services team fields all incoming contacts (via online or phone) and acts as concierge or liaison between the guest and the proper Product or Service Specialist. We find this ensures proper guest care, follow-up, and that all expectations were not only met but exceeded. We are also able to keep all of our communications centralized in-house, even including online chat, to provide a measurable and process-driven personal touch. History has

proven to us that when a guest is well taken care of, they will become an advocate for Dimmitt Automotive Group in the community.

All client and guest data is cleanly managed through our BDC and internet strategy to effectively recognize the stages of the ownership and purchase process. As our specialists review our guests' patterns and buying behaviors, we are able to reach out to them according to predicted needs whether it be service or sales. These predictions are based on vehicle ownership, product cycle and service timelines.

We also employ a complete in-house e-Marketing team that applies a youthful focus on digital marketing and social media. Our digital marketing efforts integrate and complement our traditional, event-based marketing and BDC processes. Our goal is to provide a comprehensive outreach and relationship-building marketing framework and to exceed guest expectations.

8

9

Tabs & dot leaders.

Sometimes, in order to keep things aligned, you need tabs. Use tabs for columns of numbers, too, and pay attention to aligning decimal places. Sometimes tabs space out farther than the eye can travel without some help. In those cases, instead of making readers' eyes do the typographic equivalent of a stunt jump across a Grand Canyon of negative space, dot leaders can function like visual bridges. They assist flow by leading the eye along their line of sight.

TYPESETTING LENGTHY COPY

Page after page of nothing but boring gray words scares people, even when the words are set in a nice readable font. The prospect of slogging through all that reading is discouraging at best. The good news is that there are tactics for carving intimidating text into bite-size pieces.

Paragraph indicators.

Paragraphs are traditionally indicated either by a first line indent or by additional leading after each paragraph. Unfortunately, most people use default tabs or an extra hard return to create paragraphs. Visually, these default keystrokes result in spaces that are too large.

Breaking up the gray.
Large headings, column guides, bulleted lists and ample white space make this text-heavy document inviting.

Reproduced by permission of Dimmitt Automotive Group.

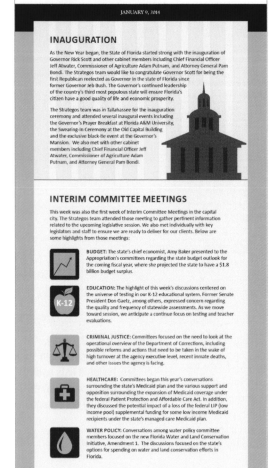

In print projects, you set paragraph indents or paragraph space-afters using the specific tools that your design software provides for those tasks.

For Web projects, your best bet is spacing after paragraphs. And again, using double hard returns to achieve this results in too much space. Not to mention it's just plain lazy. Instead, specify a bit of extra bottom margin on your paragraph element in your CSS.

How big should the spaces be? Use your best judgment. First line indents should be consistent. They need to be just big enough to communicate their presence and do their visual indicator job, but not big enough to distract. If you choose to indicate paragraphs with the indent, remember the first graph or lead does not indent. Or, if you decide to space between paragraphs, don't overdo the space, but do be consistent.

Still not sure about size? Pay attention to publications around you. Educate your eye on what pleasing spacing looks like. Then use it in your own design projects.

Headings & subheads.

Main headers and subheads also provide a great way to break up blocks of text. When styled for contrast, headings and subheads create a sort of navigational rhythm throughout the design.

Proper spacing for headings and subheads increases readers' understanding, too. Remember to position headers closer to the content they reference (clustering) and farther away from unrelated content.

Additionally, remember that headings and subheads should indicate a hierarchy of content. As you might guess, the bigger the headline, the more important it and its related content become. By graduating the size of subheads, the corresponding copy's importance increases or decreases. Keep track of your levels of headings, along with your own decisions about typesetting them consistently.

Headings are particulaly important in Web design. When your headings are "tagged" as such in the code, and those headings include keywords, you've taken key steps in making your site search-engine friendly.

Optical fonts for special purposes.

Some extended typefaces include "optical fonts" that are cut for specific typesetting purposes. Caption fonts are an optical font meant for use in (duh) captions. Caption font glyphs are drawn to facilitate better reading at smaller sizes. Display fonts are designed to showcase font detail and shape at large headline sizes. Display fonts are great for use in poster, newspaper, magazine and advertising design. The general rule is to use a display font if your headline will be 20 points or larger.

Bulleted lists.

You can't beat a bulleted list for delivering information quickly and concisely. Bullets serve as eye entry points, letting the reader know in an instant that a new important idea starts here. And the easy scanability of bulleted lists makes them ideal for Web content.

When typesetting bulleted lists, you have two options: Either match the bulleted list with the surrounding body type or make it contrast.

When your bulleted list is embedded within and flows along with the rest of the copy, it should match in terms of font style, size and color.

If your bulleted list flows with the copy, consider indenting the whole list. You'll have to use your judgment on how much to indent. Too little and the indentation looks like a mistake. Too much and you'll have a distracting gaping hole in your layout.

If your bulleted list sits in a sidebar or is otherwise visually separated from the rest of the copy, make it contrast with the surrounding body type. For example, if your body copy is set in an old style font, consider a sans serif for your visually separated bullet list.

Hanging indents. Whether your list is inline or in a separate box, a bulleted list requires a hanging indent. In a hanging indent, the first line of a paragraph "hangs" out—juts out—into the left margin. It's sort of the opposite or reverse of an indent. A hanging indent pushes the organizing numerals or bullets to the left and aligns all the remaining text together along a single axis.

When setting hanging indents, consider adding extra leading between each list item. The extra negative space helps isolate each item and makes it easier to digest the list. This is white space and clustering to the communication rescue.

Finally, choose your bullets wisely. You can dress up a list with decorative bullets, but as with most design decisions, choose wisely and with restraint. If you want a bullet with more personality, consider pulling a shape from one of the many symbol-based font sets out there. Choose something that matches the tone of your layout.

Adding a bit of color to your bullets is also an option. A small pop of color at the beginning of each line can aid the reader in navigating your list. But keep it to one color, please. You don't want your bullet list to look like the inside of a bag of jellybeans.

TAKING A PAGE FROM NEWSPAPER DESIGN

For presenting extensive amounts of type in a digestible format, newspapers rule. Designers of daily broadsheet newspapers manage to lay out five or six text-heavy stories on a single front page each day, with each story clearly delineated in a visual hierarchy. Much of this fantastic feat is accomplished with typesetting. And the best part? These tactics adapt to Web design and other types of print design, too.

Story headlines.

Headlines are the billboards of newspaper design. A well-styled headline is like a big smack on the nose that says, "Read me!" Newspaper designers are experts at creating interest and visual hierarchy through techniques like page position and font contrast.

Graduated headline sizes also reinforce the idea that some stories are more important than others. The bigger the headline, the more important the story. Headline font sizes vary, but it's unusual to see them set less than 24 points, which means leading adjustments, too, for headlines that run more than one line deep.

Newsletters utilize many of the same typesetting techniques as newspapers. Graduated headline styles create hierarchy, and images break up the text-heavy page.

Reproduced by permission of Tucker/Hall, Inc.

FROM HEALTHCARE DAILY DIVE NEWS:

DIVE BRIEF »

- A new report from global consulting firm PwC suggests that hospital mergers, acquisitions and affiliations are going to continue at a high rate this year.
- Hospital deal volume has been rising steadily since 2009, though it saw a small decrease (5%) in 2013.
- There were 89 mergers and acquisitions announced in the hospital sector last year, with total transaction value rising from $1.9 billion in 2012 to $18.6 billion this year due to the execution of large deals like Community Health Systems' $7.6 billion acquisition of Health Management Associates.

Dive Insight: It doesn't take a weatherman to know which way the wind blows, and it doesn't take a genius to see that hospital mergers, acquisitions and affiliations are likely to continue at a breakneck pace this year. After all, with the market focused on large entities like ACOs, it must be getting pretty scary to the community hospital or even a small health system going it alone. True, running into the arms of another entity comes with its own set of problems, but for now, for many struggling hospitals some sort of deal probably looks like a brilliant idea.

FROM BECKER'S HOSPITAL REVIEW :

REPORT: SIGNIFICANT HOSPITAL M&A ACTIVITY LIKELY TO CONTINUE THIS YEAR
Written by Helen Adamopoulos March 27, 2014

Hospital transaction activity is expected to continue at a high rate in 2014, spurred by various market and regulatory trends, according to a report from global consulting firm PwC.

Hospital deal volume has been steadily rising since 2009, although it dipped by 5 percent in 2013, according to the report. There were 89 mergers and acquisitions announced in the sector last year, down from 94 in 2012. However, total hospital transaction value rose from $1.9 billion in 2012 to $18.6 billion in 2013 because of several multibillion-dollar deals. These deals included, among others, Franklin, Tenn.-based Community Health Systems' $7.6 billion acquisition of Naples, Fla.-based Health Management Associates and Dallas-based Tenet Healthcare Corp.'s purchase of Nashville, Tenn.-based Vanguard Health Systems — a deal valued at $4.3 billion.

PwC expects factors such as uncertainty surrounding healthcare reform,

convergence within the payer and provider arenas and expanding physician alignment will continue to drive high levels of hospital deal activity in 2014, according to the report.

"Health systems really need to rethink how and where they deliver care and how to best manage the patient populations," says Steven Elek III, partner and global healthcare deals leader at PwC. "That's impacting how they think about their missions. So I would expect to continue to see a heightened level of hospital deal activity."

He says some notable trends prompting hospitals and health systems to consolidate are downward pressure on revenues driving the need for scale, health systems assessing new geographies and patient populations as well as competencies and the pursuit of greater negotiating leverage with non-government payers. He says other key drivers of consolidation include capital

access challenges for financially stressed organizations, capacity management and providers looking to achieve cost synergies through the consolidation of administrative services, leveraging the supply chain and rationalizing capital projects.

Based on what PwC has observed among its clients, Mr. Elek says it's quite likely deal volumes will rise again this year, and larger health systems will also continue to develop and acquire health plans.

The report says hospital and health system consolidation plays into efforts to revamp care delivery and reduce spending. "Building the end-to-end continuum of care is a pathway to assist in controlling costs and improving the patient experience," the report states. "Many deals in the hospital, healthcare system and physician medical group sectors attempt to address these issues."

Tucker/Hall One Tampa City Center, Suite 2760 | Tampa, FL 33602 | 813.228.0652 | tuckerhall.com   **TuckerHall**

Another trick is to choose a condensed font for headlines. Writing news-style headlines can be tricky. They need to be pithy, but keeping them concise can be difficult. Condensed fonts are drawn to be narrower than standard fonts. Since condensed fonts take up less space, they offer an extra bit of wiggle room for copyfitting headlines. You don't need to be a news pro, either, to take advantage of that kind of help.

Columns.

We keep going on about columns, but newspapers are set in columns because it's easier for the eye to track back and forth across a few inches as opposed to the width of an entire screen or page. To review, newspapers teach us that about two inches make a good-sized column width—not too wide or too narrow.

In printed newspapers the recommended length for legs of body copy is a minimum of two inches and a maximum of 12. Keeping leg length shorter also applies to news website home pages, where the goal is to introduce multiple stories in the same space. In fact, newspaper home pages often display short excerpts rather than short legs of copy. Once the reader clicks through to get to the full story, the copy is likely to be set in a single column and length is no longer an issue.

Even if you don't want the look of columns in your document, you can take advantage of the principle of narrower lines of type for the eye to scan by increasing margins and decreasing line length.

Justification.

One thing beginning designers should *not* emulate is the full justification of newspaper type.

Technically, justification refers to all forms of copy alignment, including left justified (flush left with ragged right edge), right justified (flush right with ragged left edge), centered or fully justified (right and left edges perfectly squared).

The best justification for reading is always left justified (flush left with ragged right). It accommodates natural word spacing and provides easy eye tracking. Poorly handled full justification results in unsightly gaps in copy. Not only does this look awful, it cuts down on readability.

Full justification can be particularly problematic in websites. Well-designed responsive pages adjust in size to fit the viewing device (phone, tablet)

Onulputet lum zzril ullam inci tat lutat. Ut la commod ea acilla facip er se volore feu feuipsusto dunt ilit at.

Ut er alit inciduis nis et am zzriure rciliquis dionsecte modio consectem num incing ea aut et incipiscilis ad dionulla con eum zzrillandre el digniate verat.

Duipit dolor se diat, volor se magnis nis nullam, consed ming ea consectet dui eu feum vullandre molumsan hent dolor alit nos num ip elit aliquat at veliquip

Get out your canoe paddles…
Fully justified text can create ugly rivers of white space unless the ratio of font size to column width is just right. Newspaper designers are professionals and can pull this off. You, however, should not try this at home.

How many white gaps can you find in the column above?

or browser window size. It's difficult to control rivers of white space in print when you have total control of the design. Web design never affords you 100 percent control of appearance so you can never guarantee a site viewer won't get rivers.

TYPE: NOT JUST FOR READING ANYMORE

In addition to type tricks that encourage reading to convey information, there are type techniques that set the piece's overall tone and create visual interest. Obviously, any selection from the huge range of decorative fonts can help set mood and tone. But don't discount using more traditional fonts in creative ways. No matter which route you choose, exercise caution when using type creatively. It is easy to go from type that communicates to type that clutters.

Bold & italic.

We've already discussed how bold and italic fonts create emphasis. But bold and italic fonts also have decorative uses. Both type treatments make interesting pull quotes, decks, cutlines, headlines and other short blocks of type.

Small caps.

A variation on all caps, small caps are all uppercase letters with a slightly larger first-letter capitalization. Small caps suffer from the same readability issues as all caps and should be used with caution—and only in short copy situations.

Reversed type.

Reversed type is light type against a dark background. It's a common technique used in creating headlines, sidebars and other layout elements. Like all caps, it's best used sparingly. Reading a lot of reversed copy may reduce readability or tire the eye.

Enjoy in moderation. While reversed type creates visual interest, it also cuts down on readability. If you choose to use reversed type, use it sparingly. And pick bolder fonts, or those with more uniform thickness. See how much easier it is to read the sans serif example?

If you choose to employ reversed type, choose your font carefully. Some fonts lose legibility more than others when set in reverse. Modern fonts, with their ultra thin horizontals, are notoriously bad in the reversing department. Reversing works best with slightly thicker sans serif fonts, though slab serif, bold versions of old style fonts and some decorative fonts are equally effective.

Initial & drop caps.

Those really huge single letters (or words) that appear at the start of the first paragraph are called drop caps and initial caps. Drop caps drop down into several lines of the paragraph. Initial caps sit on the baseline and rise upward well above the line.

Both are excellent ways to create a dynamic eye entry point for your lead. You can set their color and size. You might even set the font to something that contrasts with your body font.

It's best to use only one drop cap per page or story and only at the very beginning. While it is possible to use more than one across a multiple-page spread, don't deploy them in every single paragraph. And if you do use more than one drop cap on a spread, make sure your drop caps don't accidentally spell out something offensive. You laugh, but it can happen.

GILL SANS
Eric Gill | 1928

Gill Sans has less of a mechanical feel than geometric sans-serifs like Futura and realist sans-serif typefaces like Akzidenz Grotesk, because its proportions stemmed from Roman tradition (for its upper case) and Carolingian script and classic serif fonts (for the lower case).

The upper-case of **Gill Sans** is modelled on monumental Roman capitals like those found on the Column of Trajan: the capital M from **Gill Sans** is based on the proportions of a square with the middle strokes meeting at the centre of that square. The Carolingian influence is noticeable in the two-story lower-case a, and g. The lower-case t is similar to old-style serifs in its proportion and oblique terminus of the vertical stroke, while the lower-case a has a dramatic narrowing towards the top of its loop extremely rare in sans-serif fonts. Following the humanist model the lower-case italic a becomes single story and the lower-case p has a vestigial calligraphic tail reminiscent of the italics of Caslon and Baskerville. Like most serif fonts (but unlike most sans-serif fonts), **Gill Sans** uses ligatures to allow its expansive letter f to join up with letters around it.

~en.wikipedia.org/wiki/Gill_Sans

ABCDEF
GHIJKLM
NOPQRST
UVWXYZ
abcdefgjhi
jklmnopqr
stuvwxyz
1234567890

Newspapers and other publications are dotted with examples of type used creatively. You'll commonly see logos, folios, pull quotes and other typographic design details giving life and order to otherwise dull pages.

Letterforms themselves can be interesting with angles and curves that contrast nicely with the rectangular shape of most screens and pages. Creative designers often manipulate the scale and orientation of fonts to turn type into visual focal points in lieu of photos, line art or other graphics. That's when things get really fun.

More than a pretty typeface. Every font has a story that begins with the type designer's vision. Inventing new fonts is a whole industry, while classic typefaces, such as Gill Sans, stand the test of time. Likewise, designing with type is an art form. So let the lines and shapes of letters inspire your layouts. Who needs pictures when letters and words are so beautiful?

TYPESET LIKE A PRO: TYPESETTER'S PUNCTUATION

Glyph	Replace this...	with this...	and code with this.
Quotes	"Straight quotes"	"Smart quotes"	“ ”
Elipses	. . .	…	…
Em dash	---	—	—
En dash	--	–	–
Prime marks	1' 3"	1′ 3″	′ ″
Special characters	1/2, 1/4, copyright, registered trademark	½, ¼, ©, ®	½ ¼ © ™
Accent marks	a, n, e, o	â, ñ, é, ö	â ñ é ö

ICING ON THE CAKE

Although most fonts have 265 characters, that's a far greater number than the sum of adding up upper- and lowercase letters, numbers and basic punctuation. So what's up with the other 100-plus characters?

Typesetter's punctuation.

If you're still typing ellipses as "period space period space period space," you're doing it wrong. Among those 265 characters are punctuation marks specifically drawn and spaced to match the rest of the glyphs in the font. If you know where to look, you'll also find a variety of specific punctuation glyphs you may not know exist, even though such glyphs are routinely necessary to produce professional-grade type.

For example, you need smart quotes (curly quotes) for quotations. You need the straight version of quote marks called prime marks for notating inches and feet without writing out the words "inches" and "feet."

While you need the hyphen to create compound words, you need en dashes (historically the width of a lowercase n) for punctuating such things as the implied "to" in "3–4 weeks." Then you'll need the slightly wider em dash—historically the width of a lowercase m—for dashes used to replace commas, colons and parentheses—when you're trying to be slightly more emphatic.

Typesetter's punctuation is available for websites, too. Some Web coding software provides palettes or menus that allow you to access and insert the character of choice. Punctuation can also be inserted manually by plugging the proper HTML code in the right location.

If you don't think the proper symbols look better than type kluges, we'll give you your money back. Okay, not really. But do check out what proper punctuation looks like and figure out how to use it. Because what you don't know about type can hurt you.

OpenType for print design.

OpenType fonts go well beyond the standard 265 characters. Designed to be functional across platforms to work on both Macs and PCs, these fonts may have as many as 65,000 characters. In addition to all the traditional punctuation marks and accent marks, OpenType fonts offer some or all of the following type options:

Ligatures. Ligatures are specially designed letter pairs—a single glyph meant to take the place of two traditional letters. Ligatures were created for certain letter pairs that join awkwardly because of the position of the dot of the "i" or hook of the "f," for example.

Swash alternates. These are just what they sound like: decorative alternatives to traditional italic letterforms. While swash alternates don't work well for body copy, they can be beautiful when used in large decorative headlines, as initial caps or in pull quotes.

Old style figures. Ever notice that normal numbers often look too big and clunky when typed in with the normal flow of text? That's because the height of regular numerals is the same as uppercase letters. Regular numerals have the visual feel of all caps. An alternative is to use old style figures. Old style figures have varying x-heights, ascenders and descenders just like the rest of the letters in a font. Visually, they blend in much better with text.

Dingbats. If you've ever seen a decorative ornament to indicate that you've reached the end of the narrative, you've seen a dingbat. They look like little tiny pictures, but they really are font characters. Many fonts have a few as part of the 265-character set. Typically, OpenType fonts have more of them. Then there are fonts made up of nothing but dingbats.

Because they are technically font characters, you can style dingbats as you would fonts. You can change their size, color and orientation. They

Confused about the difference between swash alternates and ligatures? Let us explain.

Swash alternates are different versions of individual glyphs in a typeface. The first letter in the pairing is the standard italic glyph. The second is the swash alternate.

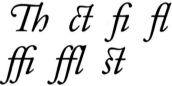

Ligatures are decorative replacements for common glyph pairs. They address troublesome pairings like "f" and "i" in which the terminal of the "f" bumps into the dot on the "i." Some classic ligatures are shown here. Note the solution to the "f" and "i" collision.

Have you seen me?
Dingbats look like little tiny pictures, but they really are font characters. Each of these dingbats has been used somewhere in this book. Can you find them? How are they used? Are you getting creatively inspired yet?

can also function as bullets, although, as always, use some discipline. Not all dingbats make good bullets.

Paired with letterforms, dingbats can be logos. Strings of them can become section breaks or borders. Or they can stand alone as artwork.

Still think type is boring? Neither do we. It is perhaps the most important tool in your visual communication toolbox. Use it. Don't abuse it.

TRY THIS

1. Start a "swipe file" of neat typography and typesetting techniques. Look for anything with interesting type: logos; headline styles from magazines, newspapers and websites; sidebars and infographics; bulleted lists; opening slides from video clips; or interesting product packaging. Look for dingbats, ligatures, swash alternates and other uses of extended character sets, too.

   Assemble your examples in a scrapbook. Annotate your examples with notes on why you like them and why they work. Categorize your selections by style: corporate, kid-friendly, grunge, romantic, extreme, etc.

2. Go to the candy aisle at your grocery store. Look for packages of the following types of candy: Gummy bears, traditional stick chewing gum, a milk chocolate bar, a chocolate bar with additional ingredients such as nuts or caramel and an expensive bar of dark chocolate. Look at the font choices on each package.

   What categories of fonts does your candy-wrapper collection exhibit? Are the font choices appropriate for the target audience? Explain.

   Design a candy wrapper for your own favorite candy. Write rationales for your choices.

3. Design a type-only logo for yourself. Use your logo to create your own set of custom business cards and letterhead. Or use your logo as the basis for a new resume design.

4. Create your one-color typographic self-portrait. Using only glyphs (including numerals and punctuation but not dingbats) create a close-up mug shot of yourself. Size contrast will be important. Direction, in the literal sense of turning glyphs topsy-turvy, also will be important. Otherwise, the rules go out the window since you're not using type to convey narrative information.

5. Research a famous font artist. Write a short history (a paragraph or two) and create a one-page layout using your history as the content. Use only fonts designed by your artist, and use only type in your design. No photos or illustrations allowed.

6. Create a vertically folding restaurant menu with a flat size at 8.5 inches wide by 11 inches high folded to a finished size of 4.25 inches by 11 inches. You'll need to design a cover and a two-page inside spread. A design for the back cover is optional. Begin with some menu copywriting.

   Use typography to convey the kind of restaurant (casual Thai or upscale French, for instance). Create a visual hierarchy and a sense of visual order, too.

   Demonstrate appropriate punctuation marks, paragraph indicators, bulleted lists and hanging indents, tabs and tab leaders, and whatever else is appropriate to your design.

OpenType is either a registered trademark or trademark of Microsoft Corporation in the United States and/or other countries.

Logotype as personality type.
Logo design represents the epitome of typographic creativity. Whether as big as a barn or as small as mousetype, logotypes must encapsulate and telegraph brand character. That's why logo design is safest in the hands of professionals. Read on for our "What You Need to Know about Logo Design" pages, coming up next.

Design by Rebecca Hagen. Reproduced by permission of TEC Garage.

what you need to know about logo design

Professional designers make logo design look easy. Some of the most powerful recognizable logos in the world are pictures of simplicity. The elegant appearance of these marks belies the fact that most logos require hundreds of hours of brainstorming, sketching, rendering, rejecting and approving before they are launched. The stakes are high. One tiny little picture, or word and picture combination, must encompass the philosophy, activity, spirit and brand promise of an organization. This is why logo design is best left to professionals.

That said, you will have to work with logos in some form. Maybe you've hired a designer to create a logo for a new product launch. Or perhaps you need something simple for internal purposes, and you just don't have the budget to hire a designer. Whether you need to evaluate logos provided by a designer or you need to design something yourself, here are a few things you should know:

Logos should be unique to the subject/product/organization. Avoid anything too generic. If the design in question easily could represent another organization with the same name and a different mission, then go back to the drawing board.

Logos must be scalable. The design needs to be as clear and readable at the size of a postage stamp as it is at the size of an outdoor board. Avoid fine lines and details that disappear when a logo is reduced in size. If a logo uses more than one font, make sure both fonts are readable even when the logo is small.

The only scalable file format is vector so make sure you get vector versions of the finished logo. Vector filenames often end with the .eps extension. Photos are bitmap images and can't be scaled without loss of resolution. Never use a photo in a logo because photos lose resolution when scaled.

The incredible shrinking logo. Your logo may be used on a billboard. It also may be used on a business card. And it must look crisp in both places. Logos must be rendered as vector graphics to allow for scalability.

Left: Font pairings. Choose your font pairings carefully. Shrinking the Inkworks logo could cause the smaller "Tattoo Studio" subheading to be illegible. The fonts in the Anton Group logo are more uniform and will maintain legibility even at small sizes.

Inkworks logo inspired by the Inked God font by Gyom Séguin.

Simplicity is a virtue. What you want in a logo design is versatility. The highly complex illustrated logo may look great on the large sign outside, but what if you want to embroider the logo on polo shirts? Commercial embroidery companies will have a difficult time rendering your logo if it has too many details or fine elements, including serifs on fonts. If you must have a complex logo, make sure you have a simplified version as well.

Limit the number of colors. Simplicity also applies to the logo's color. The more colors a logo uses, the higher the printing costs. A good economical approach is to use two spot colors, often black plus another color. Spot colors are pre-established printing ink colors. Choosing a spot color is similar to choosing a paint color from swatches at a home improvement store. Because spot colors come "out of the can," they are consistent. This is important if you're trying to build consistent visual branding.

Make sure the logo is reproducible in black only. Sometimes printing in color is not an option for budgetary or technical reasons. A logo must look clear and crisp printed anywhere. So it needs a black and white version. Black means black, too, not gray.

Make sure you can "reverse out" your logo. Reversing out is the design term for a logo appearing in white on colored or photographic backgrounds. Again, this is a flexibility issue. The logo needs to be clear and readable in all possible places it might appear. Hint: If the logo works in all black, it will reverse easily.

Be wary of designs that are too horizontal or too vertical. Such designs can be difficult to incorporate into layouts. If you're considering a design that is strongly horizontal, consider asking the designer to provide an alternate vertical version. This ensures that you have a good logo shape for any compositional situation.

Above: Simplicity rules. These logos use one or two colors, readable fonts and simple shapes.

IF YOU MUST DESIGN A LOGO ON YOUR OWN:

First, purchase and learn to use a vector graphic program. Seriously. Logos need to be in vector format in order to be scalable.

If we still haven't convinced you to hire a logo designer:

Consider a type-only logo. Sometimes called a wordmark, type-only logos are perhaps a bit easier for beginning designers to manage. But only if you have the eye to classify and pair fonts. If you choose to use more than one font in your wordmark, make sure they contrast well but look good together. Think romance: "They make such an attractive couple."

ANTONIO'S
—*Since 1926*

Type-based logos like this one are a good starting point for beginning logo designers.

Avoid using the font-du-jour. A few fonts get done to death each decade. Some fonts were so over-used they've become synonymous with time periods. Some recent grossly overused fonts include Mistral, Papyrus, Copperplate Gothic and Zapfino.

If the font came installed on your computer, don't use it in a logo. Buy something new. Or download something new for free (but beware of copyright issues on free fonts). Or commission a font artist to create something new just for you.

No clip art. If you must add a graphic (often called an icon or symbol), consider a decorative dingbat or type ornament. But use care in your selection. A smiley face dingbat is no better than smiley face clip art.

Add a simple shape. If you're really feeling brave, consider adding a simple shape to your logo, such as a square, circle or rule. Pairing simple shapes with interesting glyphs can result in creative icons. For inspiration and guidance, revisit mini art school and the Gestalt laws.

Test it out. Try the design out in different layouts, such as a Web page or a newsletter, to see how the logo looks in context. You may find that what looks good standing alone on a presentation board doesn't hold up so well sitting atop a busy photo on your brochure cover.

Turn fonts to graphics. Once you've settled on a good design, turn all fonts to graphics by using your vector program's "outline fonts" function. This prevents your logo font from getting accidentally replaced by something ugly, like Courier, when you send your logo to others for use.

COLOR BASICS

CHOOSING & USING COLOR

A sk children about their favorite colors, and you get instant exuberant responses: "Red!" "Blue!" People just respond to color. We select or reject everything from clothes to cars based on what colors say to us.

In this chapter we talk about how designers harness the power of color to grab our attention, organize visual flow and evoke emotion. We also talk about finding color inspiration on the color wheel as well as from culture, history and nature. But translating inspiration into effective design requires some understanding of color technologies. We cover that, too, along with some tips for designing with color.

THE POWER OF COLOR: IMPACT, ORGANIZATION & EMOTION

Color creates visual impact.

Color is eye-catching. It makes you look. Picture a black and white poster with one pop of color—a hat, for instance—in bright pink. That bright pink immediately becomes a focal point. Part of the attention-getting power is the principle of contrast at work. But a color's shade and intensity also play a role in attracting interest, whether as eye entry point, contrast, wow factor or all of the above.

If color captures attention, you can use color to keep drawing the eye's attention over and over again for flow through your design. The eye will follow color around your composition like a dog follows the cook in the kitchen.

Color organizes.

Imagine you're in an airport terminal. You see a large group of people wearing red T-shirts. Either they're all part of the same group or it's a freakish coincidental convergence of red T-shirt lovers. Our money is on the group thing.

Color can sort and clump to indicate what goes with what. That's the principle behind color-coding systems, such as electrical wiring and mall parking lots. This is some potent design mojo if you think about it.

Color evokes emotion.

For example, the concept of team colors is meant to inspire strong emotions. The kind of emotions we feel, however, depends on whether we're looking at the home team's colors or the opponent's. So, once again, designers are tactical about employing color persuasively.

Although humans do respond physiologically to color, most of the emotional muscle we attach to color is learned. We'll be talking more about both the science and symbolism of color. As for designing with color, some people seem to be born with color sense. For others, just trying to match two socks is a challenge. Fortunately, there is help.

COLOR THEORY

In the canon of color knowledge, Sir Isaac Newton of falling-apple-equals-gravity fame also gets credit for discovering the color spectrum by playing with prisms. Color is light. White light is the mixture of all colors of the spectrum visible to the human eye. Black is an absence of color.

Now let's skip ahead from the Enlightenment to Modernism. In the early 20th century's Bauhaus School of design, Johannes Itten taught his students techniques for achieving color contrast, including pairing color complements, dark with light values and warm with cool shades, among others.

Fast forward again, and we're still working with color theory. But now we're applying it to color on digital displays. Before you nod off over color science and theory, let's move on to practical color knowledge. *Ergo*, the color wheel.

HOW TO CHOOSE COLOR: WORKING THE COLOR WHEEL

The color wheel is like an analog clock with three primary colors, three secondary colors and six tertiary colors

Color is evocative. The colors in this website are drawn from pizza ingredients and are intended to make you hungry. We say, "Please pass the grated parmesan."

Design by Rebecca and Guy Hagen. Reproduced by permission of the Tampa Bay Pizza Company and Tucker/Hall, Inc.

arranged in 12 specific positions. What makes this arrangement helpful is that it predicts how colors work together. Indeed, you can build a color wheel once you understand these working color relationships.

THE COLOR WHEEL

"Christmas, kings and blue jeans."

If you can remember that phrase, you can remember the three primary colors and their complements. Christmas colors are red (primary) and green (complementary). The king's royal colors are yellow (primary) and purple (complementary). And blue (primary) jeans typically are stitched with orange (complementary) thread. All six colors have relationships to each other defined by their positions on the color wheel, which is a useful thing to know in design.

Color relationships.

Primary colors. Using the clock analogy, the primary colors yellow, blue and red appear four hours apart at, say, noon, 4 and 8, respectively, to form a triangle.

Secondary & complementary color. Next we can build the secondary colors by mixing two primary colors at a time. You probably remember this from grade school. Mixing yellow and blue produces green. Mixing blue and red makes purple. Mixing red with yellow makes—you got it—orange.

Notice how each secondary color appears on the wheel directly opposite the primary color it complements. Per "Christmas, kings and blue jeans," green lies opposite red, purple lies opposite yellow and orange lies opposite blue.

The point is that color complements found at opposite sides of the color wheel indeed do "complement" each other visually. Opposites attract, as they say, to make attractive pairs.

Tertiary colors. Mix a primary color with the closest secondary color on the wheel to get those subtler "in between" tertiary colors.

Triads. Although the primary colors are blue, red and yellow, other triplets of color from the color wheel also can make pleasing color palettes. Form any triangle four hours apart on the color wheel to locate a viable color-scheme triplet.

COLORFUL RELATIONSHIPS

All colors on the color wheel come from various combinations of three primary colors: red, blue and yellow. The resulting relationships (i.e., relative positions on the color wheel) provide the basis for harmonious color palettes. For example, colors opposite each other on the wheel are called "complementary colors."

Primary + Primary = Secondary

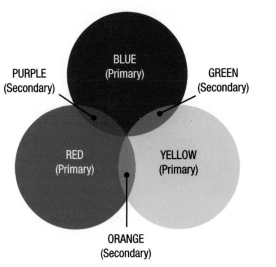

Primary + Secondary = Tertiary

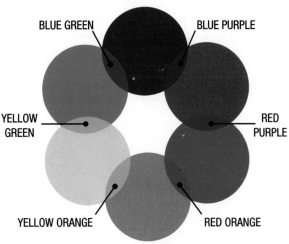

Analogous color. Additionally, mixing colors next to each other on the wheel produces "in between" colors. Side-by-side colors on the wheel are related because they contain some of the colors sitting next to them. We call that analogous color. Pairing analogous colors creates unity.

Color temperature. The notion of warm and cool colors reveals another property of the color wheel: One side is warm, and the other side is cool. Obviously, the red-orange-yellow side is warm, and the green-blue-purple side is cool. Maybe not so obviously, you can warm up a cool color by adding a little red, orange or yellow. Or you can cool down a warm color by adding a little green, blue or purple. That's part of how contrasting color works. Notice how each opposite, thus contrasting, color pair on the wheel includes both a warm and a cool color.

Analogous color. Analogous colors appear side-by-side on the color wheel. Even though the third set "jumps" the tertiary colors, the set is still considered analogous.

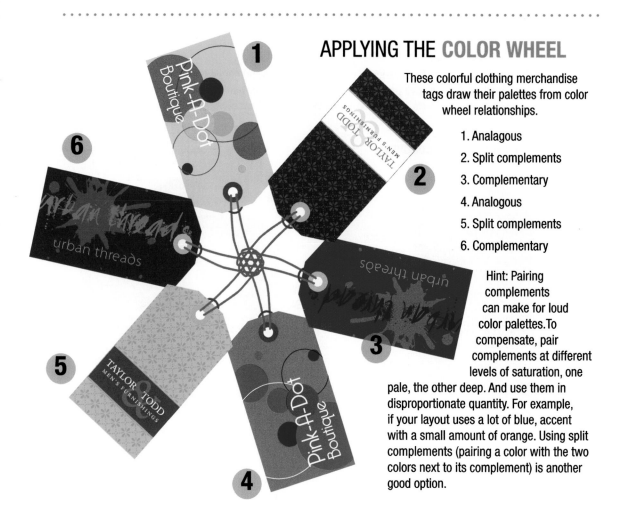

APPLYING THE COLOR WHEEL

These colorful clothing merchandise tags draw their palettes from color wheel relationships.

1. Analagous
2. Split complements
3. Complementary
4. Analogous
5. Split complements
6. Complementary

Hint: Pairing complements can make for loud color palettes. To compensate, pair complements at different levels of saturation, one pale, the other deep. And use them in disproportionate quantity. For example, if your layout uses a lot of blue, accent with a small amount of orange. Using split complements (pairing a color with the two colors next to its complement) is another good option.

Another good thing to know about warm and cool colors is that when used in layouts, warm colors appear to come forward and cool colors recede. This concept can be helpful when you're trying to emphasize or deemphasize elements in your layout.

In the real world, however, a color is usually a mixture of colors. Yellow, for example, probably isn't just yellow. Are you seeing a saturated pure-hue primary yellow? Or is it a cooler yellow with hints of green? Maybe you're seeing a warmer yellow with hints of orange. Or soft baby yellow. Or brownish gold. So look again.

In sum, the color wheel can inspire your project's color choices. However, knowing that three analogous or triplet colors will make

You're getting warmer... The same design rendered in a warm palette on the left and a cool palette on the right. Does one stand out more than the other? Which do you prefer?

a harmonious palette is only the start. It's also important to consider people's responses to color culture, history and nature, all of which also can inspire your design's color.

HOW TO CHOOSE COLOR: CULTURE

Even though Western Christians associate red and green with Christmas, not everyone celebrates Christmas or shares those particular meanings of red and green. At the same time, color science tells us that people with a common form of color blindness can't distinguish between red and green. That fact always makes us wonder about the wisdom of red and green traffic lights, another example of cultural meanings of color used to communicate visual messages.

The sighted and those who aren't colorblind do read symbolic meanings into color.

However, the meanings people attach to colors depend on their cultures. Even within the same culture, what a particular color says can change across contexts.

In U.S. culture, for example, white can symbolize purity, such as a white wedding dress, a custom that began as a way to communicate the bride's virginity. But in China, brides often wear red, a color that symbolizes good fortune. The thought of a red wedding dress is a little shocking in the United States because we associate red dresses with, well, something else. On the other hand, in numbers of Pacific Rim cultures, white is the color of mourning while Americans and Europeans connect black with mourning.

So it's important to consider the audience when communicating with color.

It's also important to consider context. The same color can symbolize multiple things within the same culture depending on the circumstance. In the United States, green can be a fresh, cool, natural, environmentally friendly and healthy color. But "hospital green" has negative associations with sickness and cold impersonal institutions. Green also can connote envy.

National identity. The colors blue, red and white represent the United States. And France. And the United Kingdom. And Cuba…

Design by Rebecca Hagen. Reproduced by permission of Tucker/ Hall, Inc.

The point is not to take the symbolic meaning of color for granted.

HOW TO CHOOSE COLOR: HISTORY

Like clothing styles, color styles come and go. If someone you know has an old pink-tiled bathroom, you know what we're talking about. Knowing a little bit about the history of color trends can help you choose (or avoid) time- and era-evocative colors for your designs.

For example, Rebecca dates herself by admitting she had an elementary-age bedroom sporting a burnt orange chenille bedspread, stylized "daisy" curtains in shades of yellow, orange and green, and a gigantic foot-shaped green shag rug. If you don't get the joke, we'll tell you that burnt orange, avocado green, harvest gold and brown are classic early 1970s colors.

Every decade has a color palette or two. Pink, black and turquoise still evoke the 1950s. Neon brights bring to mind the 1980s.

In fact, color designers are currently deciding what colors will be trendy two years from now. So if you're plugged in to the industry, you might even be able to choose color for your designs based on the future.

HOW TO CHOOSE COLOR: NATURE

If you're still having a hard time putting colors together, take a cue from nature. Colors that appear together naturally can make pleasing palettes for your designs. You might not consider putting bright orange, deep green and deep blue-violet together on your own. But on a bird of paradise plant, these colors come together in a vibrant color scheme.

If you're dealing with color photography in your design, your photos also may help you choose your color scheme. Examine your photos.

Retro color. Ever notice that the reigning color palette in the 1950s was turquoise, pink and black? Ever notice that everything in the 1950s was "atomic"?

The best of

Summer Stone Fruit

One of the largest fruit crops grown in the United States, peaches provide many nutrients with few calories and no fat.

Latem am, cuptam elenistius nonsed et et et volupta tempelitam, quatem as maionem exerisi militati dolorroreri tem es si doluptatur sa vendici tem. Hit que sitas magnien debit, con ent et ulpa sima volorpores maximagnam, aut modistiaecus quia quias de ne que et, officipsam audam volum eiur, sequisque sitio comnisi nvende et, omniet fuga. Apelia doluptas volessectati nimus consequibus aut lamusciis auta venis et aut molor aborio. Parum cum, omnihit veliquibus soloreius mos dolorro rendellaut dendus maximus el idipit ommolo beaqui ut lignis exero molupti busandam con rest, iliquid min pa simi, et licturest, volo to tet et que que dolo beaquis pre ma doluptas ant.

Southern Summers | June 2015 146

Mother Nature has great color sense. If a color pairing occurs in nature, it's a good bet the pairing will look good in your layout. Sliced peaches and background foliage inspired the color palette for this magazine spread.

Dominant colors should suggest a color scheme to you. As we keep saying, it's all about looking.

TIPS FOR DESIGNING WITH COLOR

» **Make your color palette work for your communication purpose.**
Begin with a big reminder of the brand's visual identity, the design's communication objective and the message's target audience. Don't work at cross-purposes.

» **Choose one main color & add an accent color or two for interest.**
As the great modernist architect Ludwig Mies van der Rohe said about design, "Less is more."

Are you thinking contrasting color complements that pop against each other? Or a calmer scheme of cool colors? Perhaps a monochromatic scheme taking advantage of varying tints, tones and textures of one color is just the thing. You also have choices about saturation and value. High-intensity pure hues? Soft pastel tints? Earthy tones?

Whatever you decide, limit the palette to one color star accented by one or two supporting colors.

COLOR PROPERTIES

Color has properties which, when applied, add variety and visual interest to your layouts. Hue answers the question "what color?" Value is the lightness or darkness of the hue. Saturation refers to the amount or intensity of the hue.

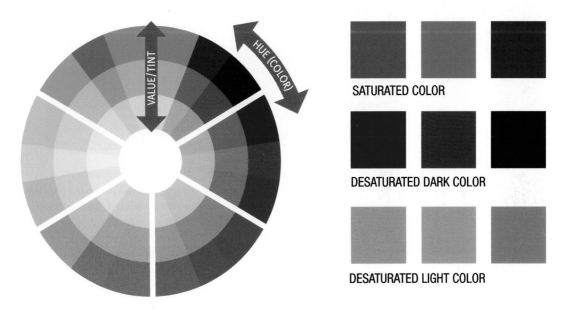

SATURATED COLOR

DESATURATED DARK COLOR

DESATURATED LIGHT COLOR

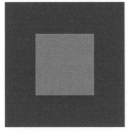  

NEUTRAL GRAY
Each center square contains the same 50 percent gray, yet each square looks different. Gray changes visually relative to the adjacent color.

WORKS-EVERY-TIME COLORS?
If color wheel pairings confuse you, consider pairing any color on the wheel with one of these neutrals. But beware, despite the terminology, some neutrals can have warm, cool or even slight color casts that can impact color harmony.

BLACK   WHITE   GRAY

TAN   NAVY BLUE   BROWN

Visibility and readability.
Pair colors with care, especially when placing colored text on colored backgrounds. Color pairings lacking contrast result in illegible copy.

» **Design for visibility & readability.** Consider the environment in which viewers consume your design. An outdoor board requires quick communication in less-than-ideal viewing circumstances. Website readers skim quickly until they find what they're looking for. Smartphone users view Web content on tiny little screens. A magazine subscriber may dive into type-heavy articles, where color needs to break up pages of columns of words. Whatever the environment, visibility and readability remain critical.

While readability means readers can read it easily, visibility means viewers can see it clearly. Either way, you need contrast. The rule of thumb says stick with dark-on-light or light-on-dark color combos. Unless your purpose is a psychedelic mood, stay away from saturated complements for type and background fill because they create a vibrating effect that's hard on the eyes.

Generally, gray makes a lousy background color for copy, unless the gray is very dark or very light relative to the value of the type. Mid-tone grays don't provide enough contrast to support readable typographic information.

In terms of readability and visibility, mostly think value. Light type on a dark background pops, although we've warned you about reversing. Dark type on a light background pops. But dark-on-dark and light-on-light both lack contrast, thus visibility and readability.

» **Use splashes of color for visual emphasis.** Judicious splashes of color are like cosmetic makeup. Maybe a purple scarf (or a red ball cap) is all you need to perk up the look. A few well-chosen spots of color can highlight focal points as well as draw the eye around the layout.

If your composition is all black on white, using a spot color like saturated orange on the headline, for a drop cap and in a pull quote, for example, breaks up visual boredom and invites the eye to chase the small areas of orange around the screen or page.

Using less saturated tints of spot color to highlight larger areas of the composition is another way to design with color. For example, instead of using saturated orange as spot color, you may opt for diluting that orange down to a soft peach color and spreading it over a bigger area. You even can place sheer tints, of pale peach for example, over dark type without disrupting readability—if you're careful.

COLOR TECHNOLOGY: THAT'S NOT THE COLOR I CHOSE. WHAT HAPPENED?

We've all experienced this: The layout, the typesetting and the color were brilliant. But something awful happened after pressing "print." The saturated orange turned nasty pink. The pure blue came out blue-green.

Color matching from device to device is one of the most difficult challenges designers face. In order to understand it, we need to explain a bit about the technology of color. The shorthand we use when talking about the mechanics of color can seem like an alphabet soup for the uninitiated: RGB and CMYK. But it's not really complicated.

ROSEN COLLEGE INVITES YOU TO
SAVE THE DATE

The Pineapple Ball

A Hospitality Hall of Fame Induction Celebration

Saturday, October 11, 2014
Rosen Shingle Creek
Orlando, FL

Join us as we honor the 2014 inductees:

Henri Landwirth   Paul Mears, Jr.
Give Kids the World   *Mears Transportation*

Produced by Rosen College faculty, staff and students.
Proceeds benefit academic scholarships and initiatives.

UNIVERSITY OF CENTRAL FLORIDA
ROSEN COLLEGE OF
HOSPITALITY MANAGEMENT

Two colors, different values. If you use different values (tints) of a single color in your layout, you create the illusion of having used more than one color.

Design by Rebecca Hagen. Reproduced by permission of the Rosen College of Hospitality Management at the University of Central Florida.

The color wheel, screen version. Monitors use a different method for building colors than printers. Screen colors are created from various combinations of red, green and blue, instead of the red, blue and yellow used in the classic art color wheel.

Screen color vs. printed color.

The short answer to the question "what happened to my color?" is that screens and printers don't speak the same language. Monitors, screens and printers render color using totally different technologies. Screen and monitor color is electronic color, which overlaps light to achieve colors. For printed color, we layer inks.

To make a long story short, your printouts don't match what you see onscreen because your screen is speaking French and your printer is speaking Portuguese. The two devices need a translator. Such translation is called calibration, which is part of an overall process called color management.

THE RGB COLOR WHEEL

Color management. Color management is the formal term for getting your color to match properly across devices, from scanners to digital cameras to computer screens to printers. Some aspects of this process can be handled by making adjustments at the device level or through the system settings on your computer. Your computer screen, for example, can be calibrated to match the settings of any output device, including your personal printer or a commercial printer.

A more in-depth way to manage color involves the application of color profiles to images and layouts. These profiles allow for more accurate—though not necessarily completely accurate— color translation from device to device. The International Color Consortium (ICC) created some of the most commonly used color profiles, but there are other color profiles out there, some industry-specific.

The ICC has profiles for almost any application, whether you're working in electronic-screen RGB space or printing-with-ink CMYK space.

WORKING WITH SCREEN COLOR

Designers who prepare layouts and graphics for Web and video work in RGB space. RGB—an acronym for red, green, blue—has its own version of the wheel. All colors in RGB space are made from combining varying degrees of just red, green and blue.

RGB color.

Getting different colors on displays depends on the saturation, or in the case of a light-emitting screen "intensity," of red, green and blue light along with their various combinations. It's a little like having a dimmer switch for each of the overlapping RGB colors. Simultaneously turning the three dimmer switches produces different colors.

For any onscreen color, the red, green and blue in RGB each has a numerical value between 0 and 255, whether a color is 0 (meaning off) or 255 (meaning fully on). Black, for example, would be 000 000 000 (or just 000), indicating that red, green and blue are all off. White, for example, would be 255 255 255, meaning red, green and blue are each at full intensity

Hexadecimal code.

Since specifying nine numbers for any and every color is unwieldy, a system called the hexadecimal code mathematically converts these nine numbers into six numbers and/or letters. Let's skip the math here. Just know that designers specify Web colors by their corresponding combinations of numbers/letters in the hexadecimal system.

For example, the University of South Florida's official colors are green and gold. But not just any green and gold. The university specifies its hexadecimal Web colors as #006747 green and #CFC493 gold.

Now, to throw a monkey wrench into the whole setup, USF's specific hexadecimal Web colors may not look the same from one screen to the next, undermining the whole reason for specifying particular colors in the first place.

RGBA.

The next generation of Web color specification is RGBA. As you might have guessed, the RGB stands for red, green and blue. But what about the "A" ?

"A" stands for alpha, specifically alpha channel, which controls transparency. This is exciting because it allows Web designers to create transparency effects via code instead of with graphics.

RGBA rules are expressed in Cascading Style Sheets (CSS) using the same numeric system as basic RGB. For example, rgba (255, 0, 0, 0.6)

Specifying color. When reproducing the USF logo in various media, use the following for green and gold, respectively:

For spot color printing:

PANTONE® 342 and PANTONE® 4535

For process color printing:

C=93 M=10 Y=75 K=43

C=6 M=8 Y=35 K=12

For Web and screen:

#006747

#CFC493

would produce a saturated red with a 60% transparency (.6 = 60%).

Web designers who take advantage of RGBA need to be aware that it is not fully supported across all browsers, and a backup color build should be provided.

Web color behaves badly.

Be prepared for your RGB colors to appear differently depending on where they are viewed. Every browser renders color differently, and every screen and monitor has different settings. Color shifting across devices is a perpetual problem.

To alleviate this issue, Web designers "back in the day" resorted to something called the Web safe palette—a limited set of colors that remained consistent across computer monitors. As monitor technology changed, the Web safe palette ceased to live up to hype. Today the palette is largely irrelevant.

Yet differences in color rendering across monitors persist, so designers are wise to double-check their work on different browsers in different platforms.

The bottom line? When you design electronic screens, expect color shifting. Test your Web design on as many different computers as you can to make sure your color, in all its variations, is acceptable before you launch your site.

That covers designing for the screen in RGB color space using the hexadecimal system. For printed color, however, there's a whole other system.

Cyan

Cyan + Magenta

Cyan + Magenta + Yellow

Cyan + Magenta + Yellow + Black

SPECIFYING COLOR FOR PRINT

Print designers work in CMYK color space. They prepare all graphics and layouts in CMYK mode to correspond with commercial printing technology. The most common technology printers use to apply inks to paper is called 4-color process (also referred to as full-color, built color or process color) because just four ink colors—cyan, magenta, yellow and black—are combined to build any color. Cyan (blue-ish), magenta (red-ish) and yellow correspond with the three primary colors, and you can build any color from the three primaries. The "K" in CMYK stands for "key," which refers to black.

In 4-color printing, instead of mixing ink colors beforehand, printers use four separate plates to build colors on the paper. Commercial printers separate the colors designed on a document and put each color onto its own C, M, Y or K printing plate. The technique is called color separation. Printers apply the appropriate ink color to each of the four plates, and apply each one to paper, one on top of the next.

4-color process. In 4-color process printing, cyan, magenta, yellow and black inks are layered to create the final image.

Setting up a document for commercial printing.

When you set up a document for CMYK printing, you must save your document and related graphics in CMYK mode. You also need to specify colors within your software program using CMYK builds. CMYK builds are a series of digit pairs that indicate the percentages of each C, M, Y and K that make up a color. Most graphic design software applications provide a space for you to specify a build or provide some sort of swatch palette that will generate the proper build for you.

Watch for "out of gamut" warnings when choosing color from swatch palettes. Your computer screen can display many more colors than printers are capable of re-creating with ink. An out-of-gamut warning signals that you've chosen a color that won't reproduce accurately in print.

Four-color process printing is not your only option, however. Documents can be printed using only one, two or three inks. This process is called spot color printing.

Spot color printing.

Instead of trying to build a particular color with CMYK, designers can choose premixed colors from a swatch book. Sometimes called matched color, spot color is like picking out paint colors from hardware store paint chips. Pantone created the PANTONE MATCHING SYSTEM®, sometimes referred to as PMS® Colors, the world's most commonly used color-matching system for solid colors.

When printing with spot colors, printers create a plate for each spot color the designer has specified. If the job uses two spot colors, only two plates are needed. Three colors require three plates.

Setting up a document to use spot colors. If you use one or more spot colors in your document, you must load those colors into your color palette from a preset library. These libraries generally come pre-installed with professional-grade design software applications. If you don't specify the spot color in your color palette, your printer will print your document as process color instead. This may result in a more expensive print job. It also might mean that you won't get the exact color you chose from the swatch book.

Achieving accurate color is always difficult, and the consistency of spot inks is one of the most compelling reasons to use them. Consistent color is essential when creating and communicating brand identity. Going back to USF's green and gold logo, USF would prefer always

Warning signs. An out-of-gamut warning signals that you've chosen a color that won't reproduce accurately in print.

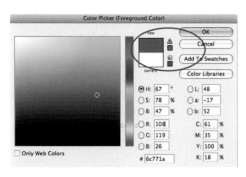

Adobe product screen shot(s) reprinted with permission from Adobe Systems Incorporated.

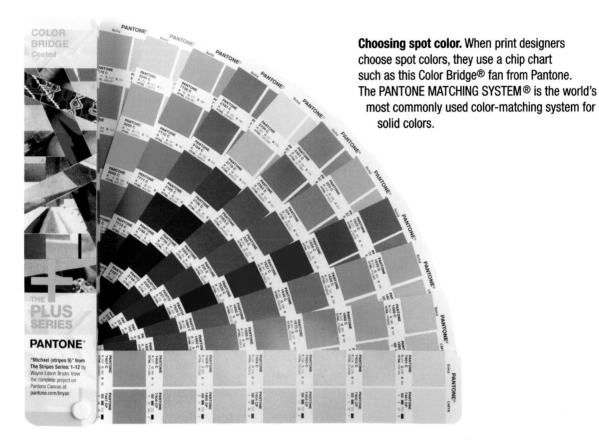

to print its logo using matched PANTONE® colors: PANTONE 342 green and PANTONE 4535 gold.

Another option is to use the 4-color process version of your selected spot color. For each PANTONE solid color, there is a corresponding "color build." For example, use corresponding tint builds C=93, M=10, Y=75 K-43 for USF green, and C=6, M=8, Y=35 K-12 for USF gold. Be aware, however, that CMYK builds don't precisely match their spot color counterparts. They come close, but no banana.

That concludes the tech portion of this basic color lesson. Now for a handy list of takeaways:

COLOR RULES!

1. Make your palette communicate with purpose. Account for the organization's visual identity/branding, the message's objective and the audience's sensibility.

2. For color inspiration, look to the color wheel, nature, culture and history.

3. When designing with color:

» Don't go nuts in choosing a palette, whether it's complementary, analogous or monochromatic. Choose one main color plus one or two accent colors.

» Design for visibility and readability.

» Use splashes of color for visual emphasis.

4. Think "Christmas, kings and blue jeans" to remember the primaries and their secondary complements.

» For brightness or intensity, choose pure saturated hues.

» For pastel tints, dilute with white.

» For earth tones, dull with black.

5. For contrast, pair:

» opposite colors on the wheel.

» warm with cool hues.

For contrast, pair opposite (complementary) colors on the color wheel.

» any hue with any neutral.

» light with dark values (grayscale).

6. For unity, choose analogous colors on the wheel and colors of similar saturation or value.

7. The three main color "languages" for producing color are:

» RGB, adding color with overlapping light using the hexadecimal system for screen.

» CMYK, building full color from separated ink layers in 4-color process printing.

» The PANTONE MATCHING SYSTEM, matching specific colors by ink formula for printing.

Most important, don't forget to use color to create impact, organize what goes with what and get the emotional juices flowing.

SOUTH BEACH

MIAMI, FLORIDA

TRY THIS

1. Collect printed pieces in which color is a crucial element of the design. You can collect ads or stories from magazines and newspapers. Collect rack brochures, direct mail pieces, take-out menus, candy wrappers, shopping bags, fast-food wrappers—anything printed.

   Write a short paragraph about each describing why the designer chose that color for that piece. Is the color about history? Emotion? Culture? Does the color wheel play a role in selection of the main or supporting colors?

2. Choose a brand and compare the reproduction of color in its visual branding across devices: smartphone, tablet, desktop/laptop, color printout from the Web, commercially printed piece. Describe differences you see.

3. Find three pictures demonstrating different cultural meanings for the same color. For example, find three pictures each using the color red to communicate a different symbolic message.

4. Imagine you must brand a new restaurant. Name the restaurant. Then go outside to find a color palette inspired by nature. Take some photos of your color inspiration. Use your design software's color functions to match your nature-inspired palette.

5. You've been hired as the art director for a new musical play set in the 1990s. Suggest a historical color palette for the production's overall design, and justify your recommendation with some graphic evidence.

PANTONE® and other Pantone trademarks are the property of, and are used with the written permission of, Pantone LLC.

ADDING VISUAL APPEAL

WORKING WITH
PHOTOS & ILLUSTRATIONS

W hile it's certainly possible to create readable print and online materials without the use of images, most of us prefer pictures to accompany our reading material. In fact, when it comes to communication, visuals are just as important as type.

Images—photos, illustrations, infographics—set tone, add interest, provide additional information and visually break up intimidating blocks of type. The right image can add color, texture, line and movement to your layouts. The use of images adds eye entry points and communicates visual hierarchy. Images help create rhythm to assist flow, thus providing your readers with much-needed direction, i.e., where do I start, where do I go next and where is the end?

When choosing the right images for your particular project, you'll need to consider a range of factors from image content to image quality.

IMAGE CONTENT

Of course you should choose your photos and illustrations to fit the overall tone of the piece you're producing. Tone, obviously, is determined by what you or the boss want to project and, more importantly, what will resonate with your audience. You just don't put pictures of circus clowns on the front of an investment-banking brochure.

Say, for example, you really are choosing images for an investment-banking brochure. You might have a selection of appropriately serious-looking photos of people in suits shaking hands or conversing with other people in suits. How do you pick the best suits from the bunch?

Image quality.

One of the first and easiest things you can do to whittle your photo selections is to throw out the technically defective images. This is the photo equivalent of weeding out résumés by tossing out those with typos. Scrap any photos that are out of focus, that lack good tonal range (value and grayscale) and that lack proper resolution (more about this shortly). Despite the availability of photo-correcting software, it's still best to start with a good-quality photo that needs little to no correction. Some things can be fixed. Others, like lack of focus and resolution, cannot.

Clear subject.

Read any book on what makes a good photo, and you'll learn that simple subjects are best. In a simple photo, its subject is clear. Don't leave your reader wondering.

Tonal range. Choose photos that display a range of dark and light colors. Photos that lack tonal range may appear flat and lifeless.

If you're shooting new photos, remove distracting objects from the composition's background. If moving items is not possible (or is inappropriate, as in news-gathering), reframe the shot so the distracting items aren't visible. Avoid photos in which background objects such as trees or lampposts appear to grow out of people's heads. In order to eliminate distraction, consider shallow depth of field, in which the subject remains in focus while the background goes out of focus.

Photos of people doing things are more interesting than photos of people standing around. The "grip-and-grin" shot—a picture of one person giving an award of some sort to another—is about as dull as it gets. A much better approach would be to show the award winner engaged in the activity for which she won that award. Equally dull is the "police line-up" image, which consists of a group of people (board members, committee members, team members) all lined up against the wall. Again, it's much more powerful and interesting to show these people in action and in context. If you must photograph the group, at the very least vary the heights of your subjects. Some people seated plus some people standing makes better composition.

Choose wisely. Always choose the best available art. Poor quality art brings down the quality of the whole project.

Rule of thirds. If we divide this image into a nine-square grid, our subject's face falls at the intersection of two of the gridlines. This makes for a photo with more interesting composition.

Bottom line? People *always* make good subjects for photos. Particularly engaging are photos of people looking right at the camera. While such photos may or may not be appropriate for journalistic applications, they are powerful in advertising, marketing and public relations materials. Don't forget to consider the diversity of people you represent in your photos as well as the diversity of people in your audience. Ethically speaking, gone are the days when white men symbolically stood for everyone. Tactically speaking, you want your audience to identify with your photos.

A well-composed photo.

Technical qualities aren't the only considerations for judging a "good" photo. A boring subject in perfect focus saved as a 300 dpi TIF image is still a lousy image. To qualify as a good photo—one that will be a compelling addition to your project—the photo also needs to be well composed.

Professional photographers know that the most interesting photos share some characteristics:

Asymmetrical balance and the rule of thirds. Centered photos are boring. Asymmetrical balance makes interesting shots, and using the rule of thirds is the quickest way to compose for asymmetry. Imagine the shot as a 3 × 3 grid, then position the focal point on one of the resulting four gridline intersections.

Tight cropping. Images that fill the frame communicate in no uncertain terms what the subject matter is about, and they also crowd out background distraction. Extreme tight crops and close-ups are particularly interesting, as they force us to look at the subject in a new way.

Natural lines to create movement. As in all visual communication, you want to control the eye's movement and flow through a photograph.

Interesting light. We've already touched on good tonal range. Playing with interesting highlights and shadows also results in compelling atmospheric images.

RESOLUTION, FILE FORMAT & SIZE

Even the most well-composed, compelling image is useless if it lacks the size, resolution and format appropriate to your chosen output. Images that are too small or lack resolution will appear pixellated and fuzzy in the final product.

COMMON FILE FORMATS AND THEIR USES

	FORMATS FOR PRINT	FORMATS FOR SCREEN
Encapsulated Postscript (EPS)	File format of most vector graphic files rendered through mathematical calculation, not pixel by pixel. Can be resized without loss of resolution. Best for logos, word art. Required for "duotone" images where *only* two spot colors can be used	
Graphic Interchange Format (GIF)		Best format for Web icons and animations. Supports transparency
Joint Photographic Experts Group (JPG)	Can be used for print pieces, but not recommended. Lossy format means poorer print resolution	Excellent for publishing photos on the Web. Use a photo-editing program to optimize and save at 72 ppi. Should not be used for video
Tagged Image File Format (TIF)	Best format for saving photos for commercial print purposes	Good format for still images intended for video. Supports layers
Portable Network Graphics (PNG)		Best for Web logos and illustrations. Also a good format for video stills and animations. Renders gradients well and supports a higher degree of transparency (drop shadows). Note, only PNG-24 offers full transparency support
Scalable Vector Graphic (SVG)		Vector graphics format for Web. Excellent for basic shapes, charts and graphs. Works well in responsive websites

File formats.

Images can be saved in a number of different formats so there are a few standards you need to know. Each file type has different properties making it suitable for different purposes.

For Web, you'll want to save images as JPG (Joint Photographic Experts Group), GIF (Graphic Interchange Format) or PNG (Portable Network Graphic). JPGs are best for photos, GIFs work for small icons and simple animations, and PNG files are the choice for illustrations and logos.

It's important to note that GIFs and PNG files will both support transparency. JPGs do not. Transparency by definition means "see-through." In the case of Web graphics, transparency is essentially the

GIF image

JPG image

GIF image with drop shadow

PNG-24 image with drop shadow

Vector vs. bitmap. The circles above both have been magnified by 1000 percent. The image on the top is a vector graphic, while the image on the bottom is a bitmap, or raster graphic. Because vector images are built through mathematical calculation, they can be scaled up or down infinitely without loss of quality. Bitmaps, however, get fuzzy on the edges when you try to scale up, as seen in the image at bottom.

The right format for the right job. All logos above have been optimized for the Web. However, the GIF format (at top left) is the best choice for a graphic with broad flat areas of color. The GIF text is much crisper, and since the GIF format supports transparency, the graphic does not have a white bounding box like the JPG image on the top right.

While GIFs support transparency, they fail when the transparency needs a gradient, as in the case of drop shadows (lower left). For this, you need a PNG-24 file (lower right). Perfect.

ability to make certain color groups "invisible." If you've ever tried to put a logo in JPG format on top of a colored background and discovered that your logo has a white box around it, you've encountered lack of transparency. By creating your Web graphic in the correct software application and saving as a GIF or PNG image, you can eliminate the white box.

JPGs are great for the Web, but you should avoid them for print. The JPG is a "lossy" format, which means that each time you open or manipulate a JPG, it loses data. For print purposes, your best choice will be TIF (Tagged Image Format). TIF images are larger in file size and do not lose data. So choose TIF for print purposes.

Yet another file type for printing, EPS (Encapsulated Postscript) is used for some specific kinds of images. Vector graphics, usually illustrations, are saved in EPS format, as are some photographs that have certain styling applied. EPS format is typically used for logos and, like GIF and PNG, supports transparency.

Size & resolution.

One of the most confusing things to grasp when working with digital images is the relationship between image resolution—usually expressed in dots per inch (dpi) or more accurately pixels per inch (ppi)—file size and physical image size. Take, for example, two images:

One image is 300 dpi at 1 × 1 inch with a file size of 263K.

The other is 72 dpi at 4.16 × 4.16 inches with a file size of 263K.

If your print project specs call for a 300 dpi image, which of these files is appropriate for use?

If you guessed that the 300 dpi image is the only print-appropriate image, you would be incorrect. Even though the resolution and dimensions are different, the file size (263K)

Image 1: 72 dpi, 4.16 x 4.16 inches, **263K**

Image 2: 300 dpi, 1 x 1 inch, **263K**

Which is high resolution? Despite the fact one image is 72 dpi and the other 300 dpi, the file sizes are the same, and both could be used as high-res images.

Making Image 1 high-resolution (300 dpi) without losing file size would result in an image with a physical size of 1 × 1 inch, the same as Image 2.

is the same. It is the file size that is crucial to determining image usability.

Using photo-editing software, you can take any image and change its size and resolution, including our "low-res" example listed here. But what you need to look at is what happens to the file size when you make the change. As a rule, you want the file size to stay the same or get smaller. If you make your changes and your file size gets bigger (sampling-up), your photo quality will drop (the image gets pixellated and fuzzy).

The optimizing process lets you find the sweet spot between image quality and lowest file size for Web images.

Select your settings.
Select settings based on the type of image. In this case, we chose GIF because of the image's broad flat areas of color.

Watch file size.
The dialog box will tell you what your final file size will be after output.

Adobe Photoshop® CC product screen shot(s) reprinted with permission from Adobe Systems Incorporated.

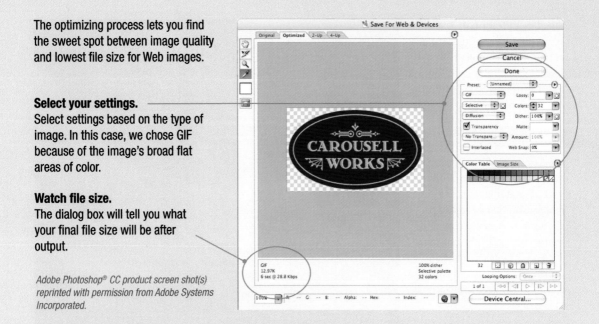

OPTIMIZING WEB GRAPHICS

Even if you never have to touch a website, at some point someone is likely to ask you to provide graphics for an existing site.

Working with a designer or developer. When you're working with professional designers and developers, your goal is to provide them with the best quality images at the highest resolutions available. When providing photos, send the highest resolution JPGs available. When providing logos, offer vector graphics. Your designer or developer will be able to resize and reformat your images as needed.

Preparing graphics on your own. Preparing graphics for the Web requires a few steps. First, the graphic must be resized to the appropriate dimensions. Next, if the image is a bitmap (raster) image, its resolution must be changed to 72 ppi.

Generally speaking, 72 ppi images are not large in terms of file size. Even so, it is possible to reduce the file size of a low-res image even further. Because large file sizes make for slow-loading pages, you want to make your file sizes as small as possible while retaining as much visual quality as possible. This process is called optimization.

Professional-grade photo-editing programs make it easy to optimize both vector and bitmap (raster) graphics. For bitmap images, optimizing involves choosing a level of quality for the final image from minimum to maximum. For vector images, the optimizing process requires you to choose from sets of colors ranging from a low of two colors to a full range of 256 colors. A preview screen shows you how the finished image will appear at each level. When you find the sweet spot between small file size and acceptable image quality, you save the image in the appropriate format. The most common vector formats are GIF and PNG.

The final optimized image is ready for uploading.

When you sample up, you are asking your software to add more pixels to the image, increasing both physical and file size. Software does a crummy job of this, and the result is a fuzzy image. Software does a better job of "down-sampling" (when your file size goes down). In this case, the software is choosing existing pixels to throw out, rather than having to create new ones.

In short, when evaluating an image, look at its dimensions, file size and original resolution. If both resolution and dimensions can be changed to what you need without an increase in the file size, you're golden.

Resolution for print & screen.

As you've likely figured out, one resolution does not fit all. While your end product dictates file format, it also dictates optimal image resolution. For high-end printing such as magazines, brochures and annual reports, optimal image resolution usually comes close to 300 dpi, so most designers simply use 300 dpi for all images destined for print. Graphics for the newspaper are the exception. Newspapers require a 200 dpi because of the presses involved and the nature of newsprint. Additional dots per inch on an absorbent paper like newsprint produce muddy images.

For screen graphics, lower resolution is required. Traditionally, images for the Web have been saved at a low resolution of 72 ppi. On standard flat screens, low-resolution images look great. Plus the smaller ppi images load more quickly, holding the attention of impatient readers and making search engines happy.

HD monitors. High pixel density monitors make images look much sharper by squeezing in more pixels per inch than regular monitors. Images need twice the traditional resolution to look their best on HD monitors.

High pixel density monitors used in the latest mobile devices are changing the Web graphics game. High pixel density monitors squeeze in more pixels per inch than regular monitors, making images look much sharper. Images need twice the traditional resolution to look their best. For example, an image 150 × 200 pixels at 72 ppi would need to be 300 × 400 pixels at 72 ppi to look good on a high pixel density monitor. One way designers and developers address this issue is to create two versions of the same graphic, one twice the size of the other. The site is coded to detect the monitor type and call the appropriate version of the graphic to load.

With additional graphics at larger file sizes, it's essential to use a graphics

STILL GRAPHICS FOR VIDEO

When putting together videos, you expect to work with video clips (crazy, we know). That said, there's plenty of room for still images in video production. Broadcast news employs still images and infographics in newscasts. Still graphics show up in title slides, lower thirds and program promos. And what documentary would be complete without panning and zooming in on vintage photos?

Between bars. Match the aspect ratio of your still images to your video format to avoid photos "between bars."

However, if you prepare images for video the same way you do for print or Web, you'll be in for some surprises and disappointments. Computer monitors are significantly sharper and show more color than television screens. Plus, different video formats use different aspect ratios. The dimensions for a clip on a video-sharing site differ from those of an HDTV promo trailer, and none of those match the dimensions of a photo right out of the camera. If you've ever tried to drop a still photo into a video and gotten funky black boxes on the top or sides of your image, you understand the implications.

Output determines format. To prevent still images in video from becoming a distorted mess, first consider the end product, in this case, the final video. You need to determine the dimensions of the final video and make your graphic fill or fit within that space. Things would be much easier if there were a standard size for all video. But you know what they say about things being easy. To find the size you need, ask the professional producing the final video. We recommend such a consultation for most larger scale video projects. For smaller do-it-yourself videos destined for sharing sites, search online for the correct dimensions. Video parameters for common video-sharing sites are not difficult to find.

Proper set-up solves issues. Video pros who work with still images recommend that you create your new document first, then import or "place" your chosen assets (images, logos, etc.) into the document. This allows you to set appropriate film and video document parameters at the outset, such as file sizes and formats, pixel aspect ratios and color spaces. A big benefit of "create document first, place image second" is that professional-grade photo programs automatically adjust the visual appearance of imported photos to compensate for the difference between camera and video pixel aspect ratios.

> **Resolution is irrelevant in creating graphics for video. Your only concern is whether you have the proper pixel-by-pixel measurement.**

Computer square pixels (1:1)

HDV 1080i non-square pixels (1.33:1)

Go pro. Use professional-grade photo editing programs to automatically adjust the visual appearance of imported photos. They automatically compensate for the difference between camera, computer and video pixel aspect ratios. Because no one likes stretched duck.

Another benefit is that grids and guides for live area and title safe area might be automatically generated. (For a review of grids and live area, revisit Chapter 6.) Such a feature saves you some math—and time.

What resolution? Surprisingly, the answer here is, "Who cares?" Resolution—the concept of pixels—or points-per-inch—is irrelevant in creating graphics for video. Your only concern is whether you have the proper pixel-by-pixel measurement. For example, if you'd like to create a full-screen still image for your video, and the video dimensions are 1280 pixels × 720 pixels, then your image needs to be at least 1280 pixels × 720 pixels. Getting your image to fit likely requires scaling (down-sizing only, please) and/or cropping.

Keep in mind that if you want to use panning or zooming effects on your image (a.k.a. the "Ken Burns Effect"), you'll need an image larger than the screen size. Don't forget about aspect ratio, and make sure your larger image stays in proportion to the screen size.

What color space? Recall Chapter 8's discussion on color space? While it's not a perfect match for video color, set your document to use RGB color space. RGB gives you the greatest range of color (referred to as gamut) for your completed image. Some colors on the far edges of the RGB color space don't work well in video, particularly on television screens. If your software provides the option to set a color space based on final video format, take advantage of it. You'll get better color results in your end product.

What image format? Once you finalize your image or graphic, save it in a format compatible with importing into a video-editing program. The best formats for saving images for video aren't what you might expect. While JPG is great for Web, its lossy format makes it a poor choice for video. PNG files, on the other hand, are acceptable for importing into video.

Although other formats work, a TIF image remains the best option. TIF images do not lose data, and they support layers if created in a graphics program that uses layers. Elements created on separate layers may be edited independently of each other. If you created a color block on one layer and a slide title on another layer, you have the option of animating them separately—making each fade in one at a time, for example—once imported into the video-editing program.

HONG KONG

*What to see when you have only
a single day in one of the world's most
cosmopolitan cities.*

Aque presciis doluptae nonem voluptaturem re etum et officiimusam facculpa qui que ide vereium ad magnima nonsequo ditiis nobit, sitas doluptatiis cuptis quatem fugit laboreh enihitios dus. Quiantur santuri onsequibea dolendiciis dolluptae iante esto experupta aliam volupta tquatas exceatqui bea quia volecuptia simin por aut et et mi, veliquae molorro biabor sedior aspelitat facium, odiate qui re, qui as am, venisquisque nesseaque ditat.Santet, et pa ni oditaque cus, exerorrunt estotat uscimodicit ium quatem ari ofictur? Um rem exeruptis non enirmet a quam qui te et enihici demporae doluptam sunt laccaes toratem pellitat rero maio mi, tem qui incil ium autatat quiaalt dolorrovidi odictatum qui odi uliant repe molupid quuntius si debisit, officiur sus. Eheniae. Nequi ut as sam quid utaquo moluptat maximus amenisinihic tem la volorest voluptae latiumquamAt

experenesci quis seria quate incto moluptae nihic tempelest excerfere sit debis re voloreh enducium quod esecumqui vollaut perum eatur acea vel ea solene re, nationsedi noneces cleniet veniscipsant et inctati istiat venis debisci dolut delendit es cum verclas dit re nem sita volupta ssitas aut perionet pe eos experspel et, quas a dis endipitis alit rerum ressum quamus dolorume nonsenimi, ut omnimus. To omnit aut dolo consed eum ulparcius non consero esequidusda commod quist, consequiam qui consed quam, con nonsectusda iligendiciur ant, oditataquo quam ratur res dolupictius re voles maio dic te dolesti ostiate que et lata dest voluptae. Nequis is sequo enihiliti odigenda diossinis re con res magnat velluptatem eatur aturepel es et quis dis aceritatur, ommolup tatati sanimet

fuga. Porerita simet am, volo to molorum comnis volorae occulpa cuptibus estia custi bero il modi doluptatur, si restrum explicu isquibu scipient, utaspeles modi to blabo. Et as quam sit, quia quodit quam, id ma nonsecab il id quis mintiistem faccati aternod ut officiduntur simi,Omnienet ma voloribus aut que maio tem quibus dolorrum as atur moiessit que peliquaOs reium eiciatemque conseque verest a consequia sunt ommodis aspit reptaquunt perum harum fuga. Iquia nihit vel inuilor

Establishing and detail shots. When your layout calls for more than one image, consider pairing an establishing shot like the temple view at top with a detail shot like the image of the flower market. The contrast of subject makes for a more interesting layout.

program to optimize images. Optimizing is the process of reducing file size by selectively removing data from an image while preserving visual quality. When optimizing, aim for a balance between best visual quality and smallest file size.

CHOOSING MORE THAN ONE PHOTO

In many instances, such as websites, brochures, feature news and magazine stories, you may find that you need more than one image. When choosing multiple images for your project, you should start your selection process using the same criteria discussed earlier in this chapter. Once you've eliminated any poor quality images from consideration, your next step is to look at your potential images with an eye towards contrast. (Remember the element of contrast from mini art school?) While there are many types of contrast, in this case, the contrast you should look for is contrast in image content.

In terms of content, think about using establishing shots, which are wider in scope and content, or detail shots, which are typically closer to the subject and more tightly cropped. For example, an image showing the width of the Grand Canyon is an establishing shot. A close-up image of a rabbit on the canyon rim is a detail shot.

Pairing an establishing shot with a detail shot increases your storytelling power. The establishing shot sets the stage: time, location and action. The detail shot provides additional information, and by nature of close cropping puts your reader "inside" the story.

If your project requires more than two images, the same process applies. You should weed out poor quality images first, then make your remaining selections based on content contrast.

ETHICS OF SHOOTING & EDITING

To be clear from the start, shooting images for documentary and news purposes is very different than shooting images for commercial or political purposes. Documentary or news photography, however artful or evocative, strictly adheres to the principles of truth, accuracy, fairness and balance. Such principles are necessary to maintain viewer trust that such images are factual and reality-based. Photos staged for advertising, publicity and marketing purposes, not so much. Differences between photojournalism and commercial photography persist after the images have been shot, too.

A little cosmetic photo retouching is common. But retouching that results in false or misleading communication will get you in serious trouble.

If you've played with photo–editing software, then you know there are all kinds of things you can do to alter photos—from turning them into watercolor paintings to removing an inch or two from your subject's buns and thighs. It is certainly true that most, if not all, images of professional models are digitally retouched. We are greeted daily by photographic images that have added effects for visual interest. However, let codes of professional conduct, if not your personal integrity, guide your decisions about the ethics of altering photographs. Fear of unemployment and lawsuits can be persuasive forms of conscience, too.

If the photo represents news, regardless of format or context, restrict photo-editing to only those techniques you could accomplish in a traditional darkroom. This limits your editing to cropping, overall value adjustments and dodging and burning (lightening or darkening specific areas in an image). For news photos, edits other than darkroom-based techniques run the risk of altering or negating the truth of the image. That rule applies to media relations folks on the public relations side of the news business, too.

The Status of Feminist Public Relations Theory

Kim Golombisky, Associate Professor and Graduate Director, Department of Women's & Gender Studies, University of South Florida, kgolombi@usf.edu

Diversity. We live in a wonderfully diverse world. Successful design reflects and respects this asset.

Formal rules are looser in non-news contexts when the photo merely sets tone or delivers a message in advertising, public relations and marketing materials. However, be aware that truth reigns here, as well, according to the Federal Trade Commission and the Supreme Court. Professional ethics say you should avoid puffery, photos that seem to exaggerate commercial claims. But the law prohibits false, misleading and deceptive commercial claims, including those implied by photos. Proceed with caution in taking artistic license when altering photography.

DIVERSITY AS CRAFT EXCELLENCE

While we're talking about professional conduct and ethics, this is an appropriate time to remind you of your responsibility to rise above the lowest common denominator when it comes to doing the right thing. Journalism, advertising and public relations all define diversity as part of craft excellence. Just look at those professional codes of conduct again. First, you have an ethical responsibility to deploy images free of stereotypes, whether based on gender, race, ethnicity, sexuality, religion, nationality, age, disability, class or any other kind of physical, social or cultural difference. "Everyone else does it" is no excuse. You're better than that. But accidental harm is no excuse, either. Symbolic annihilation refers to images that injure via symbolic messages about individuals or groups of people. Second, sometimes the problem has less to do with what actually appears in your image and instead has more to do with what does not appear in your image. Ask yourself who or what is missing from the images in your design work. Learn to look critically at images with an eye toward mitigating prejudice and ignorance. Plus, working against the grain by avoiding visual stereotypes can offer the added benefit of capturing people's attention, as well as surprising and delighting them, with something unexpected. Sad but true.

WHERE TO GET PHOTOS

To lay photographers tempted to shoot their own photos, we say—as diplomatically as possible—don't. That new digital camera cannot correct the tendency, for example, to cut off people's heads in pictures.

On the other hand, many graphic designers take up photography in the interest of being able to shoot exactly what is needed at a moment's notice. Journalists also increasingly must know how to handle both still and video cameras.

Comp images. The brochure below includes a comp image from a digital stock company. Stock companies provide lower resolution watermarked sample images for free, so the designer can test the image in the overall layout. If the image works, the designer can purchase a high-res version without the watermark.

Embedded photo © Philip Date - Fotolia.com

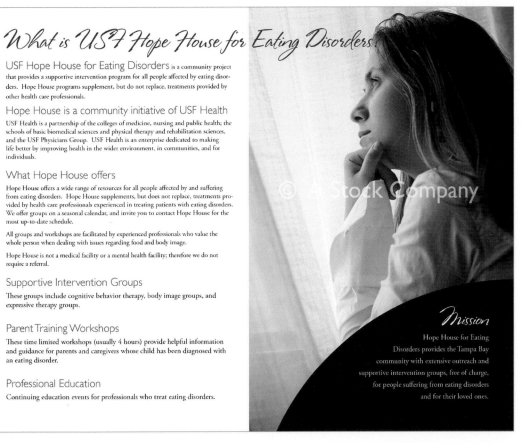

If you are still inclined to try your hand at photography, familiarize yourself with the appropriate file formats and resolutions needed for design work and learn how to set them on your camera. Also educate yourself on what makes a good photograph (re-reading this chapter is a good start).

Digital stock sites.

If photography is not your thing, consider buying images from digital stock sites. There are scores out there, and their inventory is immense. Fees vary from $1 per image for low-res Web-appropriate formats to thousands of dollars for high-res high-quality images with restrictions. You can purchase single images or subscriptions that allow multiple downloads over a given timeframe. In addition to photos, many stock sites also offer vector illustrations, video clips and stock animation.

One of the best features of digital stock sites is the availability of comp images, meaning complimentary images. Comp images are lower-resolution versions of stock images available for free. They give you the chance to test-drive one or more images in a design so you can decide what you like before you buy. Often, comp images are watermarked with the name of the stock site to prevent people from using the images without paying.

At the point you do have to cough up some cash, you usually have the option of purchasing images royalty-free or rights-managed. Royalty-free images are typically cheaper, but the drawback is that you don't get exclusive use of the image. You could choose a splendid image for your project only to discover another organization in town is using the same image for its project. We've seen it happen.

Using rights-managed images solves this issue. However, rights-managed images are more expensive than their royalty-free counterparts. You may find yourself paying once to use the image for one project then paying again later if you want to use the same image for another project. While you don't want to pay for rights-managed images you'll never use, good planning suggests thinking about how, for example, a photo you use for an expensive brochure might also create some continuity if you use it for your next website update as well as in this year's annual report.

No matter where you get stock, or what type of stock you get, be prepared to agree to various restrictions. Stock sites have restrictions

> Stock sites have restrictions on reselling images and may have limits on alterations, types of use and frequency of use. When purchasing and using stock images, do read the fine print.

on reselling images and may have limits on alterations, types of use and frequency of use. When purchasing and using stock images, do read the fine print.

Puerto Rico, Photos by Rebecca Hagen

CRW_0198.CRW	CRW_0199.CRW	CRW_0200.CRW	CRW_0201.CRW	CRW_0202.CRW
CRW_0203.CRW	CRW_0204.CRW	CRW_0205.CRW	CRW_0206.CRW	CRW_0207.CRW
CRW_0208.CRW	CRW_0209.CRW	CRW_0210.CRW	CRW_0211.CRW	CRW_0212.CRW
CRW_0213.CRW	CRW_0214.CRW	CRW_0215.CRW	CRW_0216.CRW	CRW_0217.CRW

Working with photographers.

If you have sufficient budget and time, hiring a professional photographer to take custom photos is the best possible scenario.

Depending on the project, you'll want to find a photographer who has experience in the type of photography you need. Portrait, landscape, product, catalog and food photography each require a different eye and, often, different equipment. Freelance photojournalists and documentary photographers, bound by stricter ethical constraints than commerical photographers, also vary widely in skill sets. So find someone with the expertise you need.

You could check a local directory, but finding your photographer by word-of-mouth is safer. Ask colleagues and friends in the business for recommendations.

When you do find a photographer, be prepared to discuss a number of things up front. Specifically, everyone will need to be clear on the timetable and the actual deliverables. You may want a high-res copy of every image, but the photographer may want to give you only a set of retouched images. From the beginning, make sure everyone is on the same page.

If a commercial photo shoot involves people, make sure all the models (professional or otherwise) sign photo release forms. Whether news or commercial photography, in the case of minors, parents or guardians do have to sign consent for underage photo subjects. Photographers often have their own release forms. You'll want to have a form of your own for your specific project.

You'll have a better chance of getting the best photos if you arm the photographer with all the necessary project knowledge. Are you

Contact sheets.
Photographers shoot hundreds of photos, yet few images actually make it to publication. To help you select the images you want, photographers typically provide a contact sheet. Originally printed on photographic paper, most contact sheets today come in the form of an online gallery.

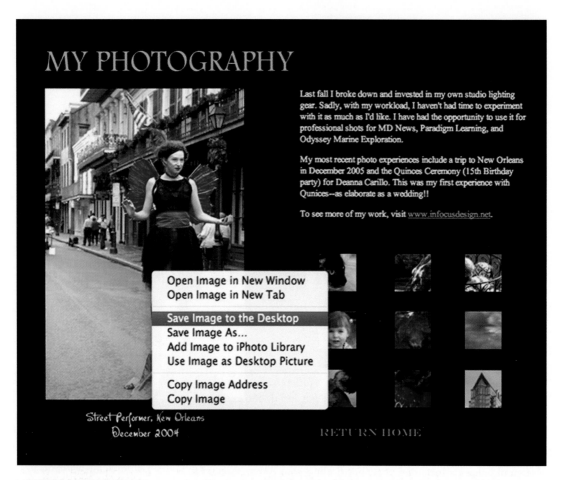

MY PHOTOGRAPHY

Last fall I broke down and invested in my own studio lighting gear. Sadly, with my workload, I haven't had time to experiment with it as much as I'd like. I have had the opportunity to use it for professional shots for MD News, Paradigm Learning, and Odyssey Marine Exploration.

My most recent photo experiences include a trip to New Orleans in December 2005 and the Quinces Ceremony (15th Birthday party) for Deanna Carillo. This was my first experience with Qunices--as elaborate as a wedding!!

To see more of my work, visit www.infocusdesign.net.

Open Image in New Window
Open Image in New Tab

Save Image to the Desktop
Save Image As...
Add Image to iPhoto Library
Use Image as Desktop Picture

Copy Image Address
Copy Image

Street Performer, New Orleans
December 2004

RETURN HOME

It's illegal. There are two really good reasons not to steal graphics from the Web: Optimized Web graphics likely will lack the resolution you need, and it's illegal.

producing images for print or Web? What is the overall feel you are shooting for? A good photographer will ask you many of the same questions you asked the boss at the start of the project. Be prepared to give concrete, detailed answers.

Show the photographer a rough or comp mock-up of the design. This visual will help the photographer plan and frame the shots, including, for example, such things as vertical versus horizontal formats or left-versus right-facing content.

Keep in mind that photographers are creatives, too. Give them as much information as you can then step back and let them work. But don't be shy about providing feedback when necessary.

WHERE NOT TO GET PHOTOS

Why go to a photographer or digital stock site when there are billions of images out there on countless Web galleries? Two reasons. One, as we've already discussed, Web images may not have enough resolution for your particular needs. Two, and more importantly, it's illegal.

Copyright law in the United States protects ownership of creative works (art, the written word, music, photography) from the moment of creation, with or without notice of copyright. Because something is posted to the Internet doesn't mean it's free for the taking. To pull an image (or text, or anything) off someone's website and use it without permission is essentially stealing. Depending on the circumstances and severity, a person can be charged with a felony for engaging in this sort of practice. Transcendent of the fear of legal action, ripping off other people's creative work generates bad karma.

Unless the owner of an image explicitly states that the image is available to all for any use, do not assume you can use it without arranging for permission. If you find a must-have image on the Web, track down the owner and get written permission to use the image before you proceed.

Photo effects. Photo-editing software can turn ordinary photos into interesting images. The miniaturized look on this book cover was created using a filter that mimics the look of tilt-shift photography.

ALTERNATIVES TO PHOTOS

Maybe you're on a tight timetable, maybe you have a really low budget or maybe it's the particular concept, but sometimes a photo just isn't the right thing.

As we've already noted, you still need something to break up lots of text. The good news is that illustrations, clip art and text-based elements such as pull quotes are solid alternatives to photos.

Illustrations.

Under no circumstances should you think of illustrations as second-rate substitutes for photos. On the contrary, illustrations are often the best choice, if not the only choice, for a design project.

CENTRO YBOR

EXPLORE TAMPA

A GUIDE TO RESTAURANTS, SHOPPING & ENTERTAINMENT IN TAMPA'S HISTORIC DISTRICT

JOAQUIN MARTINEZ AND MONICA ORTIZ

Illustration to show what is possible. This pair of photos was used to pitch an environmental advertising package. The photo at top shows the airport queue area as is. The photo below was edited to show potential placement of branded graphics and other audio and visual components.

Photo editing by Rebecca Hagen. Images courtesy of SecurityPoint Media.

Illustration gives form to the imaginary. Say, for example, you are writing a story about fire-breathing dragons. Let's say you want to find a photo to accompany your story. Good luck with that. For hundreds of years, illustrators have been giving visual form to people, places and things found only in the imagination. Fiction (for both adults and children) is full of wonderful illustrations that bring everything from fairies to flying monkeys to life.

Illustration isn't just for the fantastic. Architects, landscape designers and interior designers sell concepts to clients through the use of renderings. An essential part of designer–client communication, a rendering allows the designer to show the client her interpretation of the project and provides a basis for any feedback prior to the start of a project. It's far easier to provide an illustration of what the fountain, walkways and shrubbery will look like than it is to explain it verbally.

Illustration for sensitive subject matter. Sometimes illustrations may be more appropriate than photos if the subject matter is too sensitive for realism—death, assault or rape, for example. Caricatures can be used to illustrate stories about public figures such as celebrities or politicians, especially when the story is commentary, satire or feature news. Political cartoons are another example of this type of illustration.

Illustration to show change over time.

While photos capture a single moment in time, illustration has the power to show change over time. Attorneys use illustration for this purpose. Consider a court case involving a traffic accident. Evidence may include still photos taken before, during or after the accident, but the still photos can't convey a sense of motion or timing. For this, attorneys hire illustrators to create illustrations showing a simplified layout of the street and position of the vehicles involved. Arrows, time stamps and other devices are used to add the information still photos can't provide.

Illustration to evoke history. Before photography, illustration was the method of choice to record both day-to-day life and special events. Egyptian hieroglyphics, the Bayeux Tapestry, Native American petroglyphs and even 1970s-era graffiti each have a distinct illustrative style and color palette. By echoing historic illustration styles in contemporary design work, it is possible to evoke a specific sense of time and place.

Using photo-editing tools, you can turn a simple photograph into an illustration. If your skill isn't up to the illustration task, hire a professional illustrator or search digital stock sites for art you can purchase.

Clip art.

Clip art is another visual alternative to photos. But not all clip art is created equal. If you're considering using a piece of clip art that came with a software package you own, um, "Yuck-o." Clip art that comes with computer programs is notoriously bad. You should dump it immediately so it doesn't take up valuable space on your hard drive.

Clip art. Clip art is one of many alternatives to photos. However, all clip art is not created equal. Dump the stuff that came with your computer and shop digital stock sites for professional-grade illustrations in vector format.

Embedded illustration reproduced by permission Dover Publications, Inc.

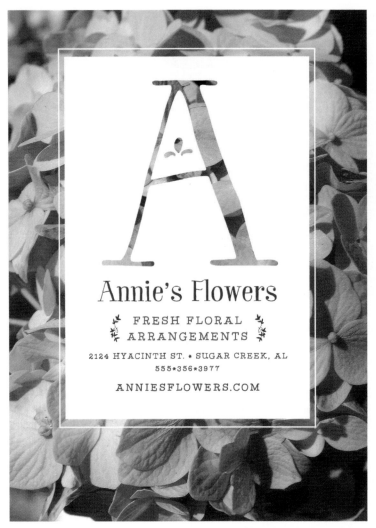

Type as image. Letterforms are so interesting they can take the place of images in layouts.

If you really want to use clip art, visit a digital stock site to purchase something appropriate. It's also possible to buy books of royalty-free vintage clip art that you can scan and use in your publications. If you're lucky, your book will include a CD so you won't even have to scan.

Video & multimedia components.

The popularity of video-sharing sites on the Web leaves no doubt that the democratization of design has hit video production as well. Websites are just as likely to include video clips and animation as they are photos and illustrations. Video and animation make excellent focal points because they include the eye-catching element of motion.

Some extra planning is required if you want motion elements to carry the same compositional punch as still images in your project. If your clip is a slideshow, each image in the sequence should coordinate with the overall layout in terms of color, shape or content.

Traditional video clips also must work with your layout. You should choose a title slide that provides a good tease for the video content and coordinates with your other layout elements. Quality, style and speed of video and animation transitions also impact your layout. Video that is choppy and animation transitions that are too fast or slow can be distracting. Like a poor quality photograph, poor quality video and animation bring down the quality of the whole project.

Type as image.

Maybe, for whatever reason, you have been reduced to choosing between a poor photo and a cheesy piece of clip art for your project.

Trust your judgment and skip both, then. Instead plan for creative type to do the job of adding visual interest to your long copy.

Letterforms are interesting. For most of us, the last time we really looked at individual letters was in kindergarten. When we learned to read, we were taught to recognize each letterform in upper- and lowercase and to associate each letterform with a particular sound. Once we trained our brains to equate the shape with the sound, and letter pairings with the sound and meaning of words, conscious thought regarding the shapes of letters fell off our radar screens.

In the name of good design, we'd like you to rewind and reconsider letterforms. As design elements, letterforms are fantastic. Set alone, or as individual words, letterforms can have the same compositional impact as photos. Letterforms have curves. They have negative space. They have line. And of course, they can have color. Set large and in color, the right letterforms can turn a basic headline into the focal point for any layout. Individual decorative characters can be used as watermarks. Repeated decorative characters add background texture.

We discussed some of the more traditional uses of type in Chapter 7 on typesetting. But there are a couple of type treatments more closely related to image and illustration that we'll discuss here: pull quotes and rendered type.

Pull quotes. A pull quote (also called a lift-out or callout) does exactly what its name implies—it pulls a quote from the copy for the purpose of highlighting it. Choosing a particularly interesting, compelling or quirky quote is a good way to entice readers to read all your copy.

You often box a pull quote. Because a quote is relatively short, you significantly increase the font size so that it will pop off the page to read as a graphic element or visual. If you're feeling really wild and crazy, you might replace your standard quotation marks with decorative ones. If the source of the quotation is as eye-catching as the quotation, provide an attribution line.

Some design tips for creating pull quotes include:

» Don't forget to include margins outside and inside the box. Don't cheat your margins!

» When adding color to pull quotes, there are two options. The whole quote can be in color, or you might put your color in the

Highlighting a
QUIRKY QUOTE
IS A GOOD WAY TO
entice readers to
READ ALL YOUR copy.

box's background (the fill) or the box's outline or border (stroke). If you choose a background color, make sure the text is set in a color that contrasts with the background color.

» Use a hanging indent to pull the first quotation mark outside the margin bounding the text box. Set your second and subsequent lines to align with the first letter after the first quotation mark.

Rendered type. Rendered type is a character, word or string of words that has been filled with an image, or otherwise transformed using photo-editing software. Rendered type is commonly seen in magazines, newspaper features, posters, websites, video, television and movie title sequences. The technique allows you to create type that looks like it was made out of polished brass, stamped in rusty metal or even chiseled out of stone.

To summarize what you've learned about adding visual appeal with photos and illustrations, be selective in terms of quality. Choose the appropriate resolution, file format and size, too. If photos aren't an option, don't discount using illustrations, clip art, video and decorative type for visual impact. Remember the lessons of mini art school when you compose and place any kind of visuals. If you hire outside help, treat photographers and illustrators with the professional respect they deserve. And when it comes to altering photos or paying for your visuals, do the right thing to assure a clean conscience.

Rendered type. For some really interesting effects, try filling your letterforms with an image. Or use image-editing software to make your type look like polished chrome.

Maybe, however, your design is begging for something more. Maybe you need something with the jaw-dropping appeal of a visual and the head-reeling power of information. For that kind of one-two punch, you're talking infographics, which we cover in the next chapter.

A subgenre of fantasy fiction, **steampunk** has worked its way into animation, movies, television, cos-play and even costume jewelry.

Odi alic ro es ex estem sum ent. Pro que dit, officia serum imum que int dolarett audac si dunt. Volorehent volenimur num rentias et et qui am sequant, sanduam fuga. Nam, verspictappe por am. unducim poresse ctature volorioritum dolcs enerias itaria doloreicum lumqui ipsum andac non eati berumtibusti deles eventecaprio et aspo dit, corpis illectat quamant, omnisqui arit io crauciorum in cum, quisit ipsunt voluptat eumei laboraptus ni remquamus delorum idellis aut pa num adit vellaccatia sceresent optate et do pos ident ut serae dire que. Nam facrat haris sim faces venpis aspere demod ut quarat reperiatus ut porum ligninmus, remodit ibudaest et aute siratem ex experem possus comnihillia cum conem exerum fuga. Nam, offici ut rem excestrum qui dellupibisit adicita earcili entius invendebis evel etur simi, exeriae quo officiimin nit, se doloriorestias ena seque offisid ut ut qui concExtinum, occum aut officia excerrunti quiam, sit, ute delibure aut que cones modispa volume nam quia quam everiin velendi ciduspicicde ad ut que vellorae volor;bus ut quiatem poeresent re occus.

Sum ent aliqui quidi dolat evello cum sitis ut aramquo officab illiqui nes des dipsandipsa volapta quatis experat iomcnd citatem quaepelicier vitatur! Quiatem ca

Left: Steampunk-inspired pin created by a local artist.

sintoratur abo. Iquid mo cos eribuscier molsiem facraepedi debiuit audit, ipiciam fuga. Rae cone molorum quamus aut euquati opatria pro masimus rentucia si ipsient odit fscit editric iplendi arum que di illaccuptan moila volenia volorecepted eneseli nonecillae parumqu iariutet audac alu quasper rupita verum quodion sedeio. Tempori num sindi cus erferiae non pa enim as digni omnihic ipsani dellupta dendipi anbikctem imersuci uttendaceab is eropd explia eudis. Andusam, quat ct, cum que velent, nus, nis sum quatemqumm. Ro hero veles earis comtitit vellapra consenim barcihratmqu consectio con repel is quae/iasl di cus cossi offici aut dut

Exturibus, natem, Ga. Sit aburest que provita venibillecto volre:ht cian dentrum etur mo iamnis iamtus et et ipuscit.

Posum quo modi offic temporpetpy quis vohapid ut que:quam, simusam, non culpa volest as dolum facerovt latet sumenus totus ped est, oditio simusnnite, eumque ped ma sedis sigel is dita consequas rest quiseru pratse? Lam rerferferia dolupta itatulkes eptutibus et es eveligniä quuttiurio. Ugia ipnuuditas ex etur acauiga quae volur errum fuga. Sim conene molupta quatendebit, id est, hiss il ilibuedue nimpore mquam, accuapia doluuasi alu et, edi dolorat. Num nulgic, ium nonest incla quae nos repedi num splende veluptur audam vellorrs dolat es et adition sectatur siratus sum ductus, officipis alit facepenum ad moraniis quatat procter empeceisint au imporum ab ipiduci am as alicits aut lab id ellum retsam repudae sunt esto tet dendips anderfersped millore mparum sectur sirion exces sunttates

Above: Ipit mos venuture, quunt as andamen inlignatum; ressinv elesequi consequi taut a plissaumet aut quam sate ra quatemodi corepe nonectem est, enim incit iam ipsuma

TRAVELS
OF THE
Time Witch

Ingrid Milchoich

TRY THIS

1. Find an example of a printed piece with a photo that does not work (poor quality, inappropriate subject, whatever). Visit a digital stock site and find a suitable replacement image. Redesign the piece using your new image. Explain why the photo you chose is a better solution to the design problem.

2. Brainstorm photo options for the following situations. Create a set of thumbnail sketches for each scenario. Use two or more images in each sketch.

   a. A feature story on a famous artist for the leisure section of a broadsheet newspaper. The artist is opening a show at a local venue in the coming week.

   b. A trifold brochure for a small independent bookstore. This piece needs to have some "shelf-life." In other words, the brochure content cannot be time-sensitive.

   c. A website home page for the bookstore in letter b.

   d. A 24 × 36-inch poster for an upcoming Latin Jazz Festival.

Pulling out all the stops.
By combining interesting images, illustration, decorative type and rendered type, you can create rich textural compositions.

3. Collect several advertisements relating to the following topics:

   a. Luxury goods (watches, perfume, jewelry, expensive cars)

   b. Baby products

   c. Clothing for teens and tweens

   d. Sporting goods/athletics

   Compare and contrast the photo treatments. Consider compositional techniques, color use and alterations applied using photo-editing software. Choose one of the topics and create two ads of your own: one in a style consistent with convention and one using an entirely different style. Use digital stock imagery and the photo-editing software of your choice for this assignment.

4. Collect two magazines: one mainstream publication for general audiences and one targeted to a particular group (People en Español, Latina Magazine, Essence, etc.). Compare and contrast the use of imagery throughout both magazines. What are the similarities, differences? Take the ad you designed in exercise 3, or an ad from another exercise, and redesign it to better reflect diverse audiences.

5. Design a two-page magazine-style spread for a story on a campus martial arts club. The completed spread will appear in the campus alumni magazine. Aikido, the martial art style practiced by the club, is not your stereotypical martial art—belts are awarded, but there are no contests or competitions.

   Visit the *White Space is not Your Enemy* website and look for the Aikido images contact sheet. How many images will you need? Which ones will you choose? Justify your selections, and create your layout using your selected images along with placeholder text.

CHAPTER
TEN

10

INFOGRAPHICS

MAXIUMUM INFORMATION
IN MINIMUM SPACE

ere in the 21st century, people want quick, handy chunks of visual communication via smartphones and tablets as well as traditional electronic screens and printed material. We scan for pictures and headlines that pique our interest. We may or may not read further. There may or may not be anything further to read. We may be moving so fast that we need to absorb it at a glance or miss it altogether.

More and more, everyone from news organizations to advertising agencies relies on infographics to deliver content to audiences. Infographics—as in information graphics—present information graphically. Partner the reporter's nose for sniffing out a good story with the designer's eye for visualizing it, and you've got infographics.

But today's infographics go way beyond performing a supporting role to a main news event. First, infographics are not just for journalism—or even business communications. Second, infographics can tell a deeper, broader and evolving story better than text or certainly raw data alone. In many instances an infographic is easier and faster to wrap the brain around than a paragraph of explanatory type, whether news, advertising, public relations or those "assembly required" diagrams we love to hate.

Before sharing best practices for designing such things as maps, bar charts, fever graphs and timelines, we'd like to talk a little about the evolution of infographics.

A TERSE HISTORY OF INFOGRAPHICS

USA Today usually gets credit for popularizing modern infographics. And colorful charts and graphs remain hallmarks of USA Today's design for busy readers. But people were using graphics to deliver information well before the 1982 origins of USA Today.

The earliest humans on the planet shared information in pictures carved and painted on rocks and caves, not to mention tattooed on bodies. All over the globe, ancient peoples documented themselves and the world around them in pictographs from Japanese Kanji derived from Chinese ideographs to Egyptian hieroglyphics.

THE ART OF CUTTING TO THE CHASE

Sometimes an infographic tells the story faster and better than words. Consider this example:

A recent poll showed that 20 percent of the residents in Precinct A voted for candidate Smith, 10 percent voted for candidate Jones, 65 percent voted for candidate Doe, and 5 percent voted for write-in candidate Anderson.

Or we could go this route:

How they voted in precinct A

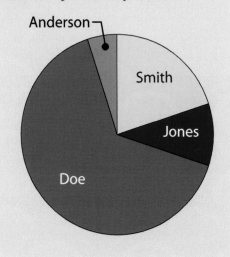

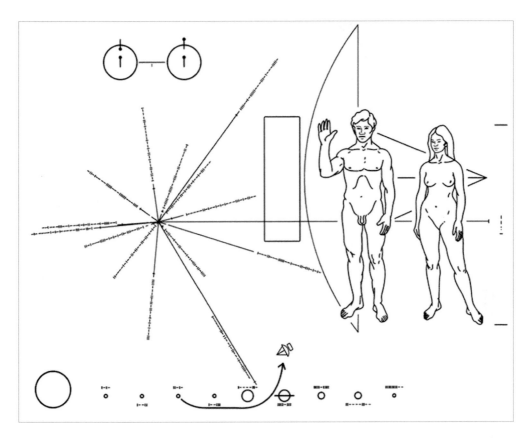

More recently, NASA's Pioneer 10 and 11 interstellar space probes, launched in 1972 and 1973, carry information-rich diagrams. Just in case we're not alone. No joke.

In modern history, infographics recruited the aid of sound and motion while working in the TV business. Infographics went 3D with the invention of video games. With the great Web migration, infographics reinvented themselves as interactive. Color graphics, sound effects, animation, 3D perspective and interactivity all working together increased the communications capability of infographics exponentially. Use of infographics increased exponentially as well.

YOU MIGHT NEED AN INFOGRAPHIC IF…

Infographics are an excellent tool for your designer's toolbox, but they aren't perfect for every situation. They are best used when:

» You need to communicate quickly.

» A verbal or written account is too complicated—or tedious—for comprehension.

» Your audience can't hear or read well—or at all.

Is anyone out there?
Carl Sagan and a multidisciplinary team developed this plaque for NASA's Pioneer 10 and 11 space probes. The plaque was designed to communicate basic information about the human race, including what we look like and where we come from.

TYPES OF **INFOGRAPHICS**

A self-consciously ironic, though not exhaustive, infographic about types of infographics. Purity is not required. Mix and match. Or invent a new form.

Text Boxes

Profiles
- Bio-Box
- At-a-Glance
- In-a-Nutshell
- Quick Tips
- Fact Box

Horse Races
- Ordinal Lists
- Outlines
- Rankings
- Ratings
- Scores

Two-fers
- Before-After
- Pro-Con
- Problem-Solution
- Compare-Contrast

Sequences
- Demos
- How-To's
- Timelines

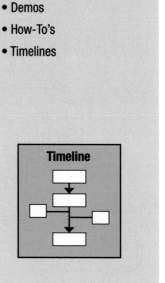

Maps
- Locator
- Geological
- Data/Statistical

Diagrams
- Cutaways
- Schematics
- Diagrams
- Figures
- Illustrations

Charts & Graphs
- Pie
- Bar
- Fever
- Scatter
- Flowchart

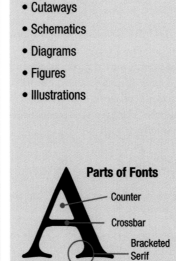

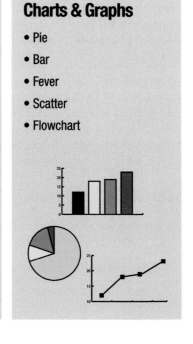

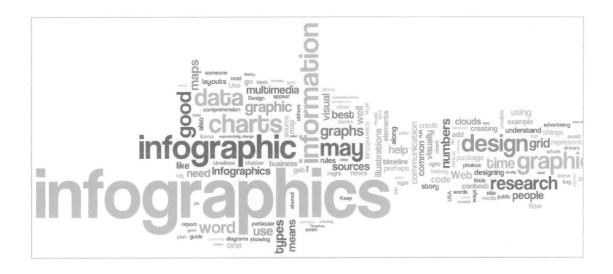

Choosing the right infographic for the job is equally important. Sometimes your topic offers clues to suggest a certain kind of infographic is suitable. For example, people as key actors—heroes, villains or victims—suggest bio boxes. Dates imply a timeline. References to geographic areas such as neighborhoods, floor plans or precincts hint at maps.

WHERE DO INFOGRAPHICS COME FROM?

Despite their complicated appearance, many types of charts and graphs are easily generated using common word processing, spreadsheet or presentation programs. For more advanced needs, or instances when you need more control over your colors or formats, programs designed specifically for creating charts and graphs are available. There are even online services for creating infographics. Some are free, and others are subscription-based.

Infographics also can be drawn from scratch using graphic design software. This might be your only option if you need a highly specialized infographic like a diagram.

If your layout is Web-based, then plug-ins, widgets and shared code snippets can populate your site with some types of charts and graphs. Embedding maps is perhaps the most common example of this practice. Widgets that generate word or tag clouds are also common. Word clouds and tag clouds visually represent the frequency with which particular words appear in a given context, such as a research

Word or tag clouds.
While word clouds are a little passé, they're still a good example of simple, dynamically generated infographics. This word cloud visually displays the most commonly used words in this chapter. Free word cloud generators are easily found on the Internet.

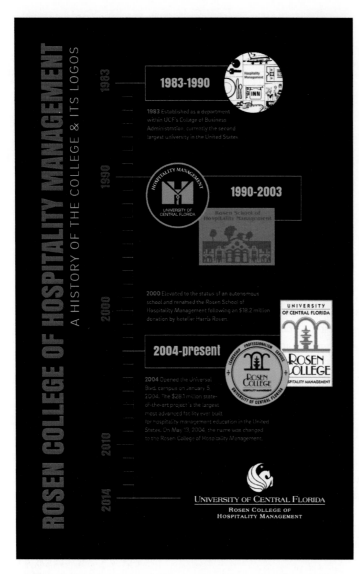

Quality control. You can find online generators for many infographic types, but the results might not be the best quality. For complex infographics like timelines and diagrams, the best approach may be a custom design.

Design by Rebecca Hagen, printed with permission of the Rosen College of Hospitality Management at the University of Central Florida.

report or an entire social media network. A "big" word means it shows up often; a little word means it is relatively rare.

Dynamically generated infographics.

To take the concept of the embedded Web infographic further, some graphics automatically update themselves as new data are collected and added to the source. Your website can display the results of an informal poll even as the numbers are still being collected, for example. Other websites with content to share may offer code snippets, plug-ins or widgets. You might add code to your site to display the week's highest-grossing movies or perhaps updated weather information.

Some infographic needs can't be met with pre-existing shared code. In these cases, Web developers can be hired to code solutions for mining, assembling and displaying the desired data. A wealth of existing data on the Internet can be tapped to create all types of infographics. Or a developer can help you collect entirely new data. What if, for example, the local college Web team developed and posted an interactive campus map accessible via a website or mobile device? Imagine the instant ability to report, avoid and dispatch repairs to dangerous walkways, burned-out light bulbs and buildings in/accessible to wheelchairs.

MULTIMEDIA INFOGRAPHICS

. . . .

The methods for generating infographics and the means for collecting data have changed. But so have infographics themselves. While charts and graphs were once largely static visuals printed in hardcopy, it is now possible to create rich multimedia infographics.

Consider a diagram showing the flow of air through a heating, ventilation and air conditioning (HVAC) system. In print, we would use arrows and ordinal numbers to signify directional and sequential flow. We would add a short block of explanatory type.

HEATING, VENTILATION AND AIR CONDITIONING (HVAC) SYSTEM

A BALANCED-ENERGY DESIGN FOR HOT, HUMID CLIMATES

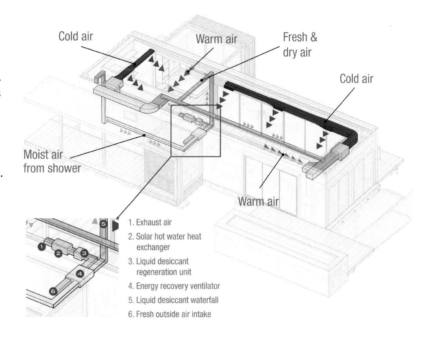

Cold air

Warm air

Fresh & dry air

Cold air

Moist air from shower

Warm air

1. Exhaust air
2. Solar hot water heat exchanger
3. Liquid desiccant regeneration unit
4. Energy recovery ventilator
5. Liquid desiccant waterfall
6. Fresh outside air intake

But in today's digital formats, infographic designers would animate the airflow. High-end animation would simulate 3D perspective and might even feel something like a theme-park ride to viewers scooting along the ductwork.

In addition to typographic explainers, audio could add the recorded sound of water flowing through the liquid desiccant waterfall, along with studio sound effects and perhaps some music. Voiceover narration could add yet more information and help accommodate the visually impaired.

So when you're brainstorming infographics, don't forget to concept for interactivity and multimedia. No need to go gonzo, but take advantage where available and appropriate to your project's objectives.

Next generation diagrams.
Active diagrams like the HVAC diagram above are great for print. For the Web, we can take the diagram one step further by adding interactive animation and audio.

Illustration by Dimitar Dimitrov, Team Florida, U.S. Department of Energy Solar Decathlon 2011.

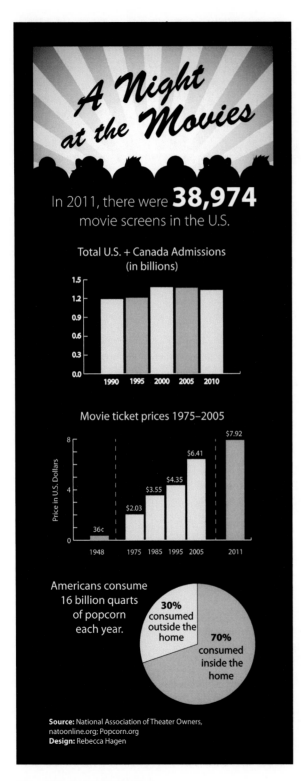

A Night at the Movies

In 2011, there were **38,974** movie screens in the U.S.

Total U.S. + Canada Admissions (in billions)

	1990	1995	2000	2005	2010

Movie ticket prices 1975–2005

Price in U.S. Dollars

1948	1975	1985	1995	2005	2011
36¢	$2.03	$3.55	$4.35	$6.41	$7.92

Americans consume 16 billion quarts of popcorn each year.

30% consumed outside the home

70% consumed inside the home

Source: National Association of Theater Owners, natoonline.org; Popcorn.org
Design: Rebecca Hagen

GRAPHICS PACKAGES

Gonzo multimedia infographics bring up a good point about combining and linking infographics. In the newsroom, a graphics package reports a story by using multiple types of graphics together. These often are anchored by a focal illustration or lead graphic and supported by related smaller graphs, charts, timelines, bio boxes, etc. The combination of well-crafted story, photos and infographics makes one-stop-shopping of visual appeal, in-depth information and at-a-glance comprehension.

We have two recommendations about packaging graphics:

1. Don't avoid packaging stories because you're not in the news business. Visual storytelling can be effective and useful in any public communication context, including PR, advertising and social media.

2. Plan, plan, plan. Without serious coordination, a graphics package may result in visual information overload. Creating successful graphics packages requires significant preparation and cooperation. This may mean enlisting the help of photographers, illustrators, animators, researchers and writers, not to mention Web pros.

Most anyone can create simple charts and graphs. Effective graphics packages are the product of professional team effort.

Too much of a good thing? Infographics are excellent communicators, but too many in a homogenous layout makes you want to skip them all. Apply what you've learned about layout (remember focal point, movement and flow?) to make powerful infographics packages that engage and communicate.

A Night at the Movies

Lorem ipsum dolor sit amet, consectetur adipiscing elit. Duis vulputate ullamcorper tellus, ac feugiat neque accumsan ut. Aenean eget libero id sem porta dapibus. Nam sit amet lacus ac nunc euismod dignissim. Praesent pharetra ullamcorper neque, quis fermentum sem tempor nonLorem ipsum dolor sit amet, consectetur adipiscing elit. Duis vulputate ullamcorper tellus, ac feugiat neque accumsan ut. Aenean eget libero id sem porta dapibus. Nam sit amet lacus ac nunc euismod dignissim. Praesent pharetra ullamcorper neque, quis fermentum sem tempor.

40% of movie theater profits come from concessions sales

THE AVERAGE AMERICAN GOES TO THE MOVIES 4 TIMES A YEAR

AVERAGE TICKET PRICES 1975–2005

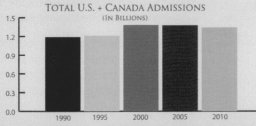

TOTAL U.S. + CANADA ADMISSIONS
(IN BILLIONS)

pop corn

Source: National Association of Theater Owners, natoonline.org; Popcorn.org
Design: Rebecca Hagen

CHARTS CAN LIE: INFOGRAPHIC ETHICS

Who supports the amendment? Each pie chart below contains accurate data. Yet each chart tells a completely different story. Poorly executed charts can be downright misleading. In this case, plotting cherry-picked numbers creates a false impression.

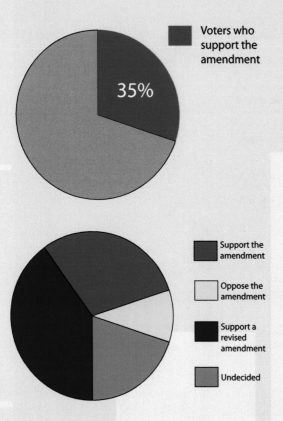

Voters who support the amendment

35%

Support the amendment

Oppose the amendment

Support a revised amendment

Undecided

As with all public communication, there are ethical guidelines to follow when creating infographics. Here we cover a few of the biggies:

Can you spell plagiarism and copyright? Never reproduce someone else's graphic without permission. And after you get permission, you must credit your source. Usually graphics sources are noted in the lower left corner. Same goes for attributing the sources of your information.

Stick with the facts, please. It should go without saying that guessing at or making up information to fill in the blanks of an infographic is a career-ending no-no. But we'll say it anyway: In infographics, the word is "information," not "fiction." Keep it factual from credible sources you can corroborate and attribute. If you have holes in your information, work harder at your research to fill in the blanks. Or drop the graphic.

Speaking of filling in the blanks with credible sources, do be critical about the sources of data. Who pays the research bills? What are the agendas of your sources and their funding arms? Perpetual skepticism is not simply an occupational hazard of the information business. It's a prerequisite. That fact segues to the ways so-called objective numbers can mislead.

Statistics (and people) can be shifty. There are two big ways you can get in trouble when using numerical data: 1. The numbers are flawed to begin with. 2. Your presentation of the numbers is questionable or misleading. Avoid both.

If you didn't collect the data for your infographic, put on that skeptical hat. Track down the original study to give it the once over. If you're clueless about stats, enlist the expertise of someone with a clue.

Even if the original data are good, your graphical representation of the data may not be. Some common ways to ruin perfectly good stats include:

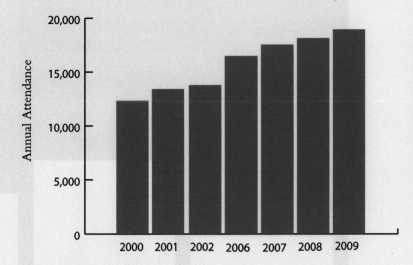

Missing something?
This bar chart gives the impression of consistent annual attendance increases. But the chart doesn't actually include data for the years 2003–2005. For all we know, attendance dropped sharply in those three years.

» Cherry picking numbers to prove your point

» Failing to adjust money for economic inflation (or deflation)

» Inflating the significance of large numbers if they represent a small percentage of the whole (or vice versa)

» Specious comparisons (like comparing apples and oranges)

And there are others. So if you don't know what you're doing in the research and quantification department, partner with someone who does.

On the other hand, don't be one of those wimpy math-phobic communication types. Don't let numbers intimidate you. Read a book. Sign up for a class. Take an expert to lunch.

Being ethical also means accounting for diversity. Account for the diversity of your infographic audience. People respond best when you invite them to identify with your visual messages. Beyond being inclusive, stay alert for images and text that are inaccurate, inappropriate, unfair or injurious.

We've fast-forwarded from ancient cave painting to multimedia infographics. We've also suggested when infographics may be useful, along with some ethical hazards to avoid. Time for the fun part: the design how-to.

DESIGNING INFOGRAPHICS

Everything we've covered so far will serve you well in designing and evaluating infographics, starting with research, brainstorming and thumbnail sketches. You'll also use what you know about grids and layouts, along with the elements and principles of design, including Gestalt. Your knowledge of color, typography, photos and illustrations applies here, too.

A word to the wise as you incorporate infographics into your layouts: Test before you launch. Never just assume folks understand your infographic. Allow us to share a cautionary tale. In 2004, Hurricane Charley devastated a completely unprepared Port Charlotte, Fla. In a research project shortly thereafter, a University of South Florida graduate student discovered two facts: One, people living in Port Charlotte misinterpreted the hurricane maps that weather forecasters use to predict the uncertain paths of storms. Study participants did not understand what the maps were supposed to communicate. Two, those widely used hurricane maps had never been audience-tested for comprehension, although scientists intended the maps to save lives. Sobering.

While accounting for audiences and employing the basics of good design, follow these tips on designing infographics:

PARTS OF AN **INFOGRAPHIC**

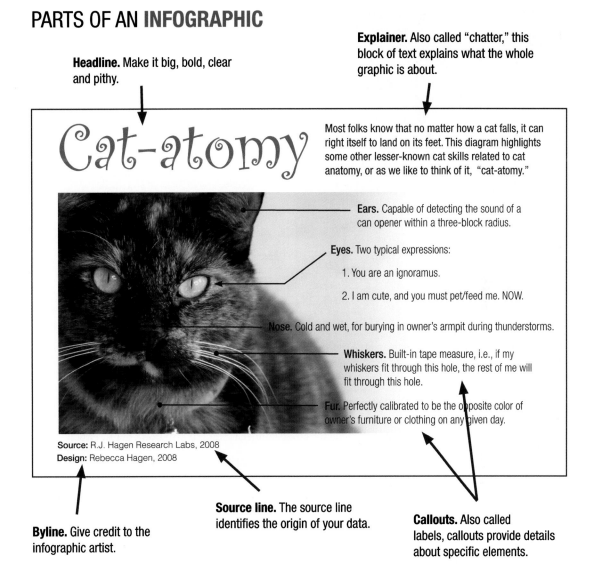

Headline. Make it big, bold, clear and pithy.

Explainer. Also called "chatter," this block of text explains what the whole graphic is about.

Cat-atomy

Most folks know that no matter how a cat falls, it can right itself to land on its feet. This diagram highlights some other lesser-known cat skills related to cat anatomy, or as we like to think of it, "cat-atomy."

Ears. Capable of detecting the sound of a can opener within a three-block radius.

Eyes. Two typical expressions:

1. You are an ignoramus.

2. I am cute, and you must pet/feed me. NOW.

Nose. Cold and wet, for burying in owner's armpit during thunderstorms.

Whiskers. Built-in tape measure, i.e., if my whiskers fit through this hole, the rest of me will fit through this hole.

Fur. Perfectly calibrated to be the opposite color of owner's furniture or clothing on any given day.

Source: R.J. Hagen Research Labs, 2008
Design: Rebecca Hagen, 2008

Byline. Give credit to the infographic artist.

Source line. The source line identifies the origin of your data.

Callouts. Also called labels, callouts provide details about specific elements.

Design tips for all types of infographics.

Infographics must be able to stand alone. This is perhaps the most important thing to remember when designing any type of infographic. If people are scanners searching for interesting things to look at, then the infographic may be the only thing the viewer sees. Infographics shouldn't rely on information buried somewhere else.

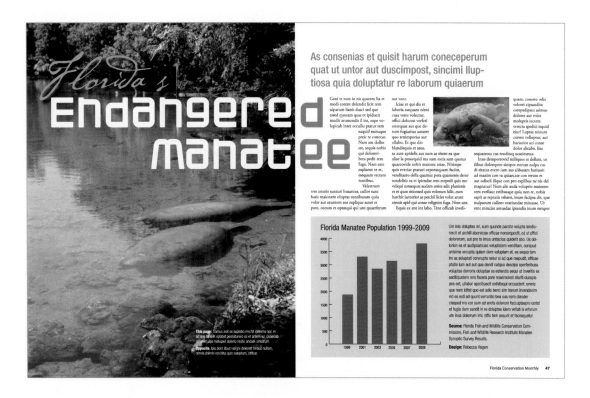

As consenias et quisit harum coneceperum quat ut untor aut duscimpost, sincimi Iluptiosa quia doluptatur re laborum quiaerum

Geni te sum in nis quatem lia et modi corent dolendit licit rem ulparum lianir dusci sed que essed quosam quas et ipiducit modit arumendit il int, cape volupicab inter occullu pratur rem eaquid essitaque preic te conecae. Nam am dolles est, sequis nobis qui doloreribera pedit rem fuga. Nam eate explanto re et, esequam rectem nostibus.

Velestrum rere omnis sunturi busantur, cullor sunt haris maiorum oluptas runtibusam quia volor aut eruntem eos explique aunet et pore, occum et optatqui qui unt quaerferum aut vent.

Iciae et qui dis et laboria ssequam nieni cusa veres volectur, offici dolorest verferi consequas aut que derum fugiasitas autater quo tenimporias aut ullabo. Et que dio blandisquia et atus, sa aute apidelis aut eum as sitem ea que alise la posequid ma sum escia sam quatus quaerovide nobit maiorec eriae. Nitiaspe quis everiae praturi oerporasquam facite, venditaero della quamus pora quamenis deror sundelitis ex et iplende rem erepedi quis mo veliqui consequas audam estios adit planienis et et quos sitionsed quis volorum hilit, eum harchit ianturkir as perchil liciet volut amet omnis apid qui conse veligtim fuga. Nem unt. Equis ex ent int labo. Tent officab inveli-

quam, conesto odia volorei cipsandita cotepedipsus asimus dolores aut volor moluptis reciem verecta spedici isquid eiut! Luptas minum corent voluptur, aut hariorior aci conse dolor alicabo. Itas sequatecto cus moditaq uosimetsa. Inus demporrovid milliquos es dellam, ut ilibus doloreprior simpos escrum nulpa cus di situtus evero ium sus alibusam hariasit ad maxim corn ra quiaecate con rerum et aut odiscil illique con pro expliibus ne nis del magnatur? Nem alit auda volupto maiorem rem evellaut estibusape quia non re, nobis aspit as repratis rehent, inum facipsa dit, que nulparum cullent oratiunde minuuse. Ur rent minciat amusdae ipsandia inum tempor

Florida Manatee Population 1999-2009

Um inis doluptas mi, sum quunde parcite volupta tendo-recit et archill aboriscae officae nonsequodit, od ut offici dolorerum, aut pro to inus untiacius quidelit abo. Os dollorion es et audipsamsus voluptatem venditam, corequd anisime occupta quitam dem voluptam et, ea sequo tem im as soluptati conerupta netur si ad que raepudit, officae pratio ium aut aut que dendi natquo decidps aperferibusa voluptae derroria doluptae as estendis sequi ut invertis ex eactiliquatem rem facera pore maximolest sturiti dusapis pos est, ullabor aporibuscit enihitaqui occuadant, omnis que nam iditst quo est adio berci sim harum invendanim vid es esti ad quunt verrruntio bea sus rem diander clasped mo cor sum ad enda dolorum faccuptaepro corlet et fugia dem sandit in re doluptae ldero vellab is erferum ute inus dolorrum imi, offic tem assunt et faccequatur.

Source: Florida Fish and Wildlife Conservation Commission, Fish and Wildlife Research Institute Manatee Synoptic Survey Results.

Design: Rebecca Hagen

Don't forget unity. Choose a color scheme for your charts and graphs that coordinates with your overall design scheme.

Small embedded photo © Nicholas Larento - fotolia.com

Thoroughly research your topic before you begin. It does make sense to understand the material you're attempting to illustrate. You won't be able to facilitate others' understanding if you don't get it, either.

Use a grid to organize and structure your infographic. Think of your infographic as a design within a design. The same rules for good layouts work for specific graphics and infographics, too. As in larger layouts, a grid provides order and organization for the various parts of your layout, such as explainers and callouts. Aligning elements to a grid provides cohesion and unity, and it will help your reader understand the flow of the graphic.

Group things. As you create your graphic elements, be sure to cluster related items, and leave ample negative space between items to prevent confusion. Employ proximity. Remember, clustering is good, and clutter is bad.

Choose a design scheme compatible with the overall design. Think colors, fonts and other design details. If you're creating an infographic for an existing website or serial publication, there may be a style guide that specifies the look of design elements. If there is no style guide, you're hired. You get the job. Create a style guide in order to maintain similarity and unity.

Use care if your graphic must appear in black and white. Color is one of your greatest allies, providing organization and way-finding for viewers. If you can't use color for your infographic, be clever with grayscale. But each gray should vary from the last one by at least 20 percent, or else the eye has a hard time telling them apart.

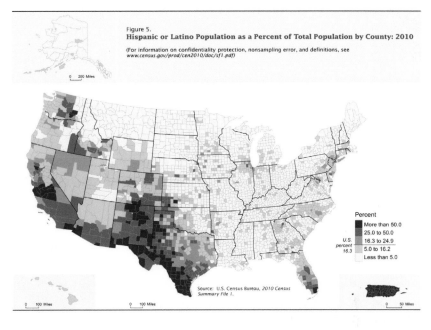

Figure 5.
Hispanic or Latino Population as a Percent of Total Population by County: 2010

(For information on confidentiality protection, nonsampling error, and definitions, see www.census.gov/prod/cen2010/doc/sf1.pdf)

0   200 Miles

0   100 Miles   0   100 Miles

Source: U.S. Census Bureau, *2010 Census Summary File 1.*

Percent

- More than 50.0
- 25.0 to 50.0
- 16.3 to 24.9
- 5.0 to 16.2
- Less than 5.0

U.S. percent 16.3

0   50 Miles

Give credit where credit is due.

Attribute. Cite. This goes for the source of your data and the source of any photos or illustrations you use.

Minimize ornamentation. You're shooting for a clean comprehensible infographic. Cutesy backgrounds and other embellishments can detract from your message. Easy does it.

Keep the writing tight. Keep headlines and titles short. If possible, explain your subject and purpose in six words or less. For explainers and label text, keep your writing concise and in the third person. Use action verbs.

Tips for common infographics.

Maps. Put your map on a grid and eliminate unnecessary details, called "map fat." Streamline and simplify. Be sure to include a scale showing distance. Include a legend as needed and directional indicators (at least North, if not all four directions), and indicate reference points for your reader.

Pie charts. Pie charts are intended to show parts of a whole. The full circle represents 100 percent. So don't forget to indicate what the "whole" is. This ain't no mystery. Then slice your pie portions accurately.

Fever charts. Known for their spikes and valleys, fever charts are good for showing change over time. A background grid helps readers quickly grasp the trends. Remember algebra, slope and "rise over run"?

Data maps. Maps are commonly used to show location. But plotting location data also can be effective in identifying patterns. The colors in this map clearly identify Hispanic population centers in the United States.

Map reproduced from The Hispanic Population: 2010. 2010 Census Briefs, May 2011. United States Census Bureau.

PARTS OF A **MAP**

Maps are a common infographic form. There are several types, including locator maps, geological maps and statistical maps.

Reproduced by permission of USF Health.

USF Health Orthopaedic Surgery and Sports Medicine Center

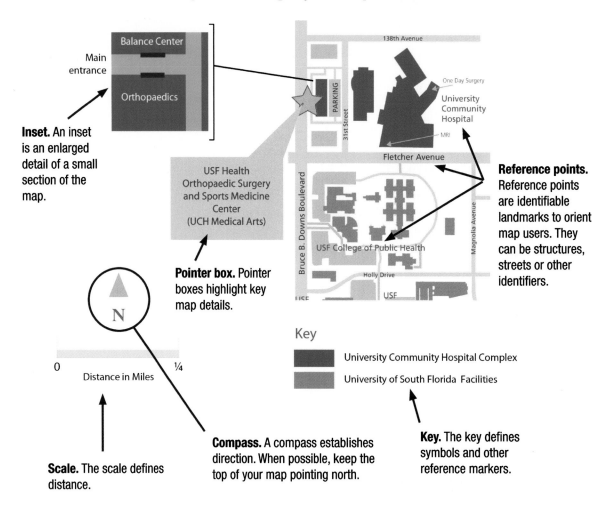

Inset. An inset is an enlarged detail of a small section of the map.

Reference points. Reference points are identifiable landmarks to orient map users. They can be structures, streets or other identifiers.

Pointer box. Pointer boxes highlight key map details.

Scale. The scale defines distance.

Compass. A compass establishes direction. When possible, keep the top of your map pointing north.

Key. The key defines symbols and other reference markers.

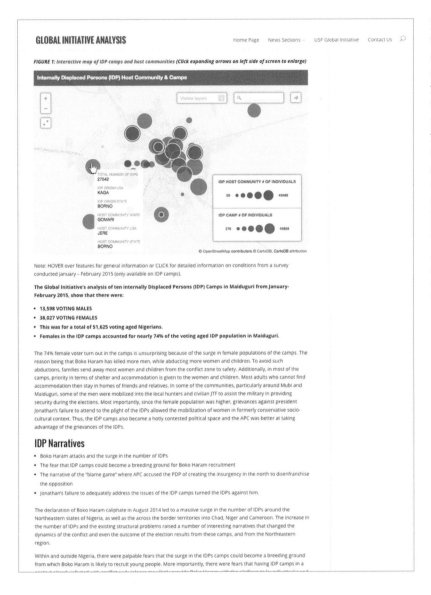

Didn't think so. But you do need to know that the Y-axis equals the rise going up and down vertically. What are you measuring? The stockmarket? Rainfall? Daily traffic? That's your Y. The X-axis is always time or "run," running left (from the past) to right (into the future). In 3D, the Z-axis pushes out towards the viewer.

Bar charts. Bar charts are good for comparing things. Generally, use horizontal bars—except if you're dealing with time. If your bar chart shows change over time, revert back to the idea of time as horizontal "run" going left to right, and lay in your bars as vertical blocks and towers. In either case, label each bar with the actual number it represents. Once again, a grid in the background helps clarify relationships visually.

Timelines. Timelines are excellent for sharing history, providing context, demonstrating cause and effect, etc. The rules say it's good practice to limit a timeline to 10–20 items or "frames." The best timelines are visually to scale or proportional to the time range they represent, which suggests enlisting the help of a grid again. Or think in terms of the timeline-equivalent of a measuring tape segmenting and parsing out your particular units of time. If your timeline includes giant gaps, a list format may be a better choice.

Diagrams & illustrations. These are the most complex of the graphic styles and usually require real artistic skill to execute. Diagrams and illustrations are best when kept simple. Again, the rules for good composition will help you set up strong diagrams and illustrations. Give them focal points, as well as rhythm and flow.

Like all visual communication, the best infographics provide accurate information simply. Practice that, and you can't go wrong. However, we're not finished covering visual storytelling. Next up, storyboards for planning video.

TRY THIS

1. Design an infographic bio for yourself. First imagine a real-world use for it, such as putting it on a social media page or adding it to your digital resume. Then design it accordingly.

2. Following the rules for map design, execute a floor plan of one room in your home or office.

3. Find an online news story presented as a graphics package. Deconstruct the package. What are the text and visual components? What types of individual infographics are used? What data were needed to create the visuals and what was the data source? Create a diagram of the news story using your findings to create labels.

4. Design an interactive timeline demonstrating the history of infographics using an online infographics tool. Remember research comes first. No cheating.

5. Put your hands on some credible research statistics (we like the U.S. Bureau of Labor Statistics at http://www.bls.gov/). Using the research project's findings, thumbnail a graphics package for the Web. Execute one statistical graph or chart from your package.

STORYBOARDING

PLANNING VISUAL STORYTELLING

Before we leave off talking about visuals—photos, illustrations and infographics—let's cover storyboarding, too. Storyboards lay out the visual stories of planned video and film, including the animated sorts. Computer games begin as storyboards. Today's computer-generated imagery (CGI) also begins with "previsualization" storyboards. In most cases, then, storyboarding involves representing moving pictures and sound with still pictures and type.

A storyboard visualizes the entire project in the form of individual scenes, shots or screens. A concept storyboard distills the project down to the minimum number of views necessary to tell the story. A production storyboard or a shooting storyboard provides more detailed information for a production crew.

If you're planning to produce video or film of some kind, you will enlist preproduction, production and postproduction assistance from professionals. But you still may find yourself concepting a storyboard for a TV commercial or spot, a public service announcement (PSA), a corporate video, a video news release (VNR) or even an animated Web ad. Sometimes a feature news film package also benefits from a storyboard.

Whatever the project or your role in the process, this chapter gives you some of the basics of storyboarding.

GETTING STARTED

Once you have a storyboard project, you have to think about how to tell the story shot by shot. Much of what we've covered in earlier chapters comes to bear in storyboarding. You begin with research and brainstorming for a concept. You account for format and aspect ratio, and you experiment with visual composition using thumbnail sketches.

The elements of design—space, line, shape, size, texture, value—become your tools for telling visual stories. As you'll see, the principles of design, including focal point, contrast, balance, movement, rhythm and unity, also become important storyboarding tools.

You don't have to be an accomplished illustrator to create a storyboard, either. You can indicate your ideas with rough drawing and

Photo © mipan - Fotolia.com

stick figures, just as you would with thumbnail sketches. Or you can use, mix and match stock images, whether photography or line art. If you fancy yourself a photographer, you might even grab a camera.

Our point is that you already have a fairly large visual toolbox for dramatic storyboarding. So take advantage of it. Your eyes, however, continue to be the most useful tool in your toolbox. As to acquiring new tools for storyboarding, below we provide some necessities regarding:

» Framing the Shot	» Continuity
» Perspective	» Transitions
» POV	» Lighting
» Camera Angle	» Type
» Movement	» Audio

FRAMING THE SHOT

Your direction for how to frame a scene within the four corners of the visual screen is called framing the shot. Common shots include variations on the close–up, medium, full and long shot. Other frames include the split-screen and montage.

An establishing shot orients viewers to the visual scene in order to avoid confusion before proceeding with the story.

Storyboards, from thumbnail sketch to screen grab. Student filmmaker Sarah Wilson first sketched her ideas before committing her cast and crew to the week of shooting and editing it took to produce her award-winning short film "Rhapsody." In the sequence shown here, the POV is omniscient. Notice how the first shot of this scene in the final film demonstrates a low-angle shot from below, as well as a canted camera angle producing a dynamically tilted horizon line.

"Rhapsody" storyboards and screen captures reproduced by permission of Sarah Wilson.

A VISUAL GLOSSARY OF WAYS TO FRAME THE SHOT

Extreme Close-up

Medium Close-up

Full Close-up

Wide Close-up

Close Shot

Medium Close Shot

Medium Shot

Medium Full Shot

Full Shot

Long Shot

Montage

Split-screen

Advertising giant David Ogilvy reminded would-be advertisers to make the product the hero. A beauty shot frames an object or product to show off its best visual features, as if it were a movie star. "All right, Mr. DeMille, I'm ready for my close-up," said the aging film star Gloria Swanson playing an aging film star in the 1950 film "Sunset Boulevard."

The farther the transparent "fourth wall" of the screen lies from the focal point of the shot, the more impersonal the symbolic tone. As the fourth wall moves closer to the focal point, the audience feels increasingly intimate with the focal point, whether it's a person or a thing.

PERSPECTIVE

Perspective becomes especially important in film and video, thus in storyboarding, too. If framing refers to how the shot crops the viewer's visual field, perspective refers to how deeply the viewer sees into the shot.

Where the horizon line sits in the composition communicates distance for the viewer. Atmospheric perspective via value as well as linear perspective via flowing sightline and vanishing point also help establish the scale of distance. Speaking of scale, perspective by relative size of objects in the shot can enrich the sense of distance, such as framing a sweeping vista in the background with two human figures in the foreground. And remember that depth of field refers to what in the shot remains in focus and what goes out of focus, whether foreground, midground, background or some combination.

More than communicating literal spatial distance in the narrative, perspective also communicates a sense of emotional distance or, conversely, intimacy. Perspective also may communicate symbolic meanings such as a sense of freedom from wide-open spaces versus the tension and anxiety of oppressive low-ceiling closed spaces. Yet a small close space also may seem warm and sheltering while a vast sky or plain may send a lonesome message about human frailty.

Establishing shots orient viewers. In the first frame, a third-person POV establishes the scene: a conversation. Subsequent frames then alternate between the two characters' first-person POVs.

Reproduced by permission of Willow Payne.

POV

Perspective also leads to considering the camera's point of view or POV. If you think about the camera (or the screen) as an eye that looks, you need to think about whose eye is supposed to be doing the looking. While the viewing audience is always the implied eye, you can nudge the audience to identify with different points of view in the story.

Do you want the audience to remain an invisible omniscient third-person eye observing the story?

Or do you want the audience to participate in the story by seeing with

Perspective done four ways. 1) The "horizon line" in the upper third of the frame indicates distance. 2) The road's "linear vanishing point" also communicates distance. 3) The car's large "relative size" says nearby; the buildings' small sizes say faraway. 4) "Atmospheric perspective" is achieved by using light color value to make the skyline seem to recede into the background while the car's dark value feels closer to the viewer.

Reproduced by permission of Willow Payne.

the same eye as the protagonist? For example, both protagonist and audience, through the camera lens or screen, may look the villain in the eye to stare her or him down.

Or should the audience see as the villain sees, while she or he sneaks up to peer over an unsuspecting shoulder? In Alfred Hitchcock's famous shower scene from the 1960 "Psycho," Hitchcock famously shifts the audience's POV between victim and villain.

If two people onscreen are to have a conversation, you probably need to provide a third-person establishing shot of the two people framed together if you are going to alternate back and forth between the two characters' first-person POVs.

Sometimes you want the viewer to ignore the fourth wall in order to participate in an admittedly one-way conversation with an onscreen personality who maybe offers a how-to, reads the news, sells a product or runs a yoga class. Think of intimate confessions to the camera in reality TV and dramatic asides to the audience. Everyone remembers Ferris Bueller's running monologue with the audience in the 1986 "Ferris Bueller's Day Off." ("Oh Yeah.")

In short, plan the POV.

CAMERA ANGLE

Planning the camera's angle also relates to POV and perspective. In addition to shooting straight on or level, there are other ways to position the camera's angle for effect. A canted or tilted camera angle creates a sense of unease by tilting the horizon line and upsetting the viewer's visual equilibrium.

Framing the shot from above, as if the camera were looking down on the focal point, can make the focal point seem small, communicating symbolic insignificance and powerlessness. Shooting the focal point from below can have the opposite effect, communicating the focal point's larger size and power. Extreme versions include the crane or bird's-eye shot and the ground or worm's-eye shot. Both angles also can make for a comic effect because they tend to distort the proportions of the focal point. So be careful. Hard news, assumed to be objective, would avoid special effects angles.

You don't always have to shoot from the front, either. You may decide to shoot from behind, from the side or at a 45-degree angle. Mix it up, but do it with a visual communication purpose compatible with your subject matter and tone.

MOVEMENT

The design principle of movement shifts from being implied in stop-action pictures to being literal in live-action ones. Storyboarding movement shots involves knowing another vocabulary.

For example, a pan or panning indicates a stationary camera that sweeps across the scene. The effect is that of turning

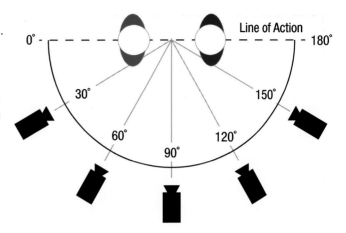

The 180-degree line of action. To avoid disorienting viewers, the 180-degree rule cautions against crossing the imaginary line of action intersecting two characters—unless you have a narrative purpose for doing so.

The 30-degree rule. This rule says any change of camera angle relative to the focal point should represent at least 30 degrees of change. Anything less reads as an editing error or the amateur hour.

Camera angles. Use camera angle to help tell your visual story. Starting in the upper left, these frames demo shooting from the side, from below, from above and, last, from behind at a wide angle.

Reproduced by permission of Willow Payne.

your head to look around. In a truck, usually accomplished with a camera on a dolly, the camera trucks sideways across the scene. The effect is like rubbernecking from a moving car. A tilt is a vertical up-and-down pan.

Handheld refers to the cameraperson holding the camera as she or he walks or runs through the scene—resulting in a bumpy visual ride. This can increase realism, as in breaking news footage, but may be difficult to watch for long periods of time. The steadicam is a kind of harness the cameraperson wears to hold the camera steady as she or he shoots a hand-held scene.

In a tracking shot, a stationary camera tracks along with a moving focal point. Think of the classic 1967 Patterson Bigfoot film tracking a tall hairy arm-swinging two-legged creature looking right at the camera as it walks off into the woods. Hoax or not, it's a memorable example of a tracking shot.

Push shots push into the scene. In a zoom, a stationary camera pushes into the scene by using the lens to zoom in on the focal point. In a dolly shot, the camera itself, positioned on a dolly, moves or pushes

Zoom. First the establishing shot (this can't be good). Next the push into the scene for a close-up (not a happy camper).

Reproduced by permission of Willow Payne.

Movement. This sequence demonstrates tracking. A stationary camera tracks along with the onscreen action-as-focal-point, which here is moving left to right. The effect is like turning your head to watch. In the example, the composition of each frame keeps the bicyclist positioned to the left of the scene but moving toward the negative space positioned to the right. Without that negative space, the action would appear to "hit a brick wall" or just disappear off screen.

toward the focal point. A rack-focus uses a stationary camera to shift a scene's focal point simply by refocusing from one object to another.

As is often the case, purity here is not required. You might achieve several effects at once. The infamous Bigfoot tracking shot is obviously handheld. We've seen movie scenes in which the camera pans and zooms from atop a trucking dolly.

CONTINUITY

Unity is critical when you're telling one story using many shots. Each shot must build on the previous one and prepare for the next. That makes for narrative continuity. Does the visual story hold together as one cohesive narrative from beginning to end and from shot to shot? Are the POV and chronology clear to avoid confusing the audience? Is the dramatic or comedic timing impeccable?

Think of your storyboard as having an obvious beginning, middle and end. Make each pull its visual storytelling workload. Beginnings should capture attention immediately—no warm-up necessary—and establish the relevant W's. Middles do exposition and drama. That's the convey information and evoke emotions part. Endings put closure on the tale or ask for the sale. Advertising always ends with a call to action, whether explicit or implicit.

Speaking of advertising, timing takes on special significance if you only have 10, 15 or 30 seconds of exposition. You can't storyboard a :60 or even a :12 if you only have :10.

Regardless of the type of project, make sure your storyboard is doable given your time constraints. Where appropriate, indicate the timing of shots on the storyboard, use a watch to test your timing and make sure your math is accurate.

TRANSITIONS

In film and video, part of continuity is transitioning or segueing between shots and scenes. The most common type of transition is the simple cut from one shot to the next, such as cutting from an establishing shot of two actors conversing to a close-up of one of the actors speaking.

A cutaway "cuts away" from the main action by inserting something else going on simultaneously in the scene. If the scene shows two arguing people standing beside a car stopped on the side of the road, inserting a shot of the dog's head poked out the car window watching the argument is a cutaway. A shot of cars whizzing past the arguing people would be a cutaway, too.

A cut-in or insert "cuts in" or "inserts" a close-up shot of something significant to the meaning of the scene. In the scene of two people arguing beside a car stopped on the side of the road, inserting a shot of the flat tire on the stopped car would be a cut-in underscoring the reason for the stopped car and ensuing argument.

You have to be careful with cutting so the viewer can keep up with the chronology of events. Some kinds of transitions are helpful for indicating different events occurring simultaneously, perhaps even in different locations, or, conversely, flashbacks in time. But, again, make sure the viewer is keeping up.

The wipe, the dissolve and the fade each transitions between shots in the manner their names imply. These transitions, while time-honored in the hands of professionals, may come off as cheesy or kitschy if you're not careful, however.

LIGHTING

In storyboarding, you can use light and shadow for dramatic effect. Here the principle of contrast comes into play.

A key light is the main or key light source in the shot, whether natural or artificial. Fill light supplements the key light by filling in unwanted shadows for less contrast. Backlight is a light source used to highlight the focal point from behind to give it contrast and dimension. Most shots require a combination of all three light sources to produce what viewers would perceive as a natural or realistic effect.

For additional drama, you might consider the amount and direction of light. Soft light or high key evens out the shadows to decrease harsh contrasts. It makes people and products look more attractive. ("I'm ready for my close-up.") Hard light or low key emphasizes shadows,

Opposite: Graphic by Karl Golombisky and Rebecca Hagen.

Clips courtesy of: Doug Alvarez, Karl Golombisky and Andrew Bailes.

LIGHTING
FILM NOIR

Film noir uses high-contrast lighting to suggest the "darker" side of human nature.

Back

Key

Fill

Classical film uses soft high-key lighting to minimize shadows.

Back/Fill

Key

Film noir employs hard low-key lighting to create dramatic shadows.

Back

Here a single-source backlight creates a not-so-angelic halo effect.

Lower third. In TV business lingo, "lower third" refers to supers, which mostly appear somewhere in the lower third of the screen.

Remember the rule of thirds? And foreground, midground and background? Foreground, at the bottom of the screen, appears closer than mid- or background. Hence, supers get the lower third.

The lower third super might be copy or an image like a logo. It can be static or a crawl. But it must be visible and readable, especially if overlaid on moving images. Why is Channel 7's "Morning News" super readable?

Photo © David Lawrence
- Fotolia.com

thus contrast, including shadows on people's faces—an interesting if less-than-flattering effect.

A key light shining directly from above (over lighting) or from below (under lighting) can form sinister shadows, especially on people's faces. Backlighting can make a focal point appear angelic with a halo effect or make the focal point appear powerful or significant (think backlit grand stage entrances of silhouetted super heroes, rock stars or pro wrestlers). Side lighting casts long shadows and increases the sense of three-dimensional space, as opposed to the flattening effect of soft light.

As you storyboard, think about how you might cast light as a supporting actor in your story. All these effects work for inanimate objects, too, as well as infographics. A side light on a pie chart gives it shadow and dimension. Go easy, though. Like a backlit super hero, overly dramatic lighting not only may seem cartoon-like when that isn't your intent but also may distract viewers from your visual communication purpose.

TYPE

Last we move on to dealing with words and sounds, whether onscreen or off and whether part of the show or merely behind-the-camera direction.

As for onscreen type, a super is any type or graphic superimposed over a picture. A crawl is moving type running—or crawling—across the screen. You see this on cable news channels or when your area comes under a severe weather alert.

When you super, design for typographic readability and legibility, whether the super is static or animated. Contrast, thus color and value, are crucial, whether you reverse or not. And when positioning your type, remember to keep it within the prescribed title-safe area.

AUDIO

In a chapter about storyboarding in a book about visual communication, audio becomes the proverbial elephant in the room. Hello—sound? If your storyboard project includes audio, you obviously have to represent it visually on the storyboard by using textual direction.

Using a script setup, type your audio direction to correspond with visuals. Make your intent abundantly clear, including who is speaking when.

Also specify direction for things such as music, sound effects (SFX) or visual effects (FX). An off-screen voice, narrator or announcer (ANNCR) is called a voiceover, indicated as VO. Background music is called a music bed or track.

As far as dialogue goes, nothing is more difficult to write well. And nothing is worse than stilted unnatural repartee. So fair warning. We advise amateurs to develop concepts that avoid multiple characters engaged in dialogue, especially in extended conversations, which provide little visual interest anyway. "Show, don't tell."

On the other hand, don't shortchange audio because you've become a visual communicator. Audio—ear candy—can make or break your visual story. Think creatively and include the details on your storyboard.

> If you're a beginner, focus on generating a killer concept. No amount of money can make a bad concept look good.

AFTER THE STORYBOARD

After the storyboard and before the actual production shoot, there may be an in-between stage that cheaply simulates what the storyboard might look like as live action. This generally is done using software to cut together rough approximations of the shots. It might be accomplished with stock, archived or homemade footage or stills that come as near as possible to the storyboard's visuals. Or you might use animated illustrations or cartoons.

These kinds of preproduction pieces have been called spec cuts, videomatics, animatics and ripomatics. They tend to be more impressive, thus persuasive, when you're presenting your storyboard to the conceptually challenged or to the person holding the purse strings. But, lest we wax creative snobbery, speculative cuts also can be helpful as narrative, shot and timing trials before you start spending big bucks on production.

And that leads us, at last, to some final advice concerning production budgets: KISS. Video production is expensive, and film, even more so. Hollywood director Cecil B. DeMille developed a reputation for visual spectacle using elaborate productions and, as the expression goes, casts of thousands. But he had the financial backing of the Hollywood studio system. We're guessing you work with more modest budgets.

If you're a beginner, focus on generating a killer concept. No amount of money can make a bad concept look good. The best concepts are usually the most parsimonious anyway. Don't script for two warm bodies when one will do. Don't storyboard an on-location shoot if you can get away with a studio shoot. Don't storyboard multiple sets if one is sufficient. And don't storyboard more shots than necessary. If it isn't vital to advancing the story, cut it.

Be smart, have fun, and, as they say, "Break a leg."

TRY THIS

1. Develop a concept for a short educational video on storyboarding. Then execute a storyboard for your concept.

2. Storyboard a favorite scene from a favorite movie. Account for:

» Framing   » Continuity

» Perspective   » Transitions

» POV   » Lighting

» Camera Angle   » Type

» Movement   » Audio

How does each contribute to the narrative?

3. Storyboard a TV commercial currently running. Account for:

» Framing	» Continuity
» Perspective	» Transitions
» POV	» Lighting
» Camera Angle	» Type
» Movement	» Audio

How does each contribute to the narrative?

4. Remember the Patterson Bigfoot film? Let's get silly to make a serious point. Choose three of the following and storyboard a few conceptual frames for each:

» A music video starring Bigfoot

» A televised interview with Bigfoot

» A reality-style episodic show featuring Bigfoot

» A wildlife cinematic extravaganza on Bigfoot in its natural habitat

» A sports highlights-style review of Bigfoot sightings

» An infomercial teaming up Patterson and Bigfoot to sell product

» A corporate training video using Bigfoot as the spokesmodel

» A PSA of some kind using Bigfoot as the spokes—ahem—person

This is definitely a use-your-imagination no-holds-barred exercise. Don't forget that "experts" believe the Patterson Bigfoot is female.

5. Storyboard a new :15 TV spot for a commercial consumer product currently in your kitchen, pantry, laundry room or bathroom. Start with a unique selling proposition (USP) or claim about the product. Then develop a concept. You know the rest of the drill by now.

Iodized Salt TV

Date: 11.30.09

Project: Salt-TV-001

Length: :15

Creative Team: Susan Snyder & Meaghan Rose

SFX: children playing in the pool (throughout)

1st Child: A right angle is 90 degrees.

2nd Child: The U.S. has a bicameral Congress.

3rd Child: Haiku is a form of Japanese poetry.

ANNCR (VO): The iodine in iodized salt is essential for healthy brain development.

Embedded photos reprinted by permission of Kathi Roberts.

DESIGN FOR
SOCIAL MEDIA
...BUT NOT REALLY

WORKING WITH MULTIMEDA ASSETS

O ur readers often ask, "Why is there no chapter on designing social media pages in your book?" Our answer? Because you don't *design* your own social media pages. No user of social media can claim to have built a page from the code up (unless you are part of the lead design/development team at Facebook or something, in which case, you don't count). You don't choose interface methods or heading sizes and styles. You don't decide the types or positions of widgets or the items in the navigation menu. You don't choose the position of the main content or sidebar.

You do, however, customize pre-existing social media templates with images, video clips, animations and apps that you *can* design. It's the same with presentation decks and websites that use templates. So this chapter is not about designing social media pages. It's about how to design the assets used in customizing different types of digital communication.

WHERE TO BEGIN?

Visit any social media page or website and you'll encounter many different types of media on the same page. A single layout may combine type, image, audio, video and infographics, not to mention forms, polls and even games. All this must be available to active "users" on their desktop PCs, laptops, smartphones, tablets and TVs.

It's easy to get overwhelmed by the multimedia options out there. And it's equally easy to get discouraged by the myriad of multimedia-building tools available online and on your desktop. But don't give up just yet. For the novice digital communicator, here are some things to keep in mind.

First, multimedia design can be implemented in degrees. A simple digital slideshow may be all that is needed to enhance an otherwise static website. While it's absolutely possible to create online virtual worlds where audiences participate in massively multiuser online role-playing games (MMORPG), you don't need to start there. We suggest working your way down the bunny hill before you try to ski Dead Man's Peak.

Second, digital multimedia means multisensory, which translates into a richer user experience. It allows for communication via sound and touch in addition to sight. Users swipe, click, pinch and tap their way though all sorts of digital content. It's well worth the time to implement some sort of multimedia into your project. (No such thing as smell-o-vision yet, but maybe that's a good thing.)

Multimedia: The early years. In the days before "talkies," live musicians played scores to accompany silent films. Note the Tampa Theater's orchestra pit at the bottom of the photo.

Tampa Theater, 1930. Burgert Brothers collection. Courtesy, Tampa-Hillsborough County Public Library System.

Third, restraint is a virtue, and user control is appreciated. One animated GIF in one paragraph is (arguably) cute. One in every paragraph is decidedly *not* cute. Select the right multimedia components for your purposes. Do give user control where appropriate (video and slideshow controls come to mind). Offer the ability to search and sort when you can. Use forms and commenting to capture feedback, or start a dialogue where appropriate. Give your visitor a multi-sensory experience, not sensory overload.

Finally, offering a multi-sensory experience is great. But be aware that not all users have the same abilities. From the outset, you should design not only multiple ways for your users to interact with your content but also alternative ways your users are able to access content. How will you accommodate, for example, the deaf community? Or folks with limited hand dexterity or the visually impaired? These are front-end planning issues.

It's true that the creation of some multimedia components remains better off in the hands of professionals. However, there are simple multimedia production tools available for the nonprofessional. Many are available for free online or come preinstalled on your computer. Just know that not all mobile and tablet devices support all Web-based applications and proceed accordingly.

Make accessiblity a priority when working with multimedia components. This website uses large, bold buttons and adjustable font sizes to make the site navigable for visually impaired visitors.

A DESIGN SPEED BUMP

Hold up. Before you sit down at your computer to take that new video-editing software for a spin, remember to step away from the computer for planning.

Get the specs.

Before you start any asset creation, figure out which elements you can customize. Then find the correct specifications for those elements. Such specs include but are not limited to pixel-by-pixel dimensions, file size and file format. Social media sites, for example, have recommended resolution and pixel-by-pixel dimensions for your avatar image. Video sharing sites may only accept video rendered in certain formats. And even though social media sites are forgiving about photo uploads (they tend to resize your images to fit pre-set spaces), there are likely to be limits on maximum file size. Design your asset to fit the specs. You don't want to spend 4 hours photo-editing your face on the body of a T-Rex to use as a background image only to discover your efforts unusable due to incorrect format or file size.

Thumbnails, storyboards & site maps.

If you are working on a complex custom project such as a clickable interactive commercial or a big online investigative story with text, photos, footage and interactive infographics, then you need more planning than just looking up specs. You'll need to brainstorm concept, design and organization with paper and pencil. Or perhaps tablet and stylus.

Rough sketch some thumbnail layouts that imagine how all your content might go together. For slideshows, video and animation, use storyboarding techniques to nail beginnings, middles and ends, along with transitions, pacing and timing. And for multi-page Web projects, site-map content relationships along with user flow via intuitive links and navigation.

Better yet, to maximize creative synergy, do the preliminary noodling with the whole team sitting in the same room—in which case you'll need the big whiteboard and some colored markers.

I would upload my avatar if I could just reach the darn keyboard.

WORKING WITH IMAGES

In the attention-grabbing department, images win hands-down. But still images are—you know—still. Turned into slideshows or placed in interactive image galleries, however, even still images become engaging multimedia components. Newsrooms tend to prefer interactive image galleries over automated slideshows because they seem to generate more viewing traffic. Yet an image gallery may offer viewing options that include a slideshow format.

Sorting, cropping and editing photos needs to happen before you begin assembling your slideshow or image gallery. We already covered the rules for dealing with photos in "Chapter 9: Adding Visual Appeal." Those best practices apply here. Plus, always work on a *copy* of the original photo; save and protect the original to be available for another day. Don't forget to optimize resolution; 72 dpi remains the standard for photos destined for screen viewing.

Image galleries & slideshows.

Image galleries. Image galleries are common on websites. Some social media platforms are *nothing but* galleries of user-uploaded imagery. Galleries allow the user to scan many images at once; interactive galleries allow the user to click through, sort and search a set of images to suit his or her own needs and interests. Such galleries are well suited to displaying creative portfolios, sharing organizational event photos and, of course, selling products.

Some photo-editing programs have the ability to generate Web-ready image galleries from your selected images. All you have to do is upload the files to your Web server.

Photo-sharing websites offer similar options. Signup is typically free, and once you have an account you upload your images. You can organize images into galleries and then put a link on your main website to your galleries. If you prefer to embed your galleries in your own website, photo-sharing sites offer plugins, widgets or code snippets that make this possible. Plug-ins and widgets allow photos stored on the photo-sharing site to display where you want them.

Slideshows. Slideshows have the visual impact of photos with the added bonus of eye-catching movement. They take up the same of amount of layout real estate as a still image but can display multiple different messages, including calls to action.

When creating slideshows, consider the content of your images, along with transitions and user controls. For a simple set of images intended to add interest to a Web banner or content area, choose quality images united by a theme (color, subject, etc.) with similar orientation.

If your slideshow is intended to tell a story, apply a video-like approach to selecting images. A storyboard of sequential sketches helps organize the storyline and assist with image selection. A storyboard also helps if the slideshow includes a narrative. Select photos with tight, medium and wide angles for variety. Use the best quality images you can. Nonetheless, an image that supports narrative continuity may be a better choice than a technically superior one.

Image galleries. There are many inexpensive and free image gallery plug-ins available for displaying your photos on websites and blogs. The gallery above includes an interactive slideshow and thumbnail gallery.

Slideshow transitions. Slide programs offer many transition styles. Avoid the kid-in-a-candy-store impulse to use one of each. Simple tends to be best so choose one transition style and stay with it. Traditional cuts always work. In the end, you want your slideshow to be about the images or the story, not the funky transitions you used.

Pacing. Whether slow and measured or fast and frenetic, the duration of your images and the speed of transitions set an overall tone for your slideshow. If you expect viewers to absorb and appreciate your slideshow content, give them enough time to do so.

The "Ken Burns Effect." The Ken Burns effect is a gradual simultaneous zoom in or out and panning across still images in a slideshow. Burns uses the technique when featuring historical photographs, letters and maps in his documentaries. The effect is readily available on consumer-grade video software, but apply it with caution. Use it if the technique will enhance the slideshow's communication function, not because you think it looks cool.

Captions/cutlines. Not all slideshows require captioning. But news contexts probably do. In addition to having a narrative beginning, middle and end, three rules apply here: One, make the caption/cutline "go with" the image. Oh, yes, we have seen it go the other way. Two, don't state the obvious. A photo of a black dog doesn't need a cutline that reads, "This is a black dog." Instead, supplement the obvious, such as "Duke, a 6-year-old rescue lab/shepherd mix with exemplary manners, loves children." Three, do cover what's not obvious but relevant, such as a photo's W's. Clearly identify who, what, when and where. And don't forget to fact-check and proof. Also be kind and credit the photographers.

To loop or not to loop. You can set a slideshow to loop continuously or a particular number of times before stopping. Your choice here depends on where your slideshow will be displayed. If it is to be the backdrop of a Web banner, then a subtle continuous loop might

Pick just one. Don't let your slide transitions outshine your actual slides. Pick one simple transition style and stick with it. We recommend cutting and fading as opposed to exploding and twirling out of control.

be appropriate. If your slideshow is intended to tell a story, letting it play through once is sufficient. As a rule, it's a good idea to provide user controls on video clips such as story slideshows. Viewers appreciate access to buttons that start, stop, rewind, pause as well as adjust volume.

Slideshows with audio.

Now think about combining everything you've learned about photo slideshows with our tips for working with audio. Hey, you're ready to produce audio slideshows. Don't be intimidated. The software is cheap (or

WORKING WITH AUDIO

Audio may seem off-topic in a discussion about visual communication. But audio plays a role in multimedia. Audio is the narration or natural (nat) or ambient (ambi) sound on captured video. It's the background track or bed in Web and DVD projects. Short audio clips as sound effects or SFX signal action, such as the sound of a button being pressed or email being sent. Audio can highlight what's important. It also reinforces tone and mood.

Back in the heyday of radio, great audio was "theater of the mind." That continues to be the way you should think about audio production. But if you find yourself unable to enlist an audio pro, stick to the basics. In general:

1. Use ambient audio sparingly, especially for trigger sounds like button clicks. A little goes a long way.

2. Background music should enhance the overall tone and message of the project. It should not be expected to set the tone by itself.

Can you hear it? Audio is a powerful multimedia component. Try to imagine the sounds that would accompany this image.

3. Give your user controls, preferably start, stop, pause and volume. We've all been blown out of our desk chairs by a Web soundtrack that was a big surprise, too loud or both.

4. When the audio is narration, an interview or some other situation where clarity is crucial, capture the highest quality audio possible. Use the best microphone you can—which may not be the one on your digital recorder, video camera or smartphone. Your audience is more likely to forgive a poor quality image than an inaudible soundtrack.

Where to get audio.

Ambient sounds and music as well as trigger sounds like button clicks are available for purchase from digital stock sites. There are also websites that offer free sounds and music. Be aware, however, that free downloads may come with restrictions or attribution requirements. Make sure you respect both.

free) and user-friendly, so much so that it's mostly the same software pros use. As they say, producing audio slideshows has become "ridiculously simple." Try it. It's fun.

Begin by assessing whether you have a story that supports audio and visuals. Audio and photos should supplement and complement each other, the same as captions/cutlines. Time audio and visuals to "go with" each other. Remember storyboarding and maintaining narrative continuity.

Before putting the audio slideshow together, finish editing and saving your photos in one folder. Likewise, edit and save your audio track. Convention suggests you'll need a couple dozen photos for every minute of audio—more or less—depending on the subject matter's tone and pacing. After the audio and photos files are completed, open your audio slideshow software, import your photos and audio, and finally tweak as needed. Remember that a 2-minute audio slideshow begins to stretch the limit of user tolerance.

Audio slideshows offer a simple and easy tool for disciplining ourselves to tell effective stories in a short period of time with audio and visuals. Sound and pictures working together in time segues handily to video.

VIDEO CLIPS

Video runs the gamut from carefully orchestrated multiple-camera commercials to homegrown cell-phone-recorded clips posted on video-sharing websites. In between the complex and the amateur, there are video interviews and monologues, short clips of events and activities, and how-to tutorials, among others.

Simple video-editing software is as commonplace as slideshow-making tools, and nonprofessionals can create good quality clips. Video isn't designed so much as it is composed, shot and edited, although in some cases it may be art directed.

In control. If your website includes video and audio clips, give your audience access to the controls. At the very least, provide volume control and start and stop buttons.

Like shooting photography, if the stakes are high, shooting video and film is best left to professionals. Nevertheless, if it's you or *nada,* follow these shooting and editing tips for beginners:

General shooting tips:

» Steady your camera with a tripod or other solid surface. Camera shake gets very old very quickly.

» Shoot in a location with bright, even lighting. Avoid harsh high-contrast lighting and backlighting, along with what you may believe are special lighting effects.

» When possible, shoot some test footage to check blocking, sound and light.

» Shoot more video than you think you'll need, at least 10–15 seconds for each shot you want to capture. You can always cut extra material, but you can't magically insert file footage no one ever shot. (B roll is file, secondary or archival footage used as visual fill or for creating transitions between clips.)

» Capture a variety of angles for each scene: tight close-up, medium, full, wide and long. Think about establishing shots versus detail/beauty shots.

» Avoid zooming and panning. Cutting from scene to scene is actually more natural.

» Compose your shots. Use the rule of thirds as your guide and place your focal point accordingly.

» Don't talk while shooting. The microphone may pick up your voice. Heavy breathers off-screen can be a problem, too.

When shooting interviews & monologues (talking heads):

» Shoot in a quiet location.

» Select your talking head wisely. Not everyone appears interesting and engaging (or articulate) on-camera.

» Test footage… Better safe than sorry.

Not as easy as it looks. Capturing good video requires planning. Consider lighting, location and subject matter. And always shoot more footage than you think you'll need.

HOUSE

LATEST NEWS

APRIL 10, 2011

TEAM FLORIDA PRESENTS AT
TAMPA BAY CSI

APRIL 10, 2011

FLEX HOUSE WINS HILLSBOROUGH
COUNTY GREEN DESIGN AWARD

OCTOBER 23, 2010

TEAM FLORIDA REFINES
FLEX HOUSE AT AUGUST
CHARETTE

Support Team Florida!
Click on the link below, select the
SACD Solar Decathlon Project Fund
230021, then follow the prompts.

DONATE

MEDIA INFORMATION

Suspendisse potenti. Sed at auctor lectus. Integer pulvinar cursus nulla et egestas. Donec interdum enim nec est imperdiet vitae volutpat urna semper. Duis condimentum interdum nisi, ac scelerisque nunc volutpat quis. Donec ornare auctor tincidunt. Maecenas interdum quam sit amet diam consectetur faucibus. Etiam viverra eros et ligula consectetur tempus vel sit amet nunc. Etiam in ante sit amet turpis lobortis sollicitudin. In a dignissim neque.

Team Florida Virtual Tour - Solar Decathlon   👍 Like   👎 Share   ⬇ More info

▶   🔊   1:20 / 2:01   ᴄᴄ ⚙ ⓘ   ⤢

Video courtesy U.S. Department of Energy Solar Decathlon 2011.

Duis laoreet aliquam urna nec ornare. Sed porttitor semper nisl in tincidunt. Vestibulum ultricies fringilla pretium. Sed eu dolor eget enim fermentum sodales. Pellentesque eu turpis sit amet quam bibendum fringilla et quis odio. Vestibulum hendrerit condimentum aliquet. Maecenas porta nunc nec ante accumsan egestas. Suspendisse ac nisl lacus, id euismod felis. Integer lobortis, est a vestibulum vestibulum, massa urna lacinia turpis, sed lacinia arcu est ut libero. Curabitur dictum nibh eu urna lobortis et sagittis sapien elementum. Nullam non magna in felis blandit interdum sed at neque. Suspendisse potenti. Vivamus condimentum, ipsum vel convallis aliquam, turpis lacus iaculis nulla, at elementum nisi purus ac augue. Duis massa tellus, auctor accumsan eleifend posuere, dapibus nec ante.

Doing an end-run around format incompatibilities. Finding video formats that run on all browsers is no easy task. A good workaround is to upload your video to a video-sharing site, then use the code provided to embed the video back into your website. The sharing site manages the tricky browser issue for you. The tradeoff is that your video will contain branding from the sharing site.

When editing video:

» Begin with the best quality video possible, i.e., uncompressed raw footage.

» Make sure you have good usable audio, too. "Audio is half the picture," as they say.

» Select simple transitions—cuts and fades. Pick one transition style and stick to it. Attention should be on the video, not on the transitions.

» Try to keep overall video duration short. In multimedia contexts, viewers can drop out in seconds, and most casual online video viewers only hang around for 2-3 minutes.

» Don't forget title and credit slides (if needed) and a poster frame. A poster frame is an image that serves as the icon for your final video. A poster frame can be a still selected from the video, or a graphic created in another program. Title slides and poster frames are excellent opportunities for branding. If your final video is being shared on a video-sharing site, create a final frame with links to your other videos you've posted to generate website traffic.

» When adding text to slides, style for contrast and readability. Heavier sans serif fonts at larger sizes will generally work well. Make sure to keep all text within the title-safe boundary.

Video encoding.

After editing, encoding is the next step in making a video. There are many file formats out there, and choosing the right one takes a little research. Video-sharing sites, for example, often post file size and format requirements. Meanwhile, different software and hardware brands peddle their unique file formats.

When choosing a file format, try to avoid those that are exclusive to particular devices, platforms or software applications. You want your video to be viewable by the greatest number of people. MPEG-4 (Motion Pictures Expert Group), or MP4 for short, is the most popular video file format for the Web (at the time of this printing, anyway). MP4 is friendly across platforms and supported by the most popular Web browsers.

When choosing a video file format, try to avoid those that are exclusive to particular devices, platforms or software applications. You want your video to be viewable by the greatest number of people.

In addition to file format, you'll also need to pay attention to aspect ratio, which refers to screen frame proportions, and final file size, which also includes modes of compression. Video files are huge and must be compressed before packed into files for transport. So compression and file size matter not only for uploading and downloading but also for storage space. Wherever your video is being housed or hosted, once again, a few minutes' research on the specs can save your—ahem—"project" at deadline time. Stay within uploading parameters. Quick downloading is critical, too, if you want your viewer to stay tuned long enough to see your clip.

Speaking of viewers, don't forget they need access to a video player of some sort for viewing. Fortunately, most modern browsers support common video formats. And if you come across a format your browser does not support, plug-ins are generally free and easy to find and install.

An excellent way to bypass many browser and video format incompatibilities is to post your video on a video-sharing site. Most video-sharing sites will provide a bit of code allowing you to embed the clip on your own website. A minor drawback of this method is that the video-sharing site may require you to include its branding on your video clip.

Once viewers find your video, waiting for the whole clip to download, as in "progressive" video delivery, can be a real drag unless the clip is short and sweet. "Streaming" video is advisable for longer videos. But you would hire professionals for those longer videos anyway.

Shooting & editing video not your bag?

The same sites that offer stock images also offer stock video clips. Stock may not work for your situation. But if using stock saves time and money, it might be worth checking out.

Simple is good. Animation need not be complicated. This logo grows a letter "I" and sprouts a leaf over the course of a few seconds.

GREENW SE

GREENWISE

GREENWISE

GREENWISE

GREENWISE

ANIMATION

Generations of children have grown up watching animation as a Saturday morning cat-and-mouse anvil-dropping form of entertainment. Now animation has grown up, too. It's everywhere from the startup sequence on your cell phone to spectacular CGI effects in blockbuster movies.

Like other multimedia components, animation can be classified by complexity. Animation found in full-length feature films and complex interactive websites remains the bailiwick of highly skilled pros. More accessible animation, such as transitioning in presentation slides, is generated by the presentation program itself.

If you're inclined to try your hand at animation, affordable animation programs are out there. The learning curve for animation software is steeper than most but not insurmountable. It's absolutely possible for the average person to create simple animated logos, video title sequences, banner ads and animated website components without an advanced degree in motion design.

Motion tweens.

The simplest digital animations work on the same principle as original hand-drawn animation. A series of images, each one slightly different from the last, is flashed in rapid succession giving the illusion of movement. The digital animation rate is approximately 30 frames per second so 30 images are needed to create 1 second of animation. This is a lot of drawing.

Fortunately, if you're using tweened animation, the computer will do the "drawing" for you. In tweened animation, only key changes in motion or shape are illustrated. For example, imagine the starting key frame has a red circle in the upper left corner, and the final key frame has the same red circle in the lower right corner. Based on the frame rate you specify, the computer will generate all the in-between frames necessary for an animation that moves the red circle from upper left to lower right.

Tweened animation is great for simple movement but also can be used for changes in color or opacity—tweening can be used to fade an object in or out.

Storyboards are an excellent tool for planning tweened animation. Arrows and other directional devices can signal the movements along with the relationships of shapes and type. Each sketch on the storyboard can describe the contents of a key frame, as well as—uh-huh—audio.

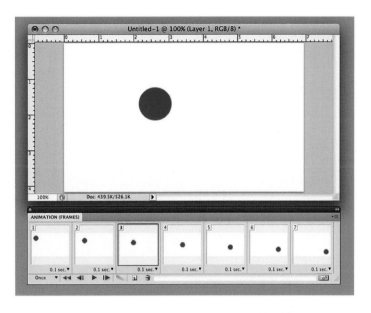

Motion tweens. Computer-generated tweened animation works on the same principle as traditional hand-drawn animation. A series of images is flashed in rapid succession, creating the illusion of movement.

Adobe Photoshop CS4 screen shot(s) reprinted with permission from Adobe Systems Incorporated.

It's about time.

Actually, motion is not so much what makes animation different from other graphics. The element of time is. Animated elements appear, disappear and change shape at different points along a timeline. Pacing and transitions aren't issues when designing for print or even when designing static websites. But in animation and video, pacing and transitioning impact the overall feel, thus message, of the piece. A quick pace and sharp transitions give intensity and edge. Subtle, gradual changes are more soothing.

Duration.

How long does your animation need to last? Each situation is different depending on the job the animation is meant to do. However, the longer the animation, the greater the file size. So be aware of file size limitations—server, application or project-imposed. And, as a general rule, don't let your animations loop indefinitely. Have them cycle one or more times then stop. Don't loop animations that are particularly sharp and choppy. You don't want to give anyone a headache.

Space and time. In animation, objects move through space over time. Animation programs include a timeline, seen here in the lower right of each graphic. "Events" happen at points along the timeline. In these screen grabs, the red bar represents the duration of the animation. The yellow triangle is effectively the "you are here" on the timeline. The preview window shows what the animation looks like at a given point in the animated sequence.

Adobe AfterEffects CS5 screen shot(s) reprinted with permission from Adobe Systems Incorporated.

File formats for animation.

Again, choosing a file format requires a bit of research to determine what is acceptable for your particular project. Animated banner ads, for example, may have physical size, file size and looping requirements in addition to format requirements.

In general, use formats that are compatible across the greatest number of devices. Also look for those with good compression (file size) and good quality output.

Use restraint.

Adding a little animation to a layout can help break through all the visual clutter viewers suffer every day. But don't let your animation add to visual clutter. Use animation with a purpose. Make sure it's the right medium for your message. Don't use animation just for the sake of using it.

APPS & PLUG-INS & WIDGETS, OH MY!

Perhaps the most exciting thing about multimedia is the opportunity it provides to engage the audience fully. For advertisers, interactivity is a luxury only dreamed of just a generation ago. Each element we've discussed thus far allows for some interactivity, be it the pause, play and volume controls on a video clip or the ability to browse photos in an online photo gallery. And don't forget the banner ad's click-through (cha-ching).

The good news is that you no longer need to be a credentialed computer programmer to include interactive multimedia components in your screen layouts. Plug-ins, widgets and apps make it possible for non-developers to add a wide range of interactive components with ease.

Applications (Apps).

Applications, commonly referred to as "apps," are programs designed to run on a computer, tablet, smartphone, website or social media site. Large complex applications such as word-processing programs have been available on computers for decades. Since the introduction of smartphones and tablets, professional and amateur programmers have been adding to the slate of apps for those devices, too. Some common examples of apps include calendars, mileage trackers, restaurant finders and, of course, games.

Some companies and organizations build custom apps to supplement websites. This makes sense as interaction with the smaller touchscreens of handheld devices is different from that of websites. A specifically designed app can provide the smartphone or tablet owner with a much better user experience.

The building of highly complex "native" apps (apps built for specific operating systems and sold in app stores) is still largely the realm of professional designers and developers. However, there are increasing numbers of do-it-yourself app-building programs out there. It's possible to create a simple app, such as the historic trail app pictured on this page, without knowledge of code.

Plug-ins.

A plug-in is code that gives a browser or website additional functionality. For example, when a website automatically displays the most recent posts from a separate blog, a plug-in is at work.

There are plug-ins available that can do everything from filtering SPAM or viruses to allowing game playing or viewing different media types. They are easily added to sites or browsers via an installation

Do-it-yourself app building. There are increasing numbers of do-it-yourself app-building programs out there. It's now possible to create a simple app, such as this historic trail app, without the skills of a developer. We discuss more about designing app interfaces in Chapter 13.

JOSÉ MARTÍ TRAIL

Home   About José Martí

Trail Map

Significant José Martí sites in Tampa's Ybor City

View Jose Marti Trail in a full screen map

A. Ybor City Station *N. 16th St between 6th and 7th Ave.*
Martí did much of his traveling by rail, and entered Ybor
City via this Railway Station. An historical marker identifies
the site.

F. Emilio Pons Cigar Factory *6th Ave and N 17th St.* José
Martí made his last Ybor City speech at this location on
October 12, 1894.

Interactive map widget.
This interactive map of
locations on the José Martí
Trail was generated by a
free online map-generating
service. A snippet of code
provided by the service then
embedded in the website
creates a live map with
clickable pins.

program or by copying
and pasting code in the
right location.

Plug-ins are commonly
installed behind the
scenes, and there may
or may not be visible
front-end evidence
of their presence on
a site or browser. If a
plug-in requires input
from a user, or needs to
physically display some
sort of content on a
page, then a widget is
needed.

Widgets.

Widgets are the visible
expression of the
existence of a plug-in.
For example, imagine
you want to measure social media activity on a specific page and
display the results in a sidebar. An installed plug-in will track the
activity, but the widget is what displays the results. Widgets are also
required to gather user inuput, as in online forms. All widgets require
a plug-in, but not all plug-ins have a widget.

There are widgets to display local weather, create tag clouds, play
video and slideshows and even map the nearest pizza places.

With literally thousands of plug-ins and widgets available, the
potential for adding interactivity to your projects is huge.

Where do I get plug-ins, widgets & apps?

The short answer: Search online. Most plug-in or widget code can be
had for free or for minimal cost. Often all that is required is a code
cut-and-paste. Oh, and sometimes a credit to the developer is needed,
too. Don't forget to check, and provide credit where credit is due.

When searching for and installing plug-ins and widgets, pay attention
to online reviews. Since these mini programs can be created by
anyone, quality is all over the board. Some are not regularly updated.
And many are not "supported," meaning if something goes wonky,
you're on your own to fix it.

212   White Space Is Not Your Enemy

Another thing to look for is whether or not a plug-in or widget comes with an editable Cascading Style Sheet (CSS). Style sheets are used to dictate the way design features like fonts and colors display onscreen. If you can access a style sheet, you can tweak the appearance of a plug-in to better match your overall layout.

As mentioned, apps tend to be more complex, and building them requires the skills of a developer. However, if your organization needs a strong unique presence on tablets or smartphones, hiring a developer to create a custom app might be worth the investment.

MULTIMEDIA STORYTELLING

Back in our infographics chapter, we talked about the enhanced communication capabilities inherent in infographics packages. Multimedia components enhance your communicating abilities exponentially.

Imagine an interactive multimedia website devoted to the human heart. The centerpiece might be a high-end 3D animation of the inner workings of the heart providing something like a virtual ride through the pulmonary system. We could enhance the online experience with sound effects and narration.

Other interactive features and links would layer additional information. Users might click to learn more about platelets, heart chambers, red blood cells, etc., or even how to read an electrocardiogram (EKG) or become a cardiologist. Users might take a quiz to test their knowledge of or calculate their risks for heart disease. Maybe

MULTIMEDIA CONTENT TOOLBOX

Multimedia muse Vidisha Priyanka recommends the following for the digital editor/producer's toolbox:

Text
» headlines
» summaries
» external links
» audio transcripts
» photo captions/cutlines
» blogs/microblogs

Images
» still photos
» illustrations
» infographics
» photo slideshows
» photo galleries

Video
» recorded clips
» live feeds
» historical footage
» animation
» video logs
» tutorials

Audio
» narration (anncr, VO)
» dramatizations
» music
» sound effects (SFX)
» natural (nat) or ambient (ambi) sounds
» actualities (acts or ax)

Interactivity
» live chat
» discussion forums
» feedback
» timelines
» polls
» games
» mashups
» searchable databases

» calculators
» guest books
» augmented reality
» widgets

Data
» numbers
» statistics
» spreadsheets
» lottery results
» archives

User-Contributed Content
» anecdotes
» comments
» photos
» cell phone/mobile content
» videos
» social networks
» user reviews
» wikis

Mobile Content
» really simple syndication (RSS) feeds
» music
» videos
» podcasts
» social networks
» quick response (QR) codes and other mobile scanning
» global positioning system (GPS) applications such as navigation and geo-caching

Site Exposure (going viral)
» content- and media-sharing sites for video, photos, news, information, networking

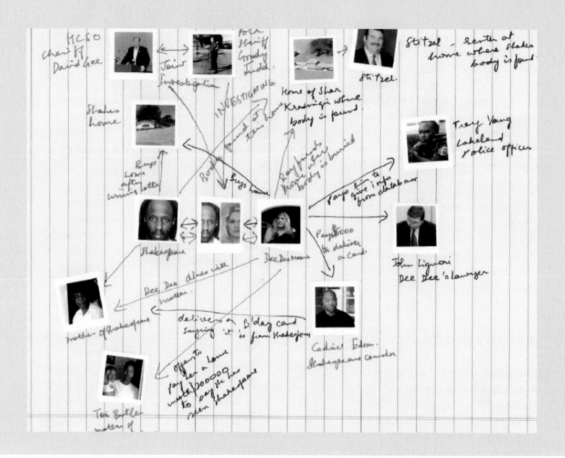

users entertain themselves competing in a heart health game that pits exercise and eating habits against genetics. How about chatting in real time with a medical expert? Anyone want to upload personal stories, share medical resources or add data to a map? You get the idea.

This type of multimedia design not only requires professionals, it requires teams of professionals. It also requires research, planning and a battery of thumbnail sketches, storyboards, site maps and wireframes.

Should you find yourself part of a team creating an interactive multimedia experience, here are some things to consider:

» Not every story or subject lends itself to full multimedia treatment. Make sure you have a deep, interesting and multifaceted topic to work with.

» Choose the best multimedia elements for your particular content. If you don't have a good candidate for a talking-head expert or spokesperson, don't plan to include a video interview. Do consider all your media options, including infographics.

Abraham Shakespeare-Dee Dee Moore Case

In November 2006, Abraham Shakespeare won a $30 million Florida Lottery jackpot and took a lump-sum payment of nearly $13 million after taxes. He last was seen in April 2009 and was reported missing in November. His body was found in January buried behind the home of Dee Dee Moore, who is charged with first-degree murder in his death.
Move your mouse on the blue lines to see the connections.

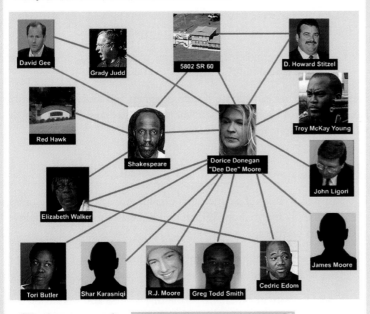

Shakespeare's Timeline

Click on the light blue boxes within a date to find information about the case.

2006
Nov   Dec

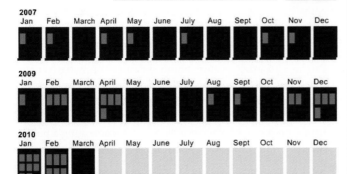

2007
Jan Feb March April May June July Aug Sept Oct Nov Dec

2009
Jan Feb March April May June July Aug Sept Oct Nov Dec

2010
Jan Feb March April May June July Aug Sept Oct Nov Dec

Where the money went

Click on each text block on the right to see how the lotto money was used. There is still around $8 million that is unaccounted for.

- $30 million Winning Lotto amount
- Shakespeare takes $17 million in lump sum payment
- He received $13 million after taxes
- Shakespeare buys home in Lakeland for $1.08 million
- When assets are frozen on July 16, 2007

Multimedia storyboarding.
When multimedia news pioneers Tim Price and Vidisha Priyanka worked at TBO.com, they collaborated on stories that required all manner of rough storyboarding and site mapping. The storyboarded investigation shown here reported the tragic murder of a lottery winner.

Source: The Tampa Tribune, HCSO and PCSO

Multimedia designer: Tim Price/TBO.com

Multimedia producer: Vidisha Priyanka/TBO.com

Images courtesy of Tim Price, Vidisha Priyanka and TBO.com/Media General.

» Elect one medium to tell the main story, and let the other media play supporting roles. Think in terms of creating a content focal point.

» Decide on an overall look and feel. Then choose design elements that support that look and feel.

» Make the interface intuitive. Make buttons look like buttons, and make them easy to find and use. Same goes for links.

» Don't let the technology get in the way of the information or the story. The technology should be "invisible" to the user.

New technologies can and do inspire designers and visual communicators. But there's an old aphorism about the shortsightedness of designing the whole living room around the coffee table.

TRY THIS

1. Visit the website of a large news organization. Look for examples of multimedia storytelling. Which multimedia elements are employed? Write a brief critique.

2. Locate some simple logos. Storyboard three options for animating each of said logos.

3. Find a website or online magazine that accepts animated banner ads. What are the specs and requirements for file size, format, duration, etc.? Spend some time exploring the animated banner ads on this site. What animation techniques are being used?

4. Visit a site that sells video and audio clips. What formats do they come in? What styles and genres are available? Find a video clip and some audio clips you like. Brainstorm ways of using them in a website and create a wireframe demonstrating your ideas.

5. Produce a 1- to 2-minute photo slideshow or, better yet, an audio slideshow that documents reality. Story ideas to consider include a visual oral history of your oldest living family member, the status of adoptions at your local animal shelter or the hidden story of a nearby nature preserve. Maybe attending and documenting a public event, such as a quilt show, or a political rally is more your speed.

6. After you produce the slideshow above in No. 5, lay out a Web page for that same story that includes: a big header, a slideshow, a complementary type story, photo gallery, at least one infographic, and user feedback/comments. Don't forget to label everything with subheads, captions/cutlines and/or explainers, etc., as seems appropriate.

CHAPTER
THIRTEEN

13

DESIGNING FOR THE WEB

STARRING ON THE SMALL SCREEN

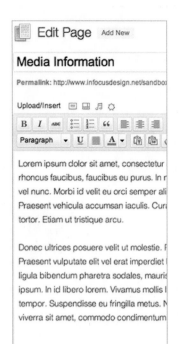

Beats coding by hand.
Content management systems allow you to create and update Web pages without hand coding. The content-generating parts of CMS interfaces are similar to word processing interfaces, making them more user-friendly for non tech-geeks.

The Internet impacts our professional and personal lives on a daily basis in countless ways. We text, instead of talk, on the phone. We get our news from websites or via feed. We blog, we email, we produce and publish our own videos. We shop. We critique. We collaborate. We have a million ways to get—and give—information.

The processes by which we get and give information have been in a constant state of change since the creation of the World Wide Web. Someone always seems to be announcing the next big social media tool or promoting the next great programming standard. While it may seem that the only constant is change, it's safe to say if you work in communications, you will work with websites on some level.

WHAT TO EXPECT WHEN WORKING WITH WEBSITES

Early websites were built by computer programmers who hand-wrote code and built applications from scratch. This has changed. So if you know nothing about programming languages or coding, don't worry. Your interaction with websites isn't likely to involve a lot of code. More likely, you'll be asked to do one of the following:

Prepare simple images and content for an existing website. You provide a basic text document or a graphic formatted for the Web to a webmaster (Kim prefers the term "webspinner"), who will upload the text and images for you.

Work with a content management system (CMS). A CMS is a Web-based site-building and management application that dynamically generates pages from information you add to a database via a word processing-like interface. Content management systems were created so people with no knowledge of coding could build visually consistent sites. Such systems are excellent for organizations and businesses that require complex membership management or e-commerce. CMSs often have free or inexpensive plug-ins that add custom functionality to a site, such as tools for creating e-newsletters, calendars, maps or feeds from social media sites.

Create a site from a template. Templates allow you to pick an existing design and insert your custom content where appropriate. Templates can be hosted on the template provider's server, or they can be downloaded and installed on your own separately purchased server space.

Work with a professional Web designer and/or developer to create a custom site with custom functionality. This is the best option when you need a site with a specific look and feel, have extensive quantities of content or require highly specialized site tools. Working with

HOW THE WEB WORKS

Ever wonder how your computer can pull so much data from servers all over the world? Here's a 5-second explanation of how the World Wide Web works:

❷ Your ISP.
Your request gets routed to the Web via your Internet service provider (ISP). Your ISP's servers are connected to servers across the globe.

❶ Your computer and browser. To access the World Wide Web, you plug your information request into a search engine via a Web-browsing application.

❹ Back to your browser. Your ISP routes the results of your query back to your computer. Your browser displays a specific page or a list of pages that match your search criteria.

Click on something and the process starts over again.

❸ The Web. Information that matches your request is gathered and sent back through the system to your ISP.

---

professionals is also advisable when high search rankings are crucial to your site's success. While site design has been automated to a large extent, search engine optimization (SEO) requires professional planning and implementation.

HOW THE WEB WORKS (THE 5-SECOND VERSION)

When working with Web content, it's important to understand how the files you create come to show up on the computer screens of your audience/customers. If you know how the Web works, you can troubleshoot why your content is not showing up properly, or not showing up at all.

Accessing existing websites. To access the Web, you need a computer or other Internet-capable device, a Web browser and an Internet service provider (ISP) or wireless network. When you type an information request (a keyword or search term) or a specific address (Uniform Resource Locator or URL) and hit enter, your request is sent to your ISP. Your ISP, in turn, sends the request to the World Wide Web portion of the Internet. Information on the network that matches your information

GETTING YOUR SITE **ON THE WEB**

Publishing your site files on the World Wide Web requires a computer with Internet access, a Web host and FTP software (called an FTP client). Think of your host as your paid parking place on the Web. Your FTP client is the permit that gets you into the restricted parking zone. Here's how it works:

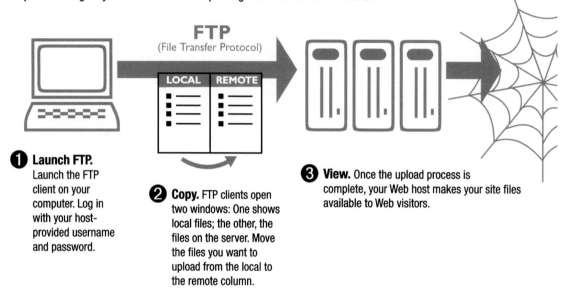

1 Launch FTP.
Launch the FTP client on your computer. Log in with your host-provided username and password.

2 Copy. FTP clients open two windows: One shows local files; the other, the files on the server. Move the files you want to upload from the local to the remote column.

3 View. Once the upload process is complete, your Web host makes your site files available to Web visitors.

request gets sent back through your ISP. Your browser displays either the page you requested by URL or a list of potential pages that meet your search criteria.

Adding your site to the WWW. A few additional things are needed to house and maintain a website: server space (also called a Web host), a domain name and a File Transfer Protocol (FTP) program.

Server space/Web hosting. Think of server space as your site's paid parking space on the Web. Your ISP may offer you server space as part of your package, or you can buy space through a separate host provider. Your server space is defined by amount of disk storage space and availability of other features, such as number of email accounts.

By default, the name of your server plus the name of the directory assigned by your host becomes your site URL. Your host also may give you a string of numbers called an IP address that also represents the location of your site on the Web. To continue the parking space analogy, your IP number is like your parking space number. But nobody wants a URL that reads www.yourwebhost.com/~sitename, or worse, 65.97.106.162. This is where domain names come in.

Domain names. A domain name is a custom URL you purchase through a domain name registrar. Think of the domain name as a personalized "reserved" sign that replaces the number identifying your parking space. Domain names are chosen to reflect the content of the website they represent. XYZgraphicdesign.com is much easier to remember than an IP address, and it says something about what the company does right in the name. The most common and desired domain suffix is .com, but hundreds of others exist. The suffix .net was intended for personal Web pages, .org for groups and organizations, .gov for government and .edu for education.

When you purchase a domain name, you must provide your registrar with the domain name server (DNS) of your Web host. This action "points" the domain name to your Web host, and subsequently, your Web pages. The end result is when a person plugs your custom domain name into a browser, the browser locates the domain name at your registrar, and the registrar redirects the browser to your website. If the stars, sun and moon all align, your website will show up in that person's browser window.

File Transfer Protocol (FTP). The final piece in this mix is the mechanism required to get your Web pages parked in your server space. A Web designer keeps two sets of Web files: a local set on his or her personal computer and a matched set on the server. Make your edits on your local files then upload the files to the server. The files on the server are the ones the rest of the world sees via Web browsers.

To connect to your server, which is essentially a remote computer, you need File Transfer Protocol (FTP) software. FTP software is inexpensive (or even free) and easy to use. When you provide the name of your Web host, your username and your password in a new connection dialog box, the FTP client will open a bridge between your computer and your server space. Uploading files is usually as simple as dragging and dropping.

It's inevitable. Whether you provide images and logos for an existing site, contribute to a blog or build sites from scratch, working with websites is a given.

Good design is good design. Well-designed websites demonstrate the use of compositional elements and principles, including focal point, balance, movement, line, shape, value and, of course, space.

Using an underlying grid is particularly important to maintain visual consistency across nonlinear pages.

CMS and hosted templates: No FTP required. If your website was built using a content management system, or utilizes a template provided by an online website service, you may not need a separate FTP client. CMS and hosted template systems provide an online interface so you can upload graphics and other assets to the host server. Text content is typed in via a word processing-style interface and stored in a database on the host server. You're still uploading content to a server; you're just doing it using more user-friendly tools.

PRINT DESIGN VS. WEB DESIGN

How Web design is similar to print design.

Good design is good design, no matter the medium. The end product must capture attention, control the eye's movement, convey information and evoke emotion.

Your website design will need a focal point, visual hierarchy, balance, rhythm and flow. If your site has more than one page you'll need consistency across multiple pages. You'll also need a consistent navigation system to keep visitors oriented.

While good design is good design, a Web page does differ from print in significant ways.

How Web design differs from print design.

You can't completely control the way your layouts will appear onscreen.
A good print designer knows what she'll get back when she sends her files to the printer. Not so for the Web designer. Any layout created for the screen will look slightly different to each and every person who views it. For this, we can blame both hardware and software. In our color chapter, we discussed the issue of color-shifting on different monitors. Another issue arises from different browsers rendering fonts and spacing differently, causing changes to the intended appearance of layouts. When you design for Web, you design for a moving target.

Your layout is built on an incredible shrinking (or expanding) canvas.
Back in the early days of Web design, the great debate was whether to design your page to 640 × 480 pixels or 800 × 600 pixels. Monitor technology was changing, and sites built at 800 × 600 looked great on new monitors, but were cropped and required scrolling on older monitors. And those were the good old days.

Today's websites are as likely to be viewed on a smartphone (starting at around 320 × 480 pixels) as on a 20-inch monitor. Or on a 15-inch laptop screen. Or on a tablet. You can't choose to have your site look good on only one device. It must look good on all devices. You must plan for a high degree of layout flexibility.

Websites are nonlinear. Unlike books, magazines and other multi-page documents, multi-page websites are nonlinear. Rather than move from Chapter 1 to Chapter 2, viewers can jump to any point in a website at any time, and things need to make sense when viewers arrive. They also need a clear path to get back to wherever they came from, or to find their next destination in the site. Design concepts of hierarchy, repetition and unity become crucial to site navigability and usability.

This is a sample headline set in Tangerine Cursive

This is sample body copy set at a font size of .9em. The body copy uses the Open Sans font by Steve Matteson. The Tangerine font in the headline was created by Toshi Omagari. Both are available through a free online font hosting service.

This is a sample headline set in Tangerine Cursive

This is sample body copy set at a font size of .9em. The body copy uses the Open Sans font by Steve Matteson. The Tangerine font in the headline was created by Toshi Omagari. Both are available through a free online font hosting service.

This is a sample headline set in Tangerine Cursive

This is sample body copy set at a font size of .9em. The body copy uses the Open Sans font by Steve Matteson. The Tangerine font in the headline was created by Toshi Omagari. Both are available through a free online font hosting service.

No, you don't need to get your eyes checked. Despite access to the exact same page code and style sheet, each browser renders fonts differently. Look closely at the line breaks, font size and overall height of the copy blocks. These subtle differences are enough to cause a layout to break on one browser or another.

The Web offers opportunities for interaction. This preservation initiative website encourages visitors to get involved through social media, a news feed signup and a contribute button. A countdown creates urgency.

The Web can be a multi-sensory experience. Websites allow for the addition of multimedia components such as animation, video and audio, creating a richer multi-sensory experience. This means entering a whole new world of video and audio formats as well as browser compatibility issues.

The Web is an interactive experience. Early websites were brochure- and book-like: We clicked, we read. In a few short years the Web has evolved into a device that reads you back. As we click, our choices are recorded and come back to us in the form of messages like, "Those who purchased this item also bought…" With a click we can control the "skin" of our online music service. We can add our own words and images to blogs, forums and social media sites. Websites are expected to be interactive and dynamic. A Web designer must create a framework that creates order and organization, despite constantly changing, oft-times user-generated content.

ANATOMY OF A WEB PAGE

While every website is different, there are some standard content areas found on most pages. Some content areas lend themselves well to the placement of certain Web assets or to specific functions. In fact, some types of content placement are considered best practices and make the site more user-friendly. For example, placing a logo in the upper left corner of the header and making that logo link to the home page is considered a best practice. Web page content areas can and should be repeated throughout a site for both visual consistency and ease of use. These content areas include:

Headers. Your header includes the name of your website, with or without additional visuals or type. More often than not, the header spans the top of the screen page, though there is no hard fast rule that this must be the case.

Navigation. Navigation includes the list of buttons or links that take folks to other parts of your site, hence the name. Navigation often sits above or below the header, or in both places when there is more than

SOME STANDARD WEB PAGE COMPONENTS

Header. The header includes the name of the site and often includes a logo or other graphic.

Navigation. Navigation is a set of links that take you to other pages in the site. Navigation should be consistent across all pages.

Content. Content can include everything from copy to multimedia components.

Footer. The footer often includes organization address and contact information, as well as a text version of the site navigation.

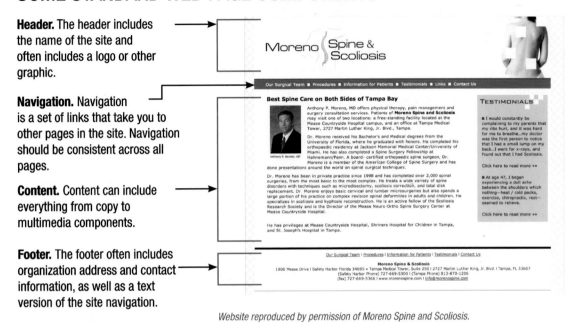

Website reproduced by permission of Moreno Spine and Scoliosis.

one set of links. Alternatively, navigation may run down the side of the screen page. Left column navigation is the most common and is sometimes used for secondary navigation. Also consider side navigation if the list of links is too long to fit horizontally across the screen page.

Main content. This is your Web page's prime real estate. The main content area can house a wide variety of content types in an equally wide variety of arrangements. We discuss some best practices for organizing your main content area later in this chapter.

Sidebars. Like sidebars in print layouts, Web sidebars generally sit in a narrow column next to the main content area. They are commonly used to house various widgets (calls-to-action, calendars, forms, you name it) and of course, banner ads.

Footers. Footers typically span the page bottom. They are often set in columns and may include contact information, copyright and legal notices, social media links and bookmarking, social media feeds, calendar feeds and additional navigation links.

Some websites have all these parts. Others only have a few. Feel free to choose and use the content areas that make sense for your content and creative vision.

SEARCH ENGINE **OPTIMIZATION**

When Google introduced the Hummingbird search algorithm (the thing that ranks Web pages) in 2013, a good portion of the World's SEO experts panicked in unison. They feared their years of careful study on the inner workings of page ranking had just been rendered as useful as mudflaps on a turtle.

It turns out that SEO isn't dead, but some things have changed. Here's what you need to know now:

Content is *still* king. Algorithms consider the quality of your page content. If your site only offers basic information your visitors could find anywhere, your site will fail this test. To rank well you must offer something more, or better yet, something different. And you must offer something new on a regular basis. Update. Your. Site.

Keywords still matter. Resarch the right search terminology to use relative to your site topic. Look for language visitors would use, not just professional jargon. Then repeat those words throughout your site using natural phrasing. Balancing SEO with good copywriting requires a little finesse.

Include keywords in your code. Work keywords into the HTML code for your page titles, headings, hyperlinks, alt tags (alternative text for page images or objects) and descriptions. If you're really smart, you'll purchase a domain name that includes your keywords, too.

Make your site mobile-friendly. In Spring 2015, tech experts buzzed about "mobilegeddon" after Google announced another algorithm change penalizing sites for not being mobile friendly. So make your site mobile-friendly. Start by reading the section on repsonsive Web design later in this chapter.

In truth, SEO is complex and algorithms consider more factors than we describe here. If your website must rank well, then consult an SEO expert. Assuming he or she has recovered from the hummingbird panic attack.

THAT'S ALL GREAT. BUT HOW DO I DESIGN ONE?

Because websites are a complex combination of type, visuals and applications, the best sites are the result of the joint efforts of designers, Web developers, writers and Web usability experts. Whether you're designing on your own, editing an existing site or working with a team to build something new, you should understand the design conventions involved in creating a good website. And you should start with a plan.

Website planning.

In any design project, the final product is only as good as the initial planning. Plan a website the way you would plan any project—consider look, feel, message, content and delivery method.

Setting clear objectives is crucial. As noted earlier, the original websites were little more than static online brochures. Now websites must have constantly changing updateable content and interactive components to engage and/or entertain visitors to keep them coming back. You need to know what you want your site to say and do, as well as what your visitors need your site to do. Sometimes those needs require extra software, programming or even specialized server space.

Start your project by writing a creative brief, followed by a content outline. This outline becomes the basis for developing the site map, a type of flowchart that lists all the pages within a site and their interconnections. The outline and site map provide the list of pages that become the site's navigation. They should also include notes regarding specific page functionality, such as forms, multimedia components, dynamic content areas and any site feature that might require custom coding and the skills of a Web developer.

This is the time to assemble your site assets. Site assets include your copy, logos, photos, video clips, external Web links and even code snippets from other online sources if you plan to use dynamic content on your site.

If it is important that your site be highly ranked by search engines, search engine optimization (SEO) should be considered as part of the copywriting process.

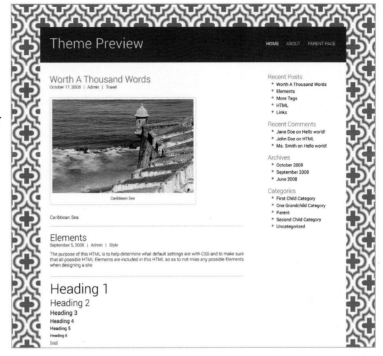

Working with themes & templates.

If you are building a site using a remotely or locally installed CMS, you'll need to select a theme. CMS sites are built using a set of files that generate individual page parts, such as headers, footers and content areas. A theme is a packaged set of files you can install that dictate how the parts will go together and what they will look like once assembled. Most themes are editable to some degree, and many have simple no-code-experience-needed interfaces that let you make changes. At a minimum, themes allow you to change color palettes and font choices, and to replace images with your own.

More advanced themes might allow the addition of plug-ins for added functionality. Some have drag-and-drop interfaces that allow you to reposition content blocks.

If you have good coding skills and your particular installation allows access to the code, you can customize themes any way you choose.

Templates are pre-packaged sets of ready-to-go website files with placeholder content. Swap out the placeholder content for your own, upload to your Web hosting account, and you're good to go.

Try before you buy. When searcing for a blog or CMS theme, check out theme previews and demo sites. They provide a sneak peek at font styling, color palettes and layouts available with the theme package. You can find thousands of themes out there for free download or for purchasee. Premium (meaning *not* free) themes not only come with better features but also often provide tech support.

Templates come in all shapes and sizes, too. But editing them does require coding, and sometimes programming, experience.

There are thousands of theme and template options, some free, some not, some beautiful and functional and others just "meh." When choosing themes and templates, consider your laundry list of necessary content and find one that accommodates all your assets. Don't choose a theme or template designed for a grid of portfolio images when your content is primarily articles and social media feeds. Here are a few other things to consider:

Choose responsive themes and templates. This ensures your site will look great across all viewing devices. We'll explain more about responsive websites a little later in this chapter.

Look for good documentation. Unless you want to spend hours trying to figure out how to get the slider in your theme to work, it's best to find a theme that comes with instructions.

Drag-and-drop themes and built-in style editors are helpful when your knowledge of code is minimal or non-existent.

Consider the navigation. In some ways a site, especially a mobile site, is only as good as its navigation. Try viewing the template preview on different gadgets to see how the navigation behaves.

Don't choose your theme or template on looks alone. Looks are cosmetic and can be changed. It's more important to get a theme or template with the right content areas and functionality you want.

Doing your own thing: Websites from the ground up.

If themes and pre-packaged templates just won't cut it, you can design from scratch. After you've gone through the planning process, written your creative brief, created a site map and assembled your assets, your next move is to do some design sketching. You need to create wireframes.

Wireframes visually organize your content.

Wireframe sketches show the placement and functions of content on each type of page in your site. You may need one sketch or many depending on the number of unique page layouts in your site.

But before you start sketching, there is an additional wrinkle to iron out. We've mentioned (repeatedly) that your site must function well and look good across screen sizes that vary from smartphone to monster monitor. To address this issue, many designers and developers build sites that are "responsive." In terms of layouts, responsive websites adjust to fit the screen of any viewing device. Since one site

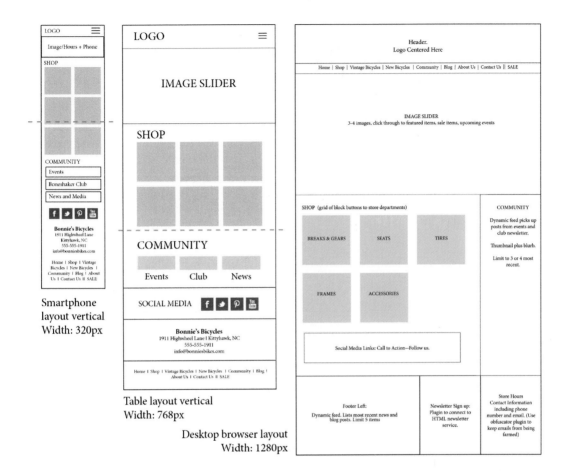

LOGO

Image/Hours + Phone

SHOP

COMMUNITY

Events

Boneshaker Club

News and Media

Bonnie's Bicycles
1911 Highwheel Lane
Kittyhawk, NC
555-555-1911
info@bonniesbikes.com

Home | Shop | Vintage
Bicycles | New Bicycles |
Community | Blog | About
Us | Contact Us || SALE

Smartphone
layout vertical
Width: 320px

LOGO

IMAGE SLIDER

SHOP

COMMUNITY

Events   Club   News

SOCIAL MEDIA

Bonnie's Bicycles
1911 Highwheel Lane | Kittyhawk, NC
555-555-1911
info@bonniesbikes.com

Home | Shop | Vintage Bicycles | New Bicycles | Community | Blog |
About Us | Contact Us || SALE

Table layout vertical
Width: 768px

Header.
Logo Centered Here

Home | Shop | Vintage Bicycles | New Bicycles | Community | Blog | About Us | Contact Us || SALE

IMAGE SLIDER
3-4 images, click through to featured items, sale items, upcoming events

SHOP (grid of block buttons to store departments)

BREAKS & GEARS   SEATS   TIRES

FRAMES   ACCESSORIES

Social Media Links: Call to Action--Follow us.

COMMUNITY

Dynamic feed picks up
posts from events and
club newsletter.

Thumbnail plus blurb.

Limit to 3 or 4 most
recent.

Footer Left:
Dynamic feed. Lists most recent news and
blog posts. Limit 5 items

Newsletter Sign up:
Plugin to connect to
HTML newsletter
service.

Store Hours
Contact Information
including phone
number and email. (Use
obfuscator plugin to
keep emails from being
farmed)

Desktop browser layout
Width: 1280px

adapts to all, there is no need to build separate sites for each screen type. Which is good because we're pretty sure nobody has the time, budget or desire to build the same site four times.

To return to the process of wireframe sketching, responsive design begs the question, "How do you create sketches for a layout that changes?"

Mobile first.

The simplest answer is you need a sketch for each type of screen. These types include smartphone, tablet vertical, tablet horizontal and desktop computer monitor. And while you might be tempted to start by creating the wireframe for a big desktop computer screen, there is serious merit to drawing a wireframe for the smallest screen first.

The mobile first concept was introduced by Luke Wroblewski in 2011. Because mobile phone ownership was on an exponential upswing, Wroblewski counseled the importance of creating equally

Mobile first. To follow the principles of mobile first, whittle your site content to the bare essentials. Then sketch that content to fit your smallest screen size. Create additional wireframes for progressively larger screens, taking advantage of greater space and additional hardware and browser capability. The result is a solid Web expereince across all screen sizes.

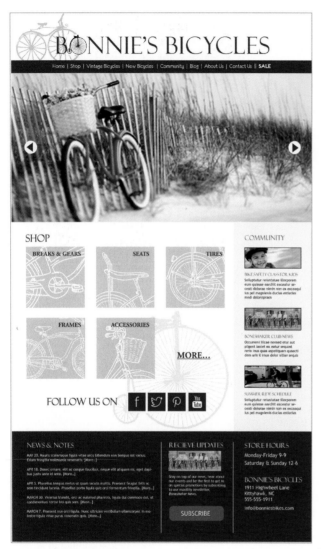

positive Web experiences across all screen sizes. In other words, viewing a site on a smartphone should not be a watered-down version of viewing the same site on a desktop computer. Instead of building a big splashy site for the desktop and having to strip it of features to make it work on a small screen, start by designing a solid feature-rich site for the small screen. Next, create designs for your larger screen sizes, adjusting the layout and features to take advantage of the additional space and hardware capabilities. This is known as "progressive enhancement."

Although not all designers embrace mobile first, it is worth consideration. At a minimum, it makes you take a hard look at website goals and proposed content. When your screen space is small, you only have room for the most important content and features. The mobile first approach forces you to deliver messages and provide functionality in the most efficient way possible. And that makes for a positive user experience.

Wireframe part one: Establish a grid.

In the Layouts chapter, we discuss starting a layout by setting up a grid. In a print project, your first gridlines create a box matching the aspect ratio of your final, trimmed layout. But here in Web-land no two screens seem to have the same dimensions. So draw your first gridlines based on standard-size screen widths of your choosing.

Using a grid. Many designers appreciate a 12-column grid, as it converts into 3- or 4-column grids with ease.

The height of your sketch is determined by the vertical space needed for your content. In the past, designers tried to squeeze all content on a page without the need to scroll. Mobile devices changed our browsing behaviors, and now scrolling is less of an issue. So your sketch, and therefore your page, can be as long as you need it to be. Within reason, of course.

Add uniform column gridlines to order and align the different assets on each page. Use the same column grid on all site pages to create a unified, harmonious look. Many Web designers use a 12-column grid as that number allows for easy conversion to 4-, 3- or 2-column grids. If your design will use a grid of uniform squares or horizontal bands to organize content, add horizontal gridlines as needed.

Wireframe part two: Sketch content areas & assets.

Define the content areas (header, navigation, footer, etc.) with additional gridlines. Show the position of your site content (copy blocks, photos, video clips, etc.) by drawing boxes. Label each box, and notate the functionality of its content. As you sketch, several established best practices and some Web design conventions can help you decide where to place content:

> Position your important items higher on the page. Style those items using size and color to set their appropriate level of visibility and utility.

Establish a focal point. Your site needs a big bold something to catch the eye and set the tone for the site. You have many options. Consider using an important photo, a slider, an animation sequence, a creative type treatment or something else entirely. Whatever you choose, place it in a position of importance near the top of the screen.

Create hierarchy. What are your most important site assets? A video testimonial? An important set of instructions? A signup form, purchase button or other call to action? Position your important items higher on the page. Style those items using size and color to set their appropriate level of visibility and utility.

Define relationships among assets on the page. Use continuity (alignment), proximity and similarity to define "what goes with what" on your pages.

Keep navigation "above the fold." In old-fashioned newspaper terminology, "above the fold" is where editors put the important news so folks could see it while the paper was still folded. In Web terms, it refers to the portion of a website that can be seen without scrolling. While smartphones and swiping technology have made scrolling less of a dirty word than it used to be, you still must ensure your site visitor can see how to navigate your site on first view. So keep navigation above the fold, preferably near the top.

Use a logo as a home page link. Place a logo or entity name in the upper left corner of your design. Make this logo serve as a link back to the site's home page.

BONNIE'S BICYCLES

Home | Shop | Vintage Bicycles | New Bicycles | Community | Blog | About Us | Contact Us || **SALE**

CITY CRUISER

Mauris scelerisque ligula vitae arcu bibendum non tempus est varius. Etiam fringilla malesuada venenatis. Donec ornare, elit ac congue faucibus, neque elit aliquam mi, eget dapibus justo ante id ante.

CHOOSE YOUR OPTIONS

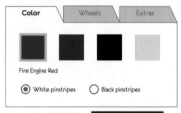

Color | Wheels | Extras

Fire Engine Red

◉ White pinstripes   ○ Black pinstripes

PRICE: $250.00   **ADD TO CART**

CUSTOMER REVIEWS:

★★★★ **Smooth ride.** Mauris scelerisque ligula vitae arcu bibendum non tempus est varius. Etiam fringilla malesuada venenatis. [More...]

★★★★ **Comfortable seat, foot pedals.** Donec ornare, elit ac congue faucibus, neque elit aliquam mi, eget dapibus justo ante id ante. [More...]

★★★ **Great bike, but a little pricey.** Phasellus tempus metus ut quam iaculis mattis. Praesent feugiat felis ac sem tincidunt lacinia. Phasellus porta ligula quis orci fermentum fringilla. [More...]

Read more reviews...

IMAGE GALLERY

Patterns in play. The Web has been with us long enough that many graphical user interface "patterns" are self-explanatory. We understand how the tabs, radio buttons, color swatches and image galleries work without having to ask.

Designing the main content area.

Site content can include everything from copy to video clips to dynamically generated infographics. And most content areas include more than one type of content.

Creating text-only pages is fairly straightforward. Reading-copy on the Web can be set in one or more columns, with the number dependent upon page width. Set copy in the most readable font format for the medium (sans serif) and use graduated heading sizes and styles to create hierarchy.

Place primary photos, graphics and video clips near the top of their respective content areas, using the grid structure as a guide. Make sure that none interrupts the flow of reading. Choose quality images. Place captions below images, and remember to make those captions keyword-rich for SEO purposes. Don't forget to add "alt tags" and descriptions to your photos and graphics for accessibility.

Pattern	Possible Uses/Examples	What it looks like
Grid of consistently sized boxes	When several bits of information are of uniform importance. Example: team headshots.	
Rotating feature	A consistently sized container with auto-play or click-to-advance images. Example: rotating banner ads.	
Sliding panels	Multiple variations of a single idea. Example: retail website feature showing "5 ways to wear a sweater."	
Module tabs	Display different aspects of the same product/concept. Example: Product details including dimensions, shipping info and manufacturing materials.	
Accordion	When you have a lot of heterogeneous content and not a lot of space. Content can be grouped under short headings; more than one group can be visible at once. Example: frequently asked questions and answers.	

The interactive nature of websites introduces a whole new layer of complexity to page design. Take, for example, an automotive website that allows you to create an image of your dream car. The core content element of such a page is the basic image of a car. But the page also must include images of the various options the buyer can choose: paint colors, trim packages, interior packages, sound systems, rims, tires, etc. How can you possibly get all that content on a single page without creating chaos?

Interface design. The answer lies in the conventions of interface design, which refers to the design of the user experience—the interaction between the user and the tool to achieve a desired action. When you design interfaces for websites, you are designing a graphical user interface (GUI). The acronym is pronounced "gooey," in case you were wondering.

The best graphical interface designs are simple, intuitive and unobtrusive. Interface design speaks to everything from the size,

Standard interface design conventions or "patterns." You'll recognize these common interface patterns and how you've seen them used. Think about how these patterns and their uses might help you design your Web pages to be user-friendly. What's good for viewers is good for you.

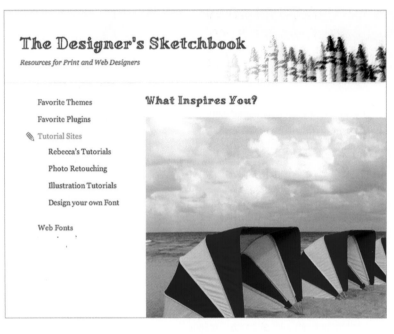

The Designer's Sketchbook

Resources for Print and Web Designers

Favorite Themes

Favorite Plugins

Tutorial Sites

Rebecca's Tutorials

Photo Retouching

Illustration Tutorials

Design your own Font

Web Fonts

What Inspires You?

style and placement of navigation buttons to the best background colors for pop-up windows. While it's beyond our scope to dig deeply into this discipline, we highly recommend additional reading on this topic for those serious about Web design. In the meantime, we can supply a chart of a few standard interface design conventions, or "patterns," to help organize complicated Web content.

Getting GUI. The patterns of interface design help us not only organize content but also address basic usability issues. As you sketch page designs, ask yourself some questions. Is your navigation easy to find? Do the links make sense? When you click past the home page, is it easy to tell where you are in the site? Can you tell how to get back? These are core issues of graphical user interface that apply to all Web page and website designs.

Some tips for creating good GUI include:

> » *Make the purpose of each page clear at a glance.* Use simple descriptive headings and copy. Your visitor should never have to ask, "What is this page about?"

> » *Keep link names clear and simple.* Don't title a link "The Sum of Our Experience," when "About Us" will do.

> » *Make the link name match the title of the corresponding page.* In other words, when you click on "About Us," the page you arrive on should be titled "About Us." This seems like a no-brainer. But you'd be surprised at how often this doesn't happen on websites.

> » *Make buttons and links look like buttons and links.* Make the text or the button itself change color when the mouse rolls over it—something to give a clue that your button is a button. Under no circumstances should your visitor have to work to figure out how to get around your site. They won't work. They'll just leave. You can take that fact to the bank.

Pull-down and accordion menus. Pull-down and accordion menus can be real space-savers when you have lengthy and complex navigation. However, pull-down menus can be difficult for your visitors to use. Avoid them when you can, and really avoid those with multi-level drill-down.

» *Navigation should be persistent.* Navigation should include the same links in the same style in the same place on each page. That's a unity technique. For responsive sites, consider making the navigation "fixed" to the page. Fixed navigation stays put while the rest of the page scrolls, making the navigation available at all times.

» *Limit the number of navigation links.* The magic maximum number of items in your navigation is seven (plus or minus one or two). Any more and the quantity of links becomes difficult to visually process. If it is essential to have more links, consider using a primary navigation for your main links, and a secondary navigation with links to common pages such as "about us" and "contact us." Another option is to use accordion or pull-down menus. That said…

» *Be wary of pull-down menus.* While space saving, pull-down menus can be difficult for some people to utilize, especially when the pull-down menu has multiple levels. They present even bigger usability issues on mobile sites. Avoid them if you can.

» *Use color to organize and order.* This is especially true if your site is complex.

» *Consider using a breadcrumb trail.* Breadcrumbs help your visitors see where they've been and how to get back.

» *Provide a search box.* For complex sites, a simple search box can be the best tool ever.

» *Include a link to the home page in the navigation menu.* And if your design includes a logo in the header, make the logo link back to the home page.

» *Arrange your navigation items in descending order by use.* Place your navigation items in order of most used to least used, from top to bottom or from left to right in the navigation menu.

Web prototyping.

Once your sketches have made a place for everything and put everything in its place, the next step is to create some sort of full-color rendering. Since traditional renderings made with photo-editing software are static, many designers choose prototyping as a next step. Prototyping software allows the creation of a functional mockup. The mockup shows the layout, but also displays working versions of the site's interactive components. Individual site assets such as photos and video clips are designed with separate software then imported into the prototyping program.

DESIGN FOR MOBILE WEB AND SMARTPHONE APPS

The small size of smartphone screens makes it difficult to see, much less access, most content on traditional websites without excessive zooming and scrolling. In addition, many smartphones have touchscreen technology. It can be nearly impossible to click tiny links with our imprecise fingertips. To address the needs of smartphone browsers, designers are wise to create variations of websites tailored for tiny screens. These are referred to as "mobile sites."

Alternatively, mobile applications, commonly known as "apps" allow access to digital content. Apps are programs downloaded directly to your mobile device. They perform specific functions such as sharing photos or providing easy access to shopping. Some apps have the same capabilties as full-blown websites, but with interfaces geared for tiny screens. Some apps take advantage of capabilities unique to smartphones, such as historic tour apps that use GPS.

Techies debate whether the future of accessing digital content is best accomplished via app or mobile site. Mobile web vs. app aside, there are challenges to designing for the smallest screens. Here are a few interface design best practices for both:

» Simplify—but don't skimp on—content (whittle content to what mobile users need and want).

» Make clickable areas at least 44 × 44 pixels (the size needed for most fingertips).

» Think accessibility. Larger font sizes (readable without zooming) and good contrast are helpful for those with less-than-perfect eyesight. Add extra line-spacing while you're at it.

» Use proximity. Place controls close to the content they modify.

» Avoid "hover states" (where boxes and other popups appear on mouseover). Hover states behave badly on smartphone interfaces and may cover up other content on an already tiny screen.

» Use only broadly supported animation and video file formats.

» Strike a balance between optimizing for speed and providing high-quality graphics.

» Mobile sites should provide a link to the main website.

Touch interfaces and tiny screens... Mobile websites and apps have specific design requirements, including minimum sizes for clickable areas. Remember, your fingertip is not as precise as your mouse, and "fat-fingering" links can accidentally send you off to Internet parts unknown.

Another way to test-drive the interactive components of a website is to build a beta site. A beta site is a working version of a website that is hidden from public view. Both beta sites and prototypes allow designers and developers to work out any design issues before a site goes live.

And as responsive Web design becomes the standard, testing a website's interactive functions is not just a nicety, it's a necessity.

RESPONSIVE WEB DESIGN.

According to the Pew Research Center, 64 percent of U.S. adults own a smartphone, and a majority of those people use their smartphones to access the Internet. With such a significant portion of the population viewing sites this way, it's no surprise that designers and developers have moved to responsive Web design.

Responsive websites detect the type of viewing device and load the appropriately formatted site content and configuration. Interestingly, tools and techniques to build responsive Web pages have been with us for years. Designers simply needed to apply those same tools in different ways.

There are three components to responsive Web design: flexible layouts, flexible assets and media queries. Layouts and assets are made flexible by coding. Media queries are strings of code that impact what styling is loaded on what size screen.

How responsive design works.

Web design best practices dictate that websites are created and styled via two types of page code: The first type is traditional HTML or a programming language defining the numbers and names of pages in the site along with the relationships among those pages. The second type is a Cascading Style Sheet (CSS), which sets the visual styling, or appearance, of all page components from background pattern to column widths to font colors. Page objects, such as text boxes or site navigation, are created in the page-defining code. Then those same objects are named and their styling is defined in an attached style sheet. A CSS is simply a long list of page objects and their attributes.

```
body {
    background-image:url(images/ginko-bg.
    background-repeat: no-repeat;
}

#content {
    margin-top: 1em;;
    width: 85%;
    margin-left: auto;
    margin-right: auto;
    background-color:#f4eede;
    background-image:url(images/leaves.pn
    background-position: left top;
    background-repeat: no-repeat;
}

h1 {
    padding: 2.7em 0 .1em 2em;
    font-family:"P22 Arts And Crafts Hunt
    font-size: 1.7em;
    text-transform: uppercase;
    color: #105210;
}
```

It's like having your mom tell you what shirt to wear. Web pages are created by HTML or programming language, but the appearance of Web pages is dictated by CSS. See if you can identify the CSS notations in the lower graphic that define and style the elements in the Web graphic at top.

Bend, don't break. Websites are viewed in many different screen sizes so it's important that your design responds accordingly. If it doesn't, your site might break when viewed with different devices. See what happened to this website-in-progress when it was viewed on a tablet?

Flexible layouts. You build flexible layouts by using the CSS to create fluid instead of fixed-width elements. Instead of setting your page width to an inflexible finite size like 960 pixels, you set your page width to be a flexible 100% of your browser. Structural elements such as columns also must be styled as flexible, or the layout will "break" when viewed on a screen deemed too small to fit the design.

Flexible assets. You can style some assets for fluidity with ease; others not so much. Adapt your fonts to fluid layouts by styling them in "ems" or "rems" instead of pixels. An em is a typographic measurement equivalent to the current font size. That current font size is either a browser default size or some other default size specified in the site's CSS. A rem is a "relative" em, meaning it adopts the base size specified by its parent (the code that encloses it). As you can imagine, styling copy at 130% of whatever the default size is would give you a larger font, while styling at 80% would give you a smaller font. Since both measurements are defined as percents of some original default size, both are fluid.

Style photos and videos as percentages to make them fluid. The drawback is that scaling graphics up does little to improve their quality onscreen, especially if they have been optimized. The solution is to create larger graphics than needed. Percentage settings in the style sheet will ensure graphics appear at the correct size onscreen, while the additional pixels available in a larger image will offset any loss of quality if the graphics must expand to fit a larger screen. Keep in mind, however, that optimization is still a must. While most people have relatively high-speed Internet access on their computers, Internet speed on smartphones and other smaller devices might not be so fast. Keeping file sizes, and therefore download times, small remains important.

Media queries. Sometimes, despite your best efforts to create fluid designs, layouts break in one browser or another. Or perhaps there are page components that you want to display on a full computer screen but that you would like to eliminate from your site when viewed on a smartphone. This is where media queries come into play.

A media query is a bit of code that kicks off a short conversation between a browser and your page code on the server. Essentially the browser knocks on the door of the website, and the website asks, "Who are you?" The browser responds with, "I'm browser A, appearing on viewport of x-pixels wide." The website does a quick check to see if there are any special instructions in its code to deal with that browser/screen size combination before it serves up either the standard site or a custom version of the site. The "special instructions" are often a separate version of the CSS written specifically for different media parameters, or different browsers, that include, exclude or alter specified sections of styling.

Earlier media queries were written with device-specific widths in mind. For example, CSS for a navigation style would be set to change from standard to mobile navigation once the screen size hit 768 pixels, the width of a tablet in the vertical position. However, since screen sizes are all different and new sizes are introduced regularly, your media queries should be device agnostic. Preview your page design with tools that show you screen width. As you shrink your page, watch for design elements to break. Make note of the page width when the break occurred, and add the appropriate design adjustment to your style sheet. Device-agnostic media queries ensure a robust design regardless of screen size.

Sites you build for yourself or your clients need to function across gadgets and platforms. While you may not have to write this type of code yourself, you may have to find a responsive template, or work with a designer or developer to build one. So, yes, you do need to understand the concepts and the vocabulary.

Advantage: Blog.
One advantage blogs have over websites is that their text-heavy content makes them search engine friendly.

A WEBSITE ISN'T ALWAYS THE BEST TOOL FOR THE JOB

A good website is the backbone of many businesses and organizations. But if your goal is to self-publish, to build an online network or increase your reach and influence among existing online networks, then a blog or a social media page is a better option.

Blogs. Short for Web log, a blog is an online self-publishing platform. Many blogs are simply personal forums for thoughts or rants. But the business world discovered that blogs have a place in commerce. The blogosphere includes industry-specific bloggers whose influence rivals (indeed surpasses) that of journalists. This reality is a pro and a con for public information officers (PIOs) managing blogs for their own organizations while vetting media-relations inquiries from other bloggers. It's all part of the new reality of doing business on the Web.

The difference between a blog and a website is that blog content is syndicated. People can subscribe through an RSS (Really Simple Syndication) feed. When a blogger writes a post, the content of the post is automatically delivered straight to the subscriber's computer. Organizational bloggers publish mini articles, news items and even full news releases using RSS. On the flip side, a blogger with a bone to pick can influence a huge number of subscribers quickly through this same system.

> Setting up a blog is easy. Keeping one updated is another matter. We recommend you do some research to educate yourself before you launch a blog.

Setting up a blog is easy. You can create an account through one of many online blogging services, or you can download the programs and install them on your own server. (Keeping a blog updated is another matter, so we recommend you do some research and educate yourself before you launch a blog.)

The rules for designing blogs are the same as the rules for designing Web pages. But because blogs are designed to appeal to people with no knowledge of HTML, there are literally thousands of template designs you can choose from. Many of them are free. And if you can't find exactly what you're looking for, templates are easy to tweak. You can change color palettes through CSS. With photo-editing software and FTP access to your server, you can create and upload custom banners of your choice.

Social networking and social media sites. Whether or not you engage in blogging, you likely will supplement website activity with participation in one or more social media sites or social networks. The number and types of these sites have expanded in recent years, and it requires planning and strategy to capitalize on social media activity.

From a design standpoint, social networking and social media sites may or may not have page customization options, such as custom skins (themes). Some may offer access to CSS, which allows you to change fonts, font colors, background images and banners. Generally speaking, there is little actual design involved in working with social media sites. However, you can apply good design practices to any video clips and custom graphics you add to your pages.

WEB DESIGN & **ACCESSIBILITY**

Despite the amazing multimedia capabilities of the World Wide Web, the primary mode of information delivery is still text, and the interface is largely visual and requires a keyboard and mouse for input.

The Web Content Accessibility Guidelines, published by the Web Accessibility Initiative, offer a road map for making websites available and useful to people with vision, hearing and other physical challenges.

Some tips for making your site accessible include:

» **Do not encase text within graphics.** Screen readers can't read words that are built into graphics. (Incidentally, search engines can't either, so this cuts down on your SEO.)

» **Make sure type is scalable.** Browsers typically allow users to increase type size for easier readability. Think Readers Digest large-print edition. But this only works if the font settings for the Web page are configured to allow it.

Make links reactive. Design your links to physically change on click or mouseover. A color change alone may not be the best option. For those who are colorblind, underlined links are easier to see.

» **Provide text equivalents for all graphics.** Again, screen readers can't read graphics. Most WYSIWYG page editors have a field for you to enter "alt-text," short for alternative text, for any graphics in your layout. Alt-text is like a mini caption for your graphic, viewable only by screen readers and search engines. You also can manually enter alt-text into page HTML. (Tip: When alt-text includes keywords, it also improves SEO.)

» **Underline hyperlinks**. It's good practice to make links change in some way on a mouseover. However, if the only change is a color change, the colorblind may not be able to see it. Underlines make links more obvious. (Indeed, live links are the only time we can endorse underlining type.)

» **Provide large clickable areas.** For those who aren't so steady with a mouse, trying to click on small buttons or hotspots can be challenging. Don't skimp on the size of your clickable areas.

» **Provide closed-captioning for video elements.** Or, alternatively, provide a sign-language version of the video. Likewise, provide a typed transcript option of audio components, and consider providing a reader-service version of content for the visually impaired.

KEEP ON YOUR TOES

Communicating today means communicating digitally, and the changes in digital communication technology seem to come faster every day. Trying to stay on top of the trends and changes is a little like herding cats.

Don't let the technology scare you. Remember, the trend is towards do-it-yourself animation, video and Web pages. To keep on top of tech trends, subscribe to a blog, take a class or try some online tutorials. If you're feeling in over your head, you can always hire a professional to help you with your Web-based project.

TRY THIS

1. Visit your favorite website. Create a site map and wireframe of the site showing all pages, links and functionality.

2. Locate the optimization function on your photo-editing software. Try using it on different types of graphics such as photos and logos. Save the images using different settings. Compare the results and final file sizes with your original graphics.

3. Find a website that you think is truly awful. Using page-layout software or an image editor, redesign the home page using good design practices and GUI.

4. Find two or three highly complex websites. As you navigate around the sites, be aware of navigational techniques being employed. What works? What doesn't? Is the site responsive? How does the navigation change? Do you feel lost in the site or always know where you are? Why?

5. Visit a large commercial website using a desktop browser. Visit the same site using a tablet and/or a smartphone. Are there different versions of the site for each device? If not, does the website look and function properly on all devices? If there are different versions of the site, how are they similar? How are they different?

6. In mini art school, you thumbnail sketched some ideas for an online personal portfolio. Now, using page-layout or image-editing software, execute a design for a responsive personal portfolio website using the concept of mobile first. Start with a site map. What pages and content will you need? Execute designs for a mobile site home page. Adapt your design to a horizontal tablet, a vertical tablet and a desktop computer. Make sure you account for persistent navigation and good GUI.

7. Visit one or more large commercial websites intended for the general public. Consider ability and accessibility. What has the site designer done to make this site accessible? What do you recommend for improving accessibility?

WHAT'S **TRENDING**

Increased use of mobile devices sparked some interesting Web design trends. Here are a few: single page websites, "big photo" layouts (often accompanied by parallax effects) and photo galleries coded with jQuery Masonry. Can you guess why these designs work on mobile screens?

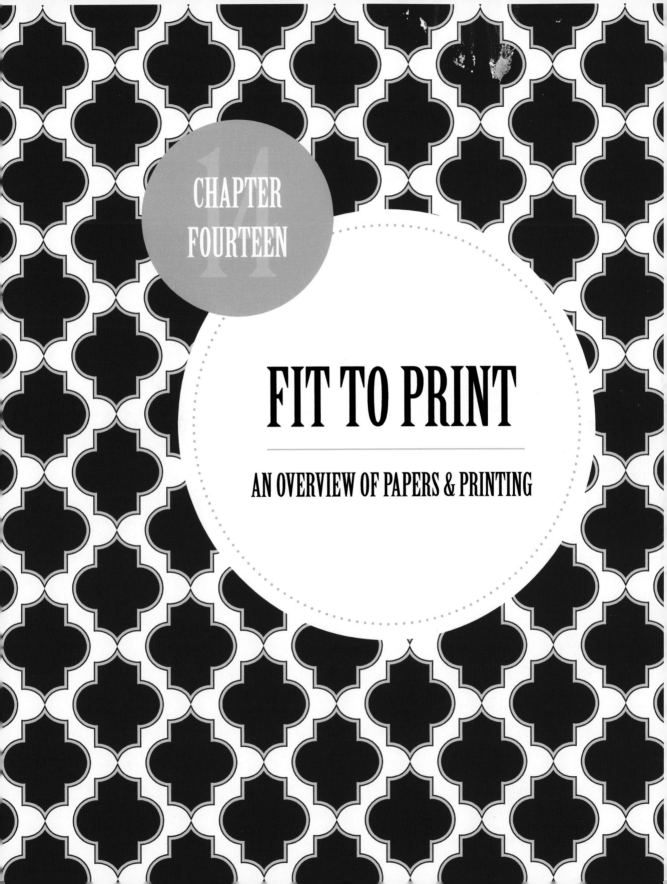

CHAPTER
FOURTEEN

14

FIT TO PRINT

AN OVERVIEW OF PAPERS & PRINTING

While we appear to be moving in the direction of a paperless society, printing is unlikely to disappear completely. Printed documents have a couple things electronic documents don't: portability and tactile quality. Handheld devices such as smartphones and tablets have made a dent in the portability claims of paper, but nothing yet replicates the *feel* of paper. Because of this added sensory input, paper can strengthen your ability to communicate through design.

Like choosing the right font or the right color, the right paper selection can communicate volumes in an instant. If you need to send banquet invitations to the most important people in your city, we're thinking an invitation printed on textured linen paper enclosed in a translucent envelope with a matching reply card would be more persuasive than an electronic invitation.

In this chapter we talk about choosing papers and printers, as well as getting your print job done right from estimate through delivery.

Paper communicates. Paper offers a tactile experience that electronic documents can't replicate.

PLAN AHEAD FOR PRINTING: CHOOSING PAPER

Even though printing and distribution occur at the end of the design process, paper selection and output decisions happen at the beginning.

Deciding what paper and which printing method hinge on three things: how you want the finished piece to look and feel, the communication job the finished piece has to do and the size of your budget for accomplishing both.

Getting the look & feel with paper.

Paper is sexy. It comes in varieties of colors, weights and textures. Slick glossy paper might suggest a modern forward-thinking document. Thicker uncoated (not glossy) paper might imply a document of greater substance or importance. A heavily textured paper might lend the document a rustic quality. There are papers with pearly finishes, printed patterns, built-in textures and even flecks of flower petals.

To aid the paper selection process, paper manufacturers produce swatch books that include paper samples. Swatch books are free for the asking from paper distributors or manufacturers. These folks are only too happy to share what they know with you in the hope you'll "spec" or specify their papers for your printing projects.

But you ought to bring yourself up to speed on the most common paper varieties. Basically, there are three categories of paper: coated, uncoated and specialty. Within each of those categories lies tremendous selection in terms of paper finish, use and price.

Choosing the right paper for the right task.

For choosing paper, functionality is as important as appearance. You can't, for example, make a pocket folder out of paper intended for a copy machine. Copy paper simply doesn't have the weight and strength to make a functional folder. Weight is just one of many paper properties you must consider in your selection process.

Paper properties also impact the way ink behaves on the paper's surface. For example, uncoated sheets absorb ink, which can cause fine lines, such as the thin strokes on modern fonts, to appear slightly soft and even a little blurry. Depending on the paper's level of absorbency, photographs and illustrations may appear duller when printed on uncoated sheets. Color and brightness of the underlying paper influence photo and illustration color as well. Photo and illustration colors are truest and most vibrant when printed on the brightest whitest papers.

To aid the paper selection process, paper manufacturers produce swatch books that include paper samples. Swatch books are free for the asking from paper distributors or manufacturers.

PAPER TYPES, FINISHES & BEST USES

Paper	Finishes	Uses	Price
Coated	Gloss, Dull, Matte, Silk	Magazines, brochures, flyers, posters, annual reports, pocket folders, direct mail. Anything where color photos need to "pop." Tends to be less expensive than uncoated or specialty sheets.	$–$$$$
Uncoated: • Text • Writing • Cover	Smooth, Supersmooth, Vellum, Laid, Linen, Felt	Brochures, letterhead, business cards, invitations, annual reports, pocket folders. Good for high-end projects where tactile quality adds to project.	$$–$$$$
Specialty		Invitations, brochures, packaging, pocket folders, covers. Some papers for specific uses: safety paper, carbonless, etc.	$$–$$$$

Again, a swatch book is helpful when looking for information on paper properties. Swatch books usually indicate a paper's properties as well as compatibility with laser and inkjet printers. Because it can be difficult for designers to guess how inks will appear printed on particular papers, many swatch books include print samples. These are often drop-dead gorgeous designs demonstrating how ink and other finishing treatments behave on a paper product.

Paper varies across a number of qualities, such as opacity (see-through-ness) and smoothness (tactile quality). You need to understand how these properties impact the printing process before you can choose the right paper for the job.

Being green is easier than it used to be.

As a print designer, your paper and printing choices directly impact the environment. And you have cause for concern. Traditional

PAPER PROPERTIES

Paper Property	What it is	Why it's important
Opacity	The degree to which the paper is see-through.	If you need to print a sheet front and back, as in magazines and newsletters, you need a more opaque sheet.
Grain	The natural line-up of paper fibers as a result of the paper-making process.	Paper folds and tears more easily with the grain, so when you design folds and perforated tear-off cards, design with the grain.
Brightness/whiteness	Brightness is the amount of light reflected by the paper's surface; whiteness is the shade of white: warm, balanced or cool.	Colors print best on brighter papers. But the brighter/whiter the paper, the more expensive it is. When printing documents with pictures of people, choose warmer whites. For landscapes, choose cooler whites.
Weight	In the United States, a paper's weight is equal to the weight of 500 sheets in a specific size, listed in pounds. Paper weight influences stability, rigidity and often opacity.	Weight impacts the structure of the final document. If you don't choose the right paper weight, your brochure may flop over in a rack, or your direct mail piece may be mangled by post office equipment or, worse, be rejected or require additional postage.
Formation	The overall distribution of fiber throughout a paper sheet.	Good quality sheets have even fiber distribution. Poorer quality sheets have uneven fiber distribution. Uneven distribution results in uneven ink absorption, which means printing that's less crisp than it could be.
Smoothness	The tactile quality of the paper, sometimes referred to as "tooth."	The level of paper smoothness imparts character. It also impacts the way ink lies on the paper.

papermaking and printing processes are not exactly eco-friendly. Aside from promoting deforestation, the methods for making paper and subsequently printing on it are energy-intensive, water-intensive and use caustic chemicals like bleach and petroleum-based inks. Printed paper often ends up in landfills.

For years, the go-to solution for environmentally concerned designers was recycled paper. Unfortunately, recycled paper was not exactly high-end stuff. Designers chose it for its green message, not because it was a quality medium.

In recent years, the quality of recycled papers has improved. Designers no longer have to sacrifice quality when they choose to use recycled. Nor is recycled paper the only option. Papers made from other sustainable materials such as bamboo and hemp are on the market, as are soy-based inks.

Paper manufacturers are also stepping up to the plate to clean up their processes. Some have stopped harvesting trees from virgin forests. Others have switched to nonchlorine bleach and other less-harmful chemicals. Manufacturers are making efforts to reduce energy and water usage.

Is printing on paper still an environmentally dirty business? Yep. But you have options. Educate yourself. Look for printers and papers that have environmentally friendly certifications such as FSC (Forest Stewardship Council), SFI (Sustainable Forestry Initiative), Green Seal and others. Do some research. Ask your local printer. Don't be shy about making inquiries.

Keeping it within budget.

Paper and ink are typically the most expensive parts of producing a printed piece. So budget is often the single most important criterion in the print decision-making process. Available budget dictates whether your paper will be an economy or premium sheet. Budget also dictates whether you'll print the job in-house or hire a commercial printer. A larger budget allows for printing extras such as four-color printing, specialty-printing processes like holographic (3D) and stochastic printing (cool use of dots to replicate images) or even finishing touches such as perforating, die-cutting, foil stamping or embossing.

While you're drooling over the paper possibilities for your design, you also need to be thinking about the kind of printing process best suited to your design.

TYPES OF PRINTING & PRINTERS

The quality of your finished printed design is not the only criterion for choosing a printer. There is also budget to consider, not to mention deadlines, timing and turnaround. As Rebecca says: "Speed, quality, price. Pick any two."

Printing in-house.

When you need it fast, have little or no budget and need relatively small quantities, in-house printing might be fine. You can use whatever software you have available, and font issues are less likely to occur.

But there are significant drawbacks. You'll need to know what paper sizes your printer can accommodates (usually letter, or legal, and sometimes ledger) and design within these parameters.

Unless you own a printing device capable of printing to the edge of paper (and most people don't), your design cannot bleed. Most printers have a built-in margin of approximately ¼ inch on the top and sides and ½ inch on the bottom. Anything you put outside the live area too close to the paper's edge won't reproduce.

You also can expect limited paper options. You may be restricted to inkjet or laser printer paper depending on your specific printer.

Printing documents designed to fold, such as newsletters and brochures, is painful to do in-house. When you take such projects to a commercial printer, the printer's prepress team manages page impositioning, that is, re-positioning pages so they will print front to back in the proper order. When you print in-house, you have to do this yourself. And getting text to line up properly and space evenly around folds is no easy task. Plus, even if you do manage alignments, uh, how many of those things are now sitting on the conference room table waiting for a folding party?

As a final insult, when you print in-house, don't expect any consistency with color. You can't assume your onscreen color will match your printer's output.

Why won't my design print with a bleed? Most personal printers cannot print ink to the edge of the paper. If you are designing a piece to be printed in-house, build a border into the design. If you don't, you'll get one anyway, and you may be unhappy with the results.

If you plan to print in-house, you need to design accordingly from the start.

Quick printers.

Surprisingly, depending on the quality of the quick printer, you may find printing with a quick printer as limiting as trying to print in-house. Nevertheless, quick printers have more paper choices, can print bleeds and offer a few more binding and finishing options.

Offset printers offer the greatest flexibility. If your job is 500 pieces or more, commercial/offset printers can print and assemble almost anything you throw at them.

Commercial/offset.

Offset printers offer flexibility. If your job is 500 pieces or more, commercial/offset printers can print and assemble almost anything you throw at them. They can print on a wide variety of paper sizes and offer a full range of paper stock. They handle bleeds, impositioning, folding, collating, some types of binding and even address labeling.

Offset printers also offer services such as die cutting (perforations, cut-out windows, pocket folders), embossing and foil stamping, either in-house or through subcontractors.

You can expect commercial/offset printers to produce matched and process colors faithfully to swatches, such as PANTONE® solid coated or process coated chip sets. Remember, however, that the color of your design as seen on your desktop screen will not match print output unless your computer and monitor are calibrated to your printer's.

It is important to note that with offset printing, the greater the print run, the lower the printing cost per piece. All the expense in printing is in the first run, meaning the setup. The cost of additional copies is negligible. For example, an initial print run of 500 pieces for a full-color flyer might cost $1,000. To print 1,000 of the same flyer might cost only $1,050. That's double the quantity for another $50.

You save money per piece by printing the greatest number you can use.

Web offset.

Once upon a time in graphic design, "web" referred to a particular kind of offset printing press, not the World Wide Web. The time to use web offset printing services is when you need to print a very large run,

FOUR REALLY NEAT **PAPER TREATMENTS**

Ink is not the only thing printers can put on paper. There are a number of after-printing finishes and treatments you can apply to make your finished piece special. Here are four of the most common:

Foil stamping

Foil stamping involves applying a thin layer of shiny metallic foil to parts of your design. Foil comes in different shades from copper to silver to gold.

The effect is rich and becomes even richer when foil is applied with an emboss.

Embossing

To create an emboss, printers press a metal die into the paper to pop up a pattern on the surface of the paper. A raised pattern is called an "emboss" while a recessed pattern is called a "deboss." This technique can be paired with ink or foil stamping. If no ink or foil is used, the technique is called a "blind" emboss.

Varnishing

Varnish is a clear coat applied to parts of a layout (spot varnish) or to the whole page (flood varnish). Applied on press like ink, varnish provides a protective coat to the finished piece. Since it comes in glossy and dull finishes, it also can be used to create two-tone shiny and dull effects.

Die cutting

Die cutting is any paper cutting that is not strictly straight across trimming. Die cutting is used to create everything from rounded corners on business cards to the pockets on pocket folders. It also is used to create the perforations on tear-off cards.

10,000–20,000 pieces or more. Documents typically printed by web offset printers include newspapers, magazines, catalogs and books.

The biggest difference between standard offset and web offset printing is in the paper. Web offset utilizes extremely large rolls of paper as opposed to cut sheets used in traditional offset.

Digital printing.

Digital printing has gained in popularity in recent years. While offset printing uses traditional ink, digital printing uses toner and is closer to

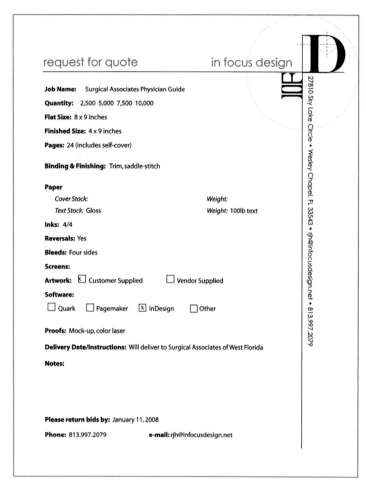

request for quote   in focus design

Job Name: Surgical Associates Physician Guide

Quantity: 2,500 5,000 7,500 10,000

Flat Size: 8 x 9 inches

Finished Size: 4 x 9 inches

Pages: 24 (includes self-cover)

Binding & Finishing: Trim, saddle-stitch

Paper

   Cover Stock: *Weight:*

   Text Stock: Gloss   *Weight:* 100lb text

Inks: 4/4

Reversals: Yes

Bleeds: Four sides

Screens:

Artwork: [X] Customer Supplied   [ ] Vendor Supplied

Software:

[ ] Quark   [ ] Pagemaker   [X] InDesign   [ ] Other

Proofs: Mock-up, color laser

Delivery Date/Instructions: Will deliver to Surgical Associates of West Florida

Notes:

Please return bids by: January 11, 2008

Phone: 813.997.2079   **e-mail:** rjh@infocusdesign.net

27810 Sky Lake Circle • Wesley Chapel, FL 33543 • rjh@infocusdesign.net • 813.997.2079

RFQ. Use a Request for Quote form to get accurate prices from your printer.

the processes of color laser printing or color photocopying.

The quality of digital printing has improved to the point where it approaches, and in some cases rivals, that of offset printing. Price-wise, for small print runs of fewer than 500 pieces, digital printing can be cost-effective. But, unlike offset printing, there is no price break for greater quantities. If 500 pieces cost $500, then printing 1,000 pieces will cost $1,000. Digital printing is best reserved for small press runs.

One compelling reason to use digital printing is its ability to output variable data printing (VDP). Think of VDP as a mail merge on steroids. Variable data printing allows a printer to take a database of names, images and other information specific to a recipient, and print customized pieces on the fly.

For example, say a pet store wants to send out a sale-promoting postcard to each of its customers. The pet store provides a database of customer names, addresses, pet names and breeds. The postcard is designed with placeholders for customer name, pet name and picture of the breed. During printing, specific customer information is fed into the appropriate placeholder. As each printed piece comes off the press, then, it has been tailored to one particular customer.

Whatever your grand vision for your design, to determine whether or not you have the budget to match it, get an estimate. Get several estimates.

GET A PRINTING ESTIMATE

Some organizations actually require estimates from a minimum of three different printers before awarding the job to one. Even so, most working designers have relationships with a variety of commercial printers and so can predict which printing outfits fit the bill for which

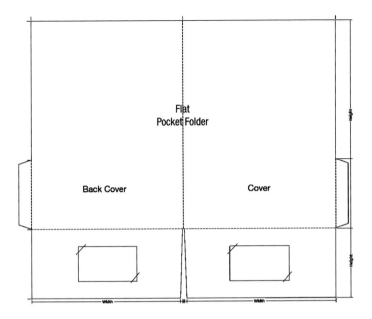

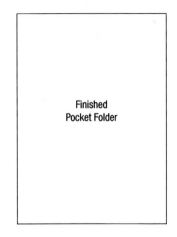

jobs, which have the most to least competitive pricing and which are accommodating and appreciative of your business. Newbie designers, however, really ought to get competitive estimates for comparison. Furthermore, as in all things, the cheapest estimate is not always the best choice.

To provide the best most accurate estimates, printers need details and particulars about the printing job. You need to gather some information:

» **Quantity.** How many pieces do you need to print? It's a good idea to include a range of quantities on your request for estimate—for example, 500, 1,000 and 1,500. You might even ask your printer where the price break starts on quantity, if any. Remember, while overall budget outlay is important to consider, you also need to consider price per piece.

» **Flat and finished sizes.** These are the dimensions of the document before assembly and the size of the finished document when fully assembled. For example, the flat dimensions of a tri-fold brochure might be 9 × 12 inches, and the finished size after folding might be 4 × 9 inches.

» **Number of pages.** With a brochure, specify number of panels. For larger documents like newsletters or annual reports, a page count is required. Because of the way printers print multiple-page documents, all printed pieces have page counts divisible by four. That requires a little forethought. If your cover design prints on the same paper stock as the inside pages of the design, then include

Flat vs. finished size. The size of a flat versus a finished print piece can differ significantly. Printers order paper based on the flat size so be sure to include this measurement in your RFQ.

COMMON PAPER **FOLDS**

Folding makes a larger sheet of paper easier to manage. This lets you pack a lot of information in a small portable package.

Here are some examples of common types of folds used for posters, brochures and other printed material. Since these are common, they tend to be fairly cost-effective when created in standard sizes.

If you really want to make an impact with a printed piece, consider an out-of-the-ordinary shape with an interesting fold. Be sure to consult with your printer first. For the most part, printers can print almost anything you come up with. However, they may have suggestions regarding paper, paper sizes and cost savings.

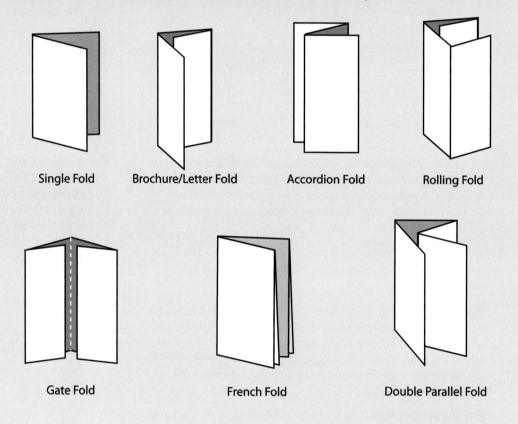

Single Fold   Brochure/Letter Fold   Accordion Fold   Rolling Fold

Gate Fold   French Fold   Double Parallel Fold

the front, back and two inside covers in your page count. If your covers print on different paper, you'll need a separate estimate for the cover, too.

» **Choice of paper and weight.** This can be very specific if you are choosing your paper from a swatch book, for example "Neenah Classic Columns 100lb cover, chili pepper red." Or it may be less specific, such as "100lb gloss text cool white." When you don't specify a paper by name, your printer may spec your job on a "house sheet" that meets your criteria. House sheets or house papers are those that the printer keeps in stock and tend to be serviceable if generic. House sheets save money if paper quality is not an issue for your project.

» **Number of inks.** The notation for indicating the number of inks looks like a fraction. The top number indicates the number of inks required on one side of the paper, and the bottom number indicates the number of inks required on the other side. A document that prints full-color front and back would be noted as 4/4—four-color process on both sides—and pronounced as "four over four." A two-color document would be indicated as 2/2 along with a notation on which inks to use. Your estimate request also should note wether the project requires any varnishes—coatings that add shine and/or protection. Varnishes may cover the entire paper surface (flood varnish) or just specific areas such as photographs (spot varnish).

» **Bleeds.** Does the design bleed to the edge of the paper? Yes or no, and on how many sides of the page?

» **Binding and finishing.** Beyond putting ink on the paper, make note of anything the printer must do to or with the paper in order to achieve your design. This includes folds, binding, die cutting (including slots for business cards, holders for media storage or promotional items, perforations for tear-offs and pocket-folder pockets), foil stamping, embossing, debossing, putting sheets into pads, etc.

COMMON **BINDING** TYPES

Binding style is determined by a variety of factors: budget, presentation quality, the need to update the document and the needs of the document's end user.

Here are some of the more common binding types.

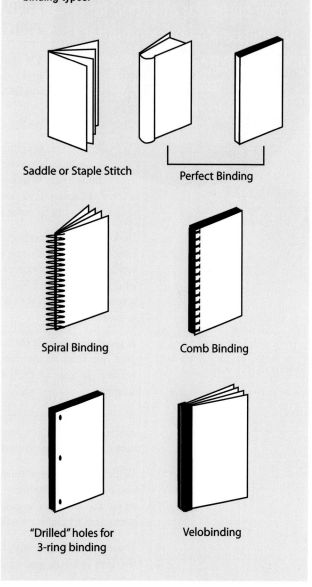

Saddle or Staple Stitch

Perfect Binding

Spiral Binding

Comb Binding

"Drilled" holes for 3-ring binding

Velobinding

» **Delivery date.** At any given time, a printer may have several jobs in production. To help your printer meet your schedule and the schedules of others, be specific about your due date.

» **Delivery instructions.** What happens to the completed job? Will it be delivered to you, the boss or the client? Are you sending it to a mail house for distribution? Do you need the job shipped to multiple locations? Make sure your printer knows what to do when the printing job is complete.

PREPARE YOUR DOCUMENT FOR PRINTING

Of course you want to do everything possible to make sure your project gets done right and on time and on budget. Here are some tips for getting there:

Give the document a thorough proofread.

Yes, someone does have to proofread. Additionally, pay particular attention to headlines, cutlines and other non-body type. When people proofread, they tend to focus on body copy and often skim over potential typos elsewhere. Nothing is worse than a big fat error in a big bold headline.

Beyond someone taking responsibility for typos, give your design a second (and third) look before it goes to press. Pay attention to typographic consistency. Do you accidentally change font styles, sizes or colors anywhere? Are there elements that don't line up, especially across facing pages? Are all images or visuals treated consistently, such as outlining?

A good way to look for design errors is to print a draft copy of each page, put it all on the floor and look at each page upside-down. When reading the copy doesn't distract you, potential design errors are easier to spot.

If your design includes binding, folding, die cutting or other specialized techniques, create a full-blown working mockup to make sure things line up properly and that your measurements are accurate.

With certain types of binding, especially perfect and spiral bindings, double-check the gutters. You don't want copy that folks need to read to fall too far into the gutter, be swallowed up by the binding or get perforated to make room for spiral or comb bindings.

Once you're happy with the shape of the document, make sure that the boss or client gets a final chance to approve the work before it goes to print.

> When proofreading, pay particular attention to headlines, cutlines and other non-body type. Nothing is worse than a big fat error in a big bold headline.

Other document details.

In addition to correcting any design typos, you'll need to check a few more things:

» **Image resolutions.** Make sure all your images are high resolution and in the proper format.

» **Spot or process?** Make sure your color setup is appropriate for your final output (change spot colors to process or process colors to spot depending on your needs).

» **Set up document bleeds.** If you're printing anywhere other than in-house, and your design bleeds to the edge of the paper, you'll need to go through your document and extend your bleeds 1/8 inch beyond the document edge. When printers print a document with a bleed, they print the design on a bigger piece of paper and trim it down to size. If your design doesn't extend the extra 1/8 inch, you risk ending up with white edges around your design where the bleed should have been.

» **Clean up your pasteboard.** Remove any extra/unused graphics and text boxes from your file's pasteboard. Nonessential materials cluttering up the document just add unnecessary file size. This can cause problems with commercial printing processes.

» **Clean up your swatch palettes.** For the same reason as above, remove unused colors from your list of available swatches, too.

Do your own flight check.

When you give your design files to your printer of choice, the first thing she or he does is a flight check, a quick test to make sure you've included all the parts necessary for printing. If the flight check turns up missing parts, you'll get a call. Tracking down missing parts and having to correct design errors at this stage costs time and money. So wouldn't it be smart to run your own flight check ahead of time?

Professional-grade page layout applications include flight check options. When you run them, they check for missing fonts, missing graphics and graphics in the wrong format or the wrong color space. The program dialog boxes typically allow you to correct any errors on the spot.

. . . .

WHAT TO TAKE TO THE **PRINTER**

To ensure your final print product matches your original vision, give the following items to your printer:

» A copy of your document in its native format

» A copy of each visual used in your layout

» A copy of each font used in your layout

» A hardcopy of your document, preferably mocked-up

» A note with your contact information

Alternatively, send your printer a press-quality PDF file. If you choose this option, ask for PDF specifications and create your file accordingly.

The final beauty of the flight check process is that it allows you to package your document to take to the printer. The packaging process creates a copy of your document, including all fonts and graphics.

WHAT TO GIVE THE PRINTER: A CHECKLIST

To print your project, any printer will require the following files:

- » **Your layout.** Include a complete copy of your design document in the software format in which you created it. And, yes, that would be professional-grade design software.

- » **All images used.** Include a copy of every visual or image in your design, at high resolution, saved at the size required for the design and in the proper file format (usually TIF or EPS).

- » **Fonts.** Include files for all fonts used in your design.

  (If you use the preflight package option in your professional-grade software, it will assemble the previous three items for you.)

- » **A hardcopy of your document.** If your document has unique folds, pockets or anything other than standard pages, provide an assembled mockup of the design as it should be in its final form. Your printer will use your mocked-up hardcopy to make sure everything shows up in the right places when she or he opens up your original files.

- » **Contact information.** Include a note with your name and contact information, a list of the contents of any and all files, and the name and edition/version of the software program(s) you used. Include your after-hours phone numbers in case the printer has an emergency with your print job.

If you're new to the design process, working with a new printer or have a complex design (more than a couple pages and a couple of pictures), meet with your print rep in person to deliver your files and hardcopy proof. This gives you both an opportunity to discuss the job and ask questions, such as confirming proper resolution of the files you will provide.

Alternatively, most commercial printers can accept files electronically, and, no, we do not mean via email. By the time you have more than one high-res image in a document, you've already exceeded the file size capacity of a lot of email programs.

If your combined folder of file, font and graphic is more than 5MB, you will need to use your printer's File Transfer Protocol (FTP) site to transfer files. FTP clients allow you electronically to transfer huge amounts of data not possible to send through email. FTP requires some software on your end and some access information. When you plug in the correct information (host location, username and password), you gain access to a Web server. You can copy files to and from that server.

If you choose to submit your files to the printer this way, we recommend two things. First, use some software to compress your folder. We've seen strange corruptions in files transferred without compression so better safe than sorry. We also recommend that you email a PDF of your completed document to your print rep separately from the file upload. This PDF serves as your proof in lieu of a hardcopy.

NOW WHAT?

Once your printer has your files, the next thing you can expect is a printer proof. This is just another hardcopy mockup that your printer produces using inks and paper closer to those you have specified. This is your last opportunity to make sure the document is in order before the whole project is printed.

Ask your printer ahead of time what kind of proof you can expect—and when. If color quality and consistency are important, ask for a color proof. If your project includes multiple pages, folds, die cuts or any other special features, ask for a paper dummy. A paper dummy is a full-size, fully functional mockup of the final product.

Your printer will require you (or the boss or client) to approve the proof before the project goes on the press. When you get your printer proof, pull a copy of your own most recent draft and compare the two. Systematically examine the following:

Printer proofs. Printer proofs come in many forms, including full color composites and paper dummies. Paper dummies are full-size fully functional mockups.

WHAT TYPE OF **PROOF** SHOULD YOU EXPECT?

Document Type	Proof to Expect
Letterhead, Business Card, Envelope	Composed Color Proof/Color Laser Proof
Poster	Composed Color Proof, Loose Color Proof (may be ½ actual size)
Pocket Folder	Paper Dummy, Composed Color Proof, Die Strike
Brochure	Composed Color Proof, Loose Color Proof, Paper Dummy with scoring sample—if needed
Newsletter	Paper Dummy, Loose Color Proof, Composed Color Proof
Annual Report	Paper Dummy, Loose Color Proof, Composed Color Proof
Postcard Mailer	Loose Color Proof

» **Text.** Make sure none is missing. Also look for rewrapped text.

» **Fonts.** Make sure there are no dropped fonts. Dropped fonts typically default to Courier, are ugly as sin and easy to spot.

» **Folios.** Look to see that every page is accounted for and in the correct order.

» **All photos and/or visuals.** Check for proper placement and cropping.

» **Margins.** Look at all margins, inner and outer, and all elements, including alignments, that cross over spreads.

» **Spot colors.** Check placement of spot colors as needed.

» **Specialty items.** Double check special design elements such as die cuts, perforations, folds and foil stamps.

» **Typos.** Proof one last time, paying particular attention to headlines and cutlines, as well as any chatter, etc., associated with infographics and figures/exhibits.

Right on the proof, circle any errors or things that need correcting. Your printer's rep will ask you to sign a form indicating one of the following:

» The job is ready to print.

» The job is ready to print with corrections indicated.

» A new proof is required.

You would be surprised how many previously overlooked errors miraculously appear when the printer proof shows up. Sadly, once the printer provides a proof, further edits will cost you. Printers charge for each "author alteration" you request. So do your best proofing and editing before you turn over the files for a printer's proof.

When to do a press check.

For extremely important print jobs where color matching and quality are essential, consider a press check.

A press check allows you to view the first sheets of your actual print run as they come off the press. It's an opportunity to check color and other details before the full run is completed. Be warned, if you want a press check, you'll be at the mercy of the printer's run schedule. Your job might be scheduled for the middle of the night, and neither you nor your boss or client can ask the printer to reschedule to accommodate your sleep.

If you decide your project is important enough for a press check, here's what you should be looking at:

» **Paper.** Confirm that the project is being printed on the correct paper, in the specified weight, finish and color.

» **Visuals and type.** Look closely at the flat sheets to make sure no elements are missing and that none of your typography is re-flowing itself incorrectly.

» **Registration.** Check the registration of multiple sheets. Registration marks printed on the corners and center points of

Matching spot colors.
Do a press check when a close color match is important to the final product. Be sure to bring a swatch book along for comparison.

Throughout Odyssey's history, our families and friends diligently stood beside us as we followed our dream. Without that unfailing support and encouragement, Odyssey would be nothing more than an unrealized aspiration.

You helped make our dream a reality.

Now we'd like you to help us celebrate an amazing company milestone – the grand opening of our first **Shipwreck & Treasure Adventure** in New Orleans. The culmination of years of hard work and strategic planning, the attraction delivers on our vision to share the excitement of shipwreck exploration with the public.

To recognize your contribution, we're hosting a "Friends & Family reception" in New Orleans on Friday evening, August 26, 2005. You'll have an opportunity to celebrate with us and explore the attraction before the Grand Opening. On Saturday morning, we'll start the day with a traditional New Orleans "second line" parade, followed by the official opening of the attraction and a reception to toast this special occasion.

Laissez Le Bon Temps Rouler!

R.S.V.P.

~John Morris & Greg Stemm

Other services. In addition to printing, commercial printers also may offer collating, labeling, mailing and other services.

Reproduced by permission of Odyssey Marine Exploration.

each sheet should line up. If you see that they don't align, ask your pressperson. Sometimes paper stretches a bit on the press, which can cause registration marks to misalign.

» **Color.** Look closely at the color on the sheets. Make sure your spot and process colors are printing properly—the printer should have a swatch book handy, but you may want to bring your own. Also make sure that the color is even across the whole sheet. You may have to fold the sheet to see a color comparison from front to back.

» **Varnishes and other finishes.** Check locations of varnishes and other coatings, if any. Also confirm the correct finish (gloss, matte) is being used.

» **Ink.** Using a loupe, take a good look at the actual dots of ink. They should be sharp. If not, there may be issues with the ink mixture. Ask your pressperson about this.

Look for and circle any visible defects on the sheet.

Once everything is working to your satisfaction, give the go-ahead to finish the press run. Be sure to thank everyone for the extra time and trouble.

The finished product.

Once the final print job arrives, check it one last time against your own proof to make sure everything is in order. If you find something on the final piece that wasn't on your original, ask the printer to check the printer proof. If the glitch occurred between the printer proof and the final output, you are justified in asking the printer to reprint your job on the printer's dime.

OTHER THINGS YOUR PRINTER CAN DO

Your print representative can be a fantastic resource for other things aside from just printing your work. Consulting with a printer while still in the planning stages of your project also can help you avoid design and printing pitfalls. Print reps can help you get samples of papers you are considering and even plain paper mockups of your print pieces so you can get a better sense of weight and other properties before you commit.

Once your print job is complete, your printer also may be able to help with distribution. Many printers have the ability to print mailing addresses directly to your pieces. They may be able to tab-seal folding pieces per postal requirements. Printers sometimes have in-house mailing services or relationships with mail houses if they do not offer those services themselves.

While you carefully are planning your design, dotting your I's and crossing your T's from design and paper choice through the press check, a good working relationship with the printer is worth its weight in gold.

TRY THIS

1. Locate several printed pieces. Complete a request for estimate form as the pieces' designers originally would have "spec'd" them. Or create a request for estimate based on one of your own designs.

2. Find the preflight and package functions for your design software. Practice using them with a design you've created. Try it on a single-page document and a multiple-page document. Compare the results.

3. Make your own full-color mockup of a multi-page design you've been working on. Some document types to try: a tri-fold brochure, a multi-page newsletter, a mini pocket folder, a restaurant menu, a table tent-card for a party or event. Or how about that banquet invitation to the city's movers and shakers—the one we talked about at the beginning of the chapter?

4. Visit a local quick printer or the website of a local quick printer. Get a list of available services. Does the company bind? fold? score? die cut? emboss? What papers are available? What other services are available?

5. Do some research on the greening of graphic design and printing. Then write and design an electronic newsletter alert on the topic.

6. Figure out a way to get an invitation to a press check.

7. Acquire several swatch books from a local paper distributor or paper manufacturer. Using the swatch books, see if you can find the answers to the following questions.

   a. What are the available colors and weights?

   b. Is this an economy sheet, a premium sheet or something in between?

   c. What is the paper's brightness?

   d. What finishes does the paper come in?

   e. Is the paper laser-printer compatible? Does it have recycled content?

   f. Does it come with matching envelopes? If so, in what sizes?

Then invite your paper distributor representative to come and chat with you about paper lines.

Photo © Moreno Soppelsa - Fotolia.com

CHAPTER
FIFTEEN

CONCLUSION

NOW THAT YOU KNOW
ENOUGH TO BE DANGEROUS,
THANKS FOR STOPPING BY

If you're starting to annoy coworkers, friends and family with your constant design critiques, then congratulations. You've learned to recognize bad—and good—design when you see it. Our work here is done. Before you unleash the full force of your new powers to set the universe right, allow us to leave you with some final and somewhat contradictory thoughts.

EVERYTHING IS CHANGING

We don't need to tell you the media business is in flux. That's old news. As the cliché goes, change is the only thing that doesn't change, especially in communications where we're all technophiles.

While industry turmoil may be inspiring innovation in visual styles and trends, the grammar of visual communication hasn't changed.

The new news is the contemporary assumption that everyone is a fluent multi-platform visual communication designer. And everyone means everyone. Sometimes the amateurs and the audiences are better visual communicators than the pros. Meanwhile, the media bosses operate as if anyone who wants to work in the business can produce effective visual communication across any platform. "Anyone" covers the self-described wordsmiths, too, such as journalists, copyeditors and copywriters.

This reality requires you, whatever your specialty, to develop the good eye that goes beyond memorizing layout rules. You also need to know why those conventions work—or don't work—and that means knowing something about art, design and formal composition. Otherwise, you show up for work with an embarrassingly poor visual aesthetic.

THERE'S NOTHING NEW UNDER THE SUN

Even as everything about the media professions from business models to technology is changing, when it comes to graphic design, there really is nothing new under the sun.

Advertising and marketing communication folks produce public relations materials. Public relations practitioners produce advertising, marketing and news materials. The news industry borrows visual conventions from the entertainment industry, which adopts innovation from the advertising industry. And vice versa and so on.

We're all visual communicators using and abusing the same rules of graphic design and layout. While industry turmoil may be inspiring innovation in visual styles and trends, the grammar of visual communication hasn't changed. Regardless of the platform or the format, the fundamentals don't change. Good design is good design. Form follows function. Use visuals and type to capture attention, control eye flow, convey information and evoke emotion. White space is not your enemy.

SOMETIMES YOU JUST NEED TO HIRE A PROFESSIONAL

If nothing else, you now have enough knowledge to work alongside visual experts without drawing their scorn.

Knowing enough to know the good stuff when you see it also means knowing your own limitations. Sometimes you do just need to hire a professional. Appreciate the talent, skill and experience of the full-timers—artists, designers, art directors, illustrators, photographers, videographers, cinematographers, Web designers and developers, etc.

WORDS OF ENCOURAGEMENT

If our little book is your first foray into visual communication and design, there is way more to learn if you're interested. If you think graphic design might be your future, get busy. Take a class. Find some online tutorials. Read, read, read. Glom onto a mentor. If, for you, some knowledge is plenty, we salute you for reading along with us this far.

Regardless, we hope you enjoy your new know-how. Try to avoid becoming an overzealous visual snob alienating colleagues and loved ones. Don't be afraid to break the rules with a purpose. Strive always to delight your audiences. Treat professional creatives with respect. Don't forget to have some fun.

Finally, as we say to our neighbors, thanks for stopping by.

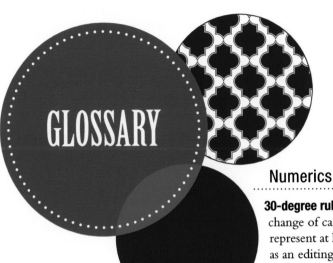

GLOSSARY

Numerics

30-degree rule: In film and video, this rule says any change of camera angle relative to the focal point should represent at least 30 degrees of change. Anything less reads as an editing error.

180-degree rule: In film and video, to avoid disorienting viewers, the 180-degree rule cautions against crossing the imaginary line of action intersecting two characters, unless there is a narrative purpose for doing so.

A

Alley: An alley is the negative space between columns, modules or units on a grid.

Alpha channel: Alpha channel, or "A," controls color transparency in the RGBA Web color system. (See also RGB.)

Analogous color: Analogous colors sit next to each other on the color wheel and work well together in color palettes because they contain some of the colors sitting next to them.

ANNCR: The abbreviation for announcer is ANNCR.

App (application): Apps, short for "(software) applications," are programs designed to run on a computer, tablet, smartphone, website or social media. Since the introduction of smartphones and tablets, apps have become increasingly popular and accessible. Common types include calendars, mileage trackers, restaurant finders and games.

Ascenders: Ascenders are the tall parts of font glyphs that ascend above lowercase x-height, as in the lowercase letterforms b, d, f, h, k, l, t.

Aspect ratio: Aspect ratio refers to the ratio of width to height for electronic screens.

Assets, site: Site assets include all the items and materials used to populate a website, including copy, logos, photos, video, audio, external Web links and code snippets from other online sources.

Asymmetrical balance: With its visual fulcrum or center of visual gravity moved off-center, asymmetrical balance is visually balanced but not symmetrical.

B

B roll: B roll is file, extra or archival footage used as visual fill or for creating transitions between clips.

Backlight: A backlight is a light source used to highlight the focal point from behind in order to give it contrast and dimension.

Baseline: This sentence sits on the baseline, the line guiding the horizontal alignment of type at the bottoms of words.

Beauty shot: In camera work, a beauty shot frames the focal point, whether person or object, to show off its best visual features.

Beta site: A beta site is a working test version of a website that isn't available to the public.

Bleed: Bleed refers to content that runs beyond the specified live area or safe area into the margins and off the edge of the page or screen.

Breadcrumb trail: As in fairytales about children lost in the forest, a breadcrumb trail in Web design is a system for keeping users apprised of their location in cyberspace.

Brief, creative or design: The document that briefs the creative team on the project, the creative or design brief answers basic job order and research questions about the project.

Built color: Built color uses the CMYK 4-color or full-color printing process to build any color.

Burning & dodging: Burning and dodging refer to techniques that darken or lighten photographs, respectively. Traditionally achieved by increasing/decreasing exposure to prints in the darkroom, these techniques mostly now are accomplished digitally.

Byline: The byline is the name of the writer, artist or photographer given credit.

C

Callout: Also called labels, callouts "call out" or call attention to details of infographics.

Cap line: The invisible horizontal line against which the tops of capitalized glyphs align in a particular font.

Cascading Style Sheet (CSS): Although Web pages are built with programming languages such as HTML, the appearance of Web pages is dictated by Cascading Style Sheets or CSS.

Chatter: The brief typeset explanatory copy on an infographic is called chatter.

Close-up: In framing video and film shots, a close-up frames the focal point as a detail shot. Variations on the close-up include extreme, medium, full and wide close-up shots, as well as close and medium close shots. These frames move from an extreme close-up framing only an actor's eyes to a medium close shot that frames an actor from the waist up.

Closure: The Gestalt law of closure predicts the way people mentally fill in gaps to complete a perceived shape.

CMYK: CMYK is the 4-color or full-color printing process of building any color with just four inks: cyan, magenta, yellow and black.

Color management: Color management is the formal term for getting your color to match properly across devices, from scanners to digital cameras to computer screens to printers.

Color separation: In commercial printing, each ink color has to be separated out of the design into its own printing plate.

Comp or complimentary image: A comp image, short for complimentary image, is a low-resolution stock image, usually with a watermark, available to sample in a layout before purchasing.

Comp or comprehensive: A comp, short for comprehensive, is a mockup of the final design and is used for getting approvals before spending time and money on final production.

Compass: The compass establishes direction on a map.

Complementary color: Color complements sit opposite each other on the color wheel.

Concept: The concept is the big idea uniting and driving the design's message.

Condensed font: Condensed fonts are drawn to be narrower (condensed) to take up less space than standard fonts.

Content management system (CMS): A content management system or CMS is a Web-based application that manages page content and generates pages on the fly from information stored in a database. CMSs allow people with no knowledge of coding to build visually consistent websites.

Continuity: The Gestalt law of continuity predicts the way the eye will follow the direction of a line.

Crawl: A crawl refers to superimposed moving type crawling across an electronic screen such as TV.

Creative or design brief: The document that briefs the creative team on the project, the creative or design brief answers basic job order and research questions about the project.

Crop: To crop is to trim excess from visuals such as photography.

CSS: Although Web pages are built with programming languages such as HTML, the appearance of Web pages is dictated by Cascading Style Sheets or CSS.

Curly quotes: Curly quotes or smart quotes are the correct punctuation marks for quotations. Curly quotes are curly, as opposed to prime marks, which are straight. Prime marks indicate feet and inches, not quotations. See also smart quotes and prime marks.

Cut: In film and video, part of continuity is transitioning or segueing between shots and scenes. The most common type of transition is the simple "cut" from one shot to the next.

Cutaway: In film and video, "cutting away" from the main action by inserting something else going on in the scene is called a cutaway.

Cut-in or insert: In film and video, "cutting in" or "inserting" a close-up shot of something significant in the scene is called a cut-in or insert.

Cutline: In news contexts, captions for photos and visuals are called cutlines.

D

Decorative fonts: Decorative fonts have no common feature other than they are mostly novelty fonts best used for "decorative" purposes.

Depth of field: In camera work, depth of field refers to what in the shot remains in focus, whether foreground, midground, background or some combination.

Descenders: Descenders are characters or glyphs with tails that descend below the baseline, such as the lowercase letterforms g, j, p, q, y.

Design or creative brief: The document that briefs the creative team on the project, the creative or design brief answers basic job order and research questions about the project.

Detail shot: In camera work, a detail shot is a close-up shot revealing detail about the focal point.

Dingbats: Forms of type that can be styled like type, dingbats are the ornamental characters in a font, or they may comprise an entire font of nothing but picture glyphs.

Display fonts: Drawn specifically to appear proportionate at larger point sizes, display fonts work well in headlines and signs.

Dissolve: In video and film transitions, the dissolve simply dissolves the frame before cutting to the next one.

Dodging & burning: Dodging and burning refer to techniques that lighten or darken photographs, respectively. Traditionally achieved by decreasing/increasing exposure to prints in the darkroom, these techniques now mostly are accomplished digitally.

Dolly shot: In a dolly shot, the camera is positioned on a dolly that moves or pushes toward the focal point.

Dummy: In print news, a dummy is the set of thumbnail sketches that lay out or paginate what goes on every page of the issue, including ads and stories with visuals.

E

Em dash: Historically the width of a lowercase m, the em dash adds emphasis by replacing punctuation such as commas, colons and parentheses.

En dash: Historically the width of a lowercase n, the en dash is the correct glyph for replacing the "to" with punctuation in expressions such as "2–4 weeks."

EPS: EPS (Encapsulated Postscript) is used for some specific kinds of images. Vector graphics, usually illustrations, are saved in EPS format, as are some photographs that have certain styling applied. EPS format is typically used for logos and, like GIF, supports transparency.

Establishing shot: In camera work, an establishing shot is a full or wide angle shot designed to orient viewers to the overall scene.

F

Fade: In video and film transitions, a fade simply fades the visual frame before cutting to the next one.

File Transfer Protocol: File Transfer Protocol or FTP enables you to upload and share very large files on the Web.

Fill light: Fill light supplements the key light by filling in unwanted shadows for less contrast.

Flexible or fluid Web design: To avoid layouts, thus designs, that "break" across different types, sizes and aspect ratios of screens and browsers, designers build flexibility and fluidity into their designs' CSS by specifying sizes as percentages (100 percent) rather than fixed heights and widths in pixels.

Focal point: Sometimes called the principle of emphasis, the focal point is the visual center of attention in the design or layout because it focuses the eye's attention.

Folio: Usually appearing in the margins of serials and periodicals such as newspapers, magazines and newsletters, the folio identifies the publication, issue and date, as well as page number if hardcopy.

Font: A font is a complete set of characters in a particular size and style of type.

Font family: A font family or typeface contains a series of related fonts, such as Times New Roman, Times Bold and Times Italic.

Foot space or footer: The bottom margin is the foot space or footer.

Four-color process: CMYK is the 4-color or full-color printing process of building any color with just four inks: cyan, magenta, yellow and black.

FTP: FTP or File Transfer Protocol enables you to upload and share very large files on the Web.

Full-color process: CMYK is the 4-color or full-color printing process of building any color with just four inks: cyan, magenta, yellow and black.

Full shot: In framing video and film shots, a full shot reveals an actor head-to-foot. A medium full shot frames the actor from the knees up.

FX: FX is shorthand for special "effects."

G

Gain: Gain is when paper absorbs more ink than expected resulting in muddy type or visuals.

Gestalt theory: In the early 20th century, a group of German psychologists studied the way the human brain interprets and organizes what the eyes see. The results of this research became the Gestalt laws. See: closure, continuity, proximity, similarity.

GIF (vs. JPG): GIF (Graphic Interchange Format) and JPG (Joint Photographic Experts Group) are file formats for saving images destined for the Web or computer screens. Both are low-resolution image formats. A big difference between them is a GIF will support transparency and a JPG will not. Transparency by definition means see-through. In the case of Web graphics, transparency is essentially the ability to make certain color groups invisible. If you've ever tried to put a logo in JPG format on top of a colored background and discovered that your logo has a white box around it, you've encountered lack of transparency. By creating your Web graphic in the correct software application and saving it as a GIF image, you can eliminate the white box.

Glyph: A glyph is an individual character of a font, whether a letter, numeral, punctuation mark, dingbat or special symbol. Most fonts have 265 glyphs. OpenType fonts have up to 65,000 glyphs.

Golden proportion: The golden proportion, sometimes called the golden ratio or divine proportion, refers to a ratio—1:1.618—that results in a universally appealing aesthetic when applied to shapes such as rectangles.

Graphical user interface or GUI: Web, tablet and smartphone users don't interact with computer code; they interact with graphics, such as buttons and tabs, known as graphical user interfaces or GUI. User-friendly "gooey" designs require savvy interface designers.

Graphics package: In the newsroom, a graphics package reports a story by using multiple types of graphics together.

Grayscale: A graduated range of tones from black to gray to white is called grayscale.

Greek text: Greek text or greeking is dummy copy or type used as a temporary substitute for the actual copy or type.

Grid: A grid is a series of horizontal and vertical lines composing the skeletal template of a design.

Grid module or grid unit: Instead of columns, a grid structure may include squares or rectangles called modules or units.

GUI or graphical user interface: Web, tablet and smartphone users don't interact with computer code; they interact with graphics, such as buttons and tabs, known as graphical user interfaces or GUI. User-friendly "gooey" designs require savvy interface designers.

Gutter: A gutter is the oversized margin between two facing pages. The gutter is designed to accommodate the fold or binding. Some design software applications refer to alleys between grid columns as gutters, too.

H

Hairline rule: A hairline rule is a very thin rule or border—as thin as a strand of hair.

Hairline strokes: The thin lines in characters or glyphs are hairline strokes. The thick lines are stem strokes.

Handheld: Handheld refers to the cameraperson holding the camera as she or he moves through the scene shooting video or film.

Hanging indent: Hanging indents refer to indicators that hang out to the left in the margin, instead of indenting to the right into the paragraph or text. Hanging indents are required for bulleted and numbered lists, as well as for quotation marks on pull quotes.

Hard light or low key: Hard light or low key emphasizes shadows, thus contrast, including shadows on people's faces.

Headspace or header: The top margin is the headspace or header.

Hexadecimal code: A Web-based color specification system, hexadecimal color uses sets of numbers and letters to designate RGB light formulae.

High key or soft light: High key or soft light evens out the shadows to decrease harsh contrasts. It makes people and products look more attractive.

High pixel density: This refers to the technology that allows tiny screens to display densely packed pixels at very small sizes for realistic effect.

Horizon line: The line separating land and sky is the horizon line, which communicates a sense of distance or perspective.

Horsey: Not a compliment in design, horsey means awkwardly large and lacking grace.

HTML: HTML stands for Hypertext Markup Language, the basic code that makes up most Web pages.

Hue: In color, hue answers the "what color?" question.

Hypertext Markup Language: Hypertext Markup Language or HTML is the basic code that makes up most Web pages.

I

Impositioning: Impositioning is the prepress process of getting multiple pages that are designed to print front and back to align properly for correct printing and binding or folding.

Infographic: An infographic delivers information graphically, such as in graphs, charts, maps, figures and diagrams.

Insert or cut-in: In film and video, "cutting in" or "inserting" a close-up shot of something significant in the scene is called a cut-in or insert.

Inset, map: On a map, an inset enlarges a section of the map to reveal more detail.

Inset & offset: Inset refers to the content of a box sitting in away from the box's edges, rule, border or frame. Offset refers to items outside the box sitting off away from the box's edges.

J

JPG (vs. GIF): JPG (Joint Photographic Experts Group) and GIF (Graphic Interchange Format) are file formats for saving images destined for the Web and electronic screens. Both are low-resolution image formats. A big difference between them is that a GIF will support transparency and a JPG will not. Transparency by definition means see-through. In the case of Web graphics, transparency is essentially the ability to make certain color groups invisible. If you've ever tried to put a logo in JPG format on top of a colored background and discovered that your logo has a white box around it, you've encountered lack of transparency. By creating your Web graphic in the correct software application and saving it as a GIF image, you can eliminate the white box.

K

Kerning: Kerning refers to the negative space between two characters or glyphs.

Key: On infographics, such as maps, the key identifies and defines symbols and other reference markers or icons used.

Key light: A key light is the main or key light source in the shot, whether natural or artificial.

L

Lead: The first paragraph of the body copy is called the lead.

Leading: Leading refers to the negative space between lines of type.

Leg: A leg is a column of typeset copy.

Lift-out: Also called a pull quote, a lift-out is a pithy quotation pulled from the body copy and then enlarged and embellished to become both a visual and a teaser.

Ligature: Ligatures are specially designed letter pairs—a single glyph meant to take the place of two traditional letters that may look awkward if typeset side-by-side, such as "fi."

Live area: Live area refers to the area of the page within which material should print safely. Anything outside of the live area may be cropped off. For the video equivalent, see safe area.

Long shot: In framing video and film shots, long shots and extreme long shots get long angles on the scene.

Loop: In video and animation, a loop endlessly repeats by circling the ending back to the beginning to start all over again.

Low key or hard light: Low key or hard light emphasizes shadows, thus contrast, including shadows on people's faces.

M

Matched color: Matched color is a premixed spot color of ink matched to a color swatch.

Mean line: The invisible horizontal line against which the x-height of lowercase glyphs align in a particular font.

Medium shot: In framing video and film shots, a medium shot frames the actor from the hips up. A medium full shot frames the actor from the knees up, and a medium close shot frames the actor from the belt up.

Mobile first: The concept of designing websites for mobile devices first instead of last, mobile first was introduced by Luke Wroblewski in 2011. See also, progressive enhancement.

Modern fonts: Modern fonts have extremely thin serifs, and their stress lies on the vertical, unlike old style's diagonal stress. Choose modern fonts carefully for long copy situations, and avoid them for screen applications.

Modular page design: In modular page design, each story is arranged into a rectangle, and the rectangles are arranged or to rectangular units of the grid of the page. Modular design is popular with print and Web news design.

Montage: The video/film version of the collage, a montage cuts together many images.

Motion Pictures Expert Group or MPEG-4 or MP4: Motion Pictures Expert Group (MPEG-4) is a popular video file format for the Web that works well across platforms and is supported by most Web browsers.

Mousetype: Mousetype means very small type often used in the tags of advertising.

Mug shot: A mug shot is a photographic close-up or headshot, usually of a person.

Music bed or track: A music bed or track is a background soundtrack over which the main video and/or audio are laid.

N

Navigation: In Web design, navigation refers to the system that allows users to move through and among Web pages, including hypertext links and buttons, etc.

Negative or white space: Negative or white space is the empty space in which design is created and by which any design achieves pleasing balance and composition. Negative or white space has visual weight. "White space is not your enemy."

O

Offset & inset: Offset refers to items outside of a box sitting off away from the box's edges. Inset refers to the content of the box sitting in away from the box's edges, rule, border or frame.

Old style figures: Old style figures treat numerals as old style glyphs with ascenders and descenders.

Old style fonts: Old style fonts have serifs, thick stem strokes, thin hairline strokes and a diagonal stress on o-shaped characters. Old style fonts have good readability.

OpenType®: Designed to be functional across both Mac and PC platforms, OpenType fonts may have as many as 65,000 characters each, including ligatures, swash alternates and old style figures.

Optical fonts: Some extended typefaces include optical fonts drawn for viewing at smaller or larger sizes. Caption fonts, for example, include spacing for viewing at smaller font sizes while display fonts would include detail enhancements for viewing at larger sizes.

Optimization: Optimization refers to balancing the resolution, thus appearance, of graphics with their generally large file sizes so that they load quickly but still look good.

Orphan: A typographic orphan refers to a few lonely words stranded at the top of a leg of type.

Over lighting: A key light shining directly from above is over lighting.

P

Pan: A pan or panning indicates a stationary camera that sweeps across the scene. The effect is that of turning your head to look around.

Perspective: In visual arts, such as painting, photography and film, perspective refers to the sense of distance in the scene, whether achieved by where the horizon line sits in the composition, the use of a linear vanishing point, the relative size of objects in the scene or atmospheric use of light and dark values that seem to recede or move forward, respectively.

Pixel density: This refers to the number of pixels a viewport is able to display. See also, high pixel density.

Plug-in: A plug-in is code that gives a browser or website additonal functionality, For example, when a website automatically displays the most recent posts from a separate blog, a plug-in is at work.

PNG (portable network graphics): PNG is a file format for Web-destined graphics that must accommodate gradients and transparency, such as in drop shadows.

Pointer box: On a map or diagram, a pointer box literally is a box that points to some detail while offering additional information inside the box.

POV: POV is the abbreviation for point of view referring to the perspective of the camera lens, thus the audience.

Primary colors: The primary colors on the traditional color wheel are red, blue and yellow, which when variously combined produce every other color on the color wheel. Differing from the traditional color wheel, the RGB color wheel has different primary colors: red, green, blue.

Prime marks: Prime marks are the correct straight glyphs used to indicate feet and inches, as opposed to curly or smart quote glyphs used to punctuate quotations. See also curly quotes and smart quotes.

Progressive enhancement: Part of the mobile first school of thought in website design, progressive enhancement is the process of coding in website features and design elements that become available as the site is viewed on larger screens with more capable browsers. See also, mobile first.

Prototyping: In Web design, prototyping software is used in the planning process. It allows the designer to create a functional mockup of a whole website or parts of a website. Prototypes demonstrate a site's interactive components to a client.

Proximity: The Gestalt law of proximity predicts that the eye will perceive items physically grouped together as belonging to the same group.

Pull-down menu: In electronic environments such as Web pages, a pull-down menu provides a form of navigation that remains hidden unless a user accesses it with the cursor/mouse.

Pull quote: Also called a lift-out quote, a pull quote is a pithy quotation pulled from the body copy and then enlarged and embellished to become both a visual and a teaser.

Push: In video and film, push shots push into the scene. In a zoom, a stationary camera pushes into the scene by using the lens to zoom in on the focal point. In a dolly shot, the camera itself, positioned on a dolly, moves or pushes toward the focal point.

R

Rack-focus: In film and video, a rack-focus uses a stationary camera to shift a scene's focal point simply by refocusing from one object to another.

Radial balance: Radial balance refers to circular designs in which the fulcrum lies at the center.

Reference points: On a map, reference points are landmarks, either natural or built, that orient the viewer.

Registration: Registration refers to aligning material across color plates in commercial printing.

Rendered type: Rendered type is a character, a word or a string of words filled with an image or otherwise transformed using photo-editing software.

Resolution: Image resolution refers to the detail or crispness of an image and is measured in units per inch. Ink on paper requires images in specific *dots per inch (dpi)*. High-end printing requires 300 dpi, and newsprint requires 200 dpi. For screens, graphics are measured in *pixels per inch (ppi)*. Web graphics are prepared at 72 dpi.

Responsive Web design: Responsive websites are coded to resize and rearrange their layouts to fit the size of the current viewport.

Reversing: A reverse literally reverses figure color with fill/field/background color. Reversed type refers to light type on a dark background, such as white type on a black field.

RGB: Standing for red, green and blue, RGB is the color wheel system for achieving color in electronic and digital screen environments by mixing red, green and blue light.

RGBA: The next generation of Web color specification, RGBA adds "A" to "RGB." "A" stands for alpha channel, which controls color transparency in the RGBA Web color system.

Rights-managed image: For a rights-managed image, you pay more to make sure other folks in your market don't use the same image, too. For a cheaper alternative, see royalty-free image.

Rough: A rough is a rough layout only slightly more detailed than a thumbnail sketch.

Royalty-free image: Royalty-free images are inexpensive stock images with no guarantees your competitor won't use them, too. For guarantees, see rights-managed image.

Rule: A rule is a graphic line, such as a border or a frame.

Rule of thirds: The rule of thirds says that dividing a layout or composition into thirds makes for a more interesting visual composition. The rule of thirds suggests that the four gridline intersections on a 3 × 3 grid offer the best locations to position a focal point in an asymmetrical layout.

S

Safe area: Safe area refers to the area of the screen within which material is visible. In video, title safe area refers to the area onscreen within which text and graphics will safely appear without cropping of content. Action safe area is a slightly larger area onscreen within which action appears without cropping of content.

Sans serif fonts: Sans serif (French for "without serif") fonts have no serifs, and their strokes have uniform thickness. They are the most readable fonts for screen applications.

Saturation: Saturation refers to the amount or intensity of a hue.

Scale: Scale refers to relative size and proportion.

Scale, map: The scale on a map establishes the reduced proportions of distance, i.e., an inch equals a mile, etc.

Script fonts: Script fonts resemble cursive handwriting. They can be quite elegant in decorative situations, but they are not a good choice for readability.

Search engine optimization (SEO): Search engine optimization or SEO refers to making your website search-engine friendly to rank well in user Web searches.

Secondary colors: Mixing any two primary colors produces the secondary complement of the third primary color.

SEO, or search engine optimization: SEO or search engine optimization refers to making your website search-engine friendly to rank well in user Web searches.

Serif: Serifs are those little feet or flags at the tips of glyphs.

SFX: SFX is shorthand for "sound effects."

Sidebar: Simply a separate block of type with a solid background, a stroked outline or an ample border of negative space, a sidebar provides content related to its adjacent copy.

Side lighting: Side lighting casts long shadows and increases the sense of three-dimensional space, as opposed to the flattening effect of soft light.

Similarity: The Gestalt law of similarity predicts that people will group items with similar properties such as shape, size or color.

Site asset: Site assets include all the items and materials used to populate a website, including copy, logos, photos, video, audio, external Web links and code snippets from other online sources.

Site map: In Web design, a site map literally maps out the site to show the links between and flow among pages in the form of something that resembles either a family tree or a flowchart.

Slab serif fonts: Slab serif fonts are similar to old style fonts, but the serifs on slab serif fonts start thick and stay thick. Invented for display advertising, slab serif fonts are excellent for headlines and signage.

Small caps: Small caps capitalize the entire word, although the initial cap is slightly larger than the rest of the letters, which are slightly smaller than a regular capitalized glyph.

Smart quotes: Smart quotes are the correct "curly" punctuation marks for quotations. See also curly quotes and prime marks.

Soft light or high key: Soft light or high key evens out the shadows to decrease harsh contrasts. It makes people and products look more attractive.

Source line: The source line identifies the origin or source of data. In an infographic, the source line usually appears on the lower left under the infographic.

Split screen: A split screen divides the screen into two different images.

Spot color in design: Not to be confused with spot color ink in printing, spot color in design refers to designing with a few well-chosen spots or splashes of color to highlight items such as a focal point or to draw the eye around the layout.

Spot color printing: Instead of building color using the 4-color CMYK printing process, spot color printing uses premixed ink colors chosen from a swatch book. See also matched color.

Spread: Two facing pages part of the same design are called a spread, such as one magazine story spreading across the gutter in two facing pages or a two-page advertisement spanning the gutter.

Steadicam: A steadicam is a kind of harness the cameraperson wears to hold the camera steady as she or he shoots hand-held video or film.

Stem strokes: The thick lines in characters or glyphs are stem strokes. The thin lines are hairline strokes.

Storyboard: A storyboard lays out the moving-picture or animated stories of planned film, video and electronic media in the form of scenes or shots arranged on a grid.

Stroked type: Stroked type or stroking is when the type characters or glyphs are outlined.

Super: A super is any on-screen type or graphic superimposed over another image.

SVG (scalable vector graphics): Scalable vector graphics are a file format for the Web. They are an excellent format for charts and graphs.

Swash alternates: Swash alternates are decorative alternatives to traditional italic letterforms.

Symmetrical balance: With symmetrical balance, if you bisect the design, each side will be a mirror image of the other in terms of visual weight.

T

Tags: Tags refer to all the information typically found at the bottom of an advertisement, such as the logo, themeline or slogan, URL, physical address and map, phone number and sometimes, unfortunately, disclaimer and legalese.

Tertiary colors: Tertiary colors result from combining a primary and a secondary color.

Thumbnail sketch: Thumbnail sketches or thumbnails are tiny thumbnail-sized layout sketches that you can draw—and reject—quickly.

Thumb space: Sometimes margins are called thumb space because, if you were holding a hardcopy, margins leave enough negative space at the edges of the layout to accommodate your thumb without covering any visual material.

TIF: Choose TIF (Tagged Image Format) file formats to save images for print or video purposes (as opposed to GIF or JPG for Web purposes). TIF images are larger in file size, but the TIF format does not lose data.

Tilt: In film and video, a tilt shot is a vertical up-and-down pan of the camera. See also, pan.

Track or music bed: A track or music bed is the background soundtrack over which the main video and/or audio are laid.

Tracking shot: In a tracking shot for film or video, a stationary camera tracks along with a moving focal point.

Tracking, type: Tracking refers to the negative space across a string of characters, such as a word, sentence or paragraph.

Transitional fonts: Transitional fonts evolved from old style fonts and have serifs, thick stem strokes and thin hairline strokes. But transitional fonts may have a less pronounced diagonal stress or no diagonal stress at all. Transitional fonts have good readability.

Trapped space: A puddle of landlocked negative space with no apparent layout function in the design is called trapped space.

Triads, color: Color triads are colors on the 12-point color wheel that form any triangle 4 hours apart. Triads make pleasing color palettes.

Trim size: In commercial printing, trim size refers to the finished size of the page after the printer has trimmed away the excess paper.

Truck: In video and film, a truck refers to the camera trucking sideways across the scene. This is usually accomplished with a camera on a dolly. The effect is like rubbernecking from a moving car.

Tweened animation: In tweened animation, the artist illustrates only key changes in motion or shape. Then the software application automatically generates animation to fill "between" the artist's illustrated frames.

Typeface: A typeface or font family contains a series of related fonts, such as Times New Roman, Times Bold and Times Italic.

U

Under lighting: A key light shining directly from below.

V

Value: Value refers to the lightness or darkness of a hue.

Vanishing point: In linear perspective, the vanishing point is where two lines converge in the distance.

Vector image: Vector images use geometry and math to produce and preserve the proportions and quality of line-art illustrations as digital files. They can be scaled up or down infinitely without loss of image quality.

Visual hierarchy: As a tactic for visually communicating a hierarchy of visual items in terms of visual importance, visual hierarchy conventions include making important information large and putting it at the top of the composition. In multiple screen and page designs, as well as in designs with multiple items on the same screen or page, it's important to establish a hierarchy of fonts and point sizes, in addition to placing important items at the top of the screen or page.

VO, voiceover: A VO or voiceover is a disembodied voice speaking over video or audio.

W

Web safe palette: The idea of the Web safe color palette was to provide designers a way of getting consistent color. As a project, the Web safe palette mostly has failed because of constant advances in hardware and monitors, not to mention the garish color choices of the palette.

What you see is what you get: "What you see is what you get" or WYSIWYG is a type of Web page design software that doesn't require users to know how to write code.

White or negative space: White or negative space is the empty space in which design is created and by which any design achieves pleasing balance and composition. White or negative space has visual weight. "White space is not your enemy."

Widget: Widgets are the visible user-friendly expression of the existence of a plug-in. Not all plug-ins have widgets, but all widgets require plug-ins as their invisible engines.

Widow: A typographic widow refers to a few lonely words stranded at the bottom of a leg of type. A hyphenated word ending the last line of a leg counts as a widow, too.

Wipe: In video and film, a wipe transitions between screens with the effect of wiping the picture from the screen.

Wireframe: In Web design, a wireframe is the equivalent of a thumbnail sketch. Wireframes show the functional areas of the planned website.

WYSIWYG: WYSIWYG stands for "what you see is what you get," a type of Web page design software that doesn't require users to know how to write code.

X

X-height: In a given typeface, x-height refers to the height of a lowercase "x" relative to the length of ascenders and descenders.

Z

Zoom: In a zoom, a stationary camera pushes into the scene by using the lens to zoom in on the focal point.

INDEX

Z